Regulating for Equitable and Job-Rich Growth

Edited by

Colin Fenwick

Head, Labour Law and Reform Unit, International Labour Office, Switzerland

Valérie Van Goethem

Labour Law Officer, Labour Law and Reform Unit, International Labour Office, Switzerland

Edward **Elgar**
PUBLISHING

Cheltenham, UK • Northampton, MA, USA

International Labour Office
Geneva, Switzerland

Published by
Edward Elgar Publishing Limited
The Lypiatts
15 Lansdown Road
Cheltenham
Glos GL50 2JA
UK

Edward Elgar Publishing, Inc.
William Pratt House
9 Dewey Court
Northampton
Massachusetts 01060
USA

In association with
International Labour Office
4 route des Morillons
CH-1211 Geneva 22
Switzerland
ISBN 978-92-2-129646-1 (paperback)

A catalogue record for this book
is available from the British Library

Library of Congress Control Number: 2017947260

This book is available electronically in the **Elgar**online
Economics subject collection
DOI 10.4337/9781788112673

MIX
Paper from
responsible sources
FSC
www.fsc.org   FSC® C013056

ISBN 978 1 78811 266 6 (cased)
ISBN 978 1 78811 267 3 (eBook)

Typeset by Servis Filmsetting Ltd, Stockport, Cheshire
Printed and bound in Great Britain by TJ International Ltd, Padstow

Contents

Contributors

David Bailey is Professor of Industrial Strategy at Aston Business School at Aston University, UK. His research interests include the areas of international business, industrial policy, economic and industrial restructuring, regional economic development policy and globalization. Professor Bailey has published extensively in international journals, including the *Journal of Industry, Competition and Trade, Cambridge Journal of Regions, Economy and Society* and the *European Journal of Industrial Relations*. He also been the recipient of funding grants, including an Economic and Social Research Council (ESRC) project on examining the labour market status of MG Rover workers four years after plant closure, for which he was Principal Investigator. He also has a substantial international media profile and has twice served as Chair of the Regional Studies Association.

Fabio Bertranou is Director of the International Labour Organization (ILO) Decent Work Team and Country Office for the Southern Cone of Latin America. His fields of specialization are labour market analysis, social protection, social security and pensions. He holds a PhD in Economics and a Graduate Certificate in Latin American Public and Social Policy Studies from the University of Pittsburgh, USA.

Luis Casanova is Technical Officer of the Decent Work Country Programme at the ILO Office for Argentina. His areas of expertise are labour market analysis and social protection. He is an economist from the National University of Cuyo, Argentina, and holds a Master's Degree from National University of La Plata/CEDLAS (Centro de Estudios Distributivos Laborales y Sociales), Argentina.

Sara Charlesworth is based at the School of Management and the Centre for People, Organisation and Work at the Royal Melbourne Institute of Technology (RMIT) University in Australia. Her research is concerned with gender (in)equality in employment, including pay inequity, discrimination and insecure work at the labour market, industry and organizational levels. The current focus of her research is low-paid and precarious work and, in particular, front-line care work.

Colin Fenwick is Head of the Labour Law and Reform Unit at the International Labour Office in Geneva, Switzerland, where he was previously a Labour Law Specialist. Before joining the ILO he was an Associate Professor at Melbourne Law School, where he served as Director of the Centre for Employment and Labour Relations Law, and as a joint Editor of the Australian Journal of Labour Law. He retains an honorary position at Melbourne Law School, at the rank of Associate Professor. His research explores the effects of labour law as a policy instrument for labour market regulation, with a particular focus on developing economies. He edited *Human Rights at Work: Legal and Regulatory Perspectives* (Hart Publishing, 2010, with T. Novitz) as well as *Labour Regulation and Development: Socio-Legal Perspectives* (Edward Elgar Publishing and ILO, 2016, with S. Marshall). He has also published articles in leading law journals.

Mark Freedland is Emeritus Professor of Employment Law at the University of Oxford, UK. His university teaching has been in the fields of labour law, international and European employment law, and comparative public law. He is an Honorary Queen's Counsel, and a Fellow of the British Academy. He is also an Emeritus Research Fellow in Law at St John's College, Oxford. He has acted as the Director of Graduate Studies for the Oxford Law Faculty, and as Director of the Oxford Institute of European and Comparative Law. In previous years he has held visiting professorships in France at the Universities of Paris I, and Paris II of which he holds an Honorary Doctorate, and he currently holds an Honorary Professorship in the Faculty of Laws of University College London, UK. He has written a number of works in the fields of labour law and public law. He has recently been acting as the Editor-in-Chief of a general treatise on the law, *The Contract of Employment*, which was published in May 2016 by Oxford University Press.

Valérie Van Goethem is a Labour Law Officer in the Labour Law and Reform Unit at the International Labour Office in Geneva, Switzerland. She also worked as a Legal Officer in the International Labour Standards Department on issues related to freedom of association, collective bargaining and collective labour law. Before joining the ILO, she was a Researcher at the University of Louvain (UCL/CRIDHO), Belgium, where her research focused on the relationship between market mechanisms and fundamental rights, both at the level of inter-individual relationships and at the level of the intergovernmental relationships in the EU context. She co-edited *International Labour Organization (ILO)* (Wolters Kluwer, 2016, with J.M. Servais).

John Grundy is a postdoctoral researcher affiliated with the Department of Political Science at York University, Toronto, Canada. His expertise lies in the areas of labour standards enforcement and unemployment policy. His work appears in journals such as *Economy and Society, Economic and Industrial Democracy, Citizenship Studies, Canadian Public Administration* and *Canadian Public Policy*.

Maarten van Klaveren is an economist, and until his retirement in 2016 was Senior Researcher at the Amsterdam Institute for Advanced Labour Studies (AIAS), University of Amsterdam, the Netherlands, and a senior consultant at STZ Consultancy and Research, Eindhoven, the Netherlands. As a researcher, he has taken part in many European and worldwide research projects. In recent years he has co-authored *Empowering Women in Work in Developing Countries* (Palgrave Macmillan, 2012), *Multinational Companies and Domestic Firms in Europe* (Palgrave Macmillan, 2013), and *Minimum Wages, Collective Bargaining and Economic Development in Asia and Europe* (Palgrave Macmillan, 2015).

Byung-Hee Lee is a Research Fellow at the Korea Labor Institute, Republic of Korea. His research interests include informal and non-regular work, the working poor, economic inequality and labour market institutions. He has published books and articles in the research areas of labour economics and social policy, including 'Labor income share and income inequality in Korea' (Korea Labor Institute Working Paper 2016-01, 2016), and 'Low wages and policy options in the Republic of Korea: Are policies working?' (2012), *International Labor Review*, **151** (3), 243–59 (with Deok Soon Hwang).

Riani Rachmawati is the Human Resources (HR) Director of the University of Indonesia. She also leads a team that provides HR advice and business consultancy for companies, private or government-owned, in Indonesia. She completed her PhD thesis at the University of Birmingham, UK, on the activities and effectiveness of trade unions in multinational companies in Indonesia.

Jill Rubery is Professor of Comparative Employment Systems at Alliance Manchester Business School, University of Manchester, UK, and Director of the Work and Equalities Institute at Manchester. Her research focuses on the interdisciplinary comparative analysis of employment systems. See, for example, G. Bosch, S. Lehndorff and J. Rubery (eds), *European Employment Models in Flux* (Palgrave, 2009), D. Anxo, G. Bosch and J. Rubery (eds), *The Welfare State and Life Transitions* (Edward Elgar Publishing, 2010), and M. Karamessini and J. Rubery (eds), *Women and Austerity: The Economic Crisis and the Future for Gender Equality* (Routledge, 2013).

Alex de Ruyter is a Professor and Director of the Centre for Brexit Studies at Birmingham City University, UK. He has published more than 60 research outputs in the time since he completed his PhD in 2002. He has published in leading international journals such as the *International Journal of Human Resource Management*, *Urban Studies* and the *European Journal of Industrial Relations*, and presented at numerous international conferences. He has also been the recipient of funding grants, including ESRC-sponsored projects examining the labour market status of MG Rover workers four years after plant closure, and flexible staffing practices in UK nursing and social care. His main research interests are in labour markets, globalization, Brexit and economic development.

Muhammad Irfan Syaebani is a Researcher at the Department of Management in the Faculty of Economics and Business at the University of Indonesia.

Mark P. Thomas is Associate Professor in the Department of Sociology and Director of the Global Labour Research Centre at York University, Toronto, Canada. His current areas of research include the enforcement of employment standards legislation in Canada, and labour, austerity and populism in urban North America. Thomas is the author of *Regulating Flexibility: The Political Economy of Employment Standards* (McGill-Queens, 2009), co-author of *Work and Labour in Canada: Critical Issues*, 3rd edition (Canadian Scholars Press, 2017), and co-editor of *Interrogating the New Economy: Restructuring Work in the 21st Century* (University of Toronto Press, 2010) and *Power and Everyday Practices* (Nelson, 2012). His work has also been published in journals including *Antipode*, *Economic and Industrial Democracy*, *Economic and Labour Relations Review*, *Labor Studies Journal*, *Journal of Industrial Relations* and *Studies in Political Economy*.

Kea Tijdens is a sociologist and Senior Researcher at the Amsterdam Institute for Advanced Labour Studies (AIAS), University of Amsterdam, the Netherlands. She is the scientific coordinator of the continuous *WageIndicator* web survey on wages and working conditions as well as of the current European EDUWORKS, BARCOM and SERISS projects. In recent years she co-authored *Empowering Women in Work in Developing Countries* (2012) and *Multinational Companies and Domestic Firms in Europe* (2013), and articles in *Human Resources for Health*, *Journal of Official Statistics*, *IZA Journal of Migration*, *IZA Journal of Labour Economics* and *World Development*.

Ana Maria Vargas-Falla is Research Director at the Swedish International Centre for Local Democracy (ICLD), and Affiliated Researcher at the

Department of Sociology of Law at Lund University, Sweden. She holds a PhD in Sociology of Law from Lund University and the University of Milan, Italy. Her doctoral research looked at how legal institutions influence the well-being of informal workers. She is interested in understanding the relations between law, social norms and the well-being of disadvantaged groups in society. Her current areas of research include: decent work for informal workers, well-being and life improvements, equal rights for immigrants, and local democracy in post-conflict countries.

Leah F. Vosko, FRSC (Fellow of the Royal Society of Canada), is Professor of Political Science and Tier 1 Canada Research Chair in the Political Economy of Gender and Work at York University, Toronto, Canada. Her current research focuses on employment standards enforcement and access to labour rights and protections among temporary migrant workers. She is author of *Managing the Margins: Gender, Citizenship and the International Regulation of Precarious Employment* (Oxford University Press, 2010) and *Temporary Work: The Gendered Rise of a Precarious Employment Relationship* (University of Toronto Press, 2000), and co-author of *Self-Employed Workers Organize: Law, Policy, and Unions* (McGill-Queen's University Press, 2005). Her most recent co-edited collection, *Liberating Temporariness? Migration, Work and Citizenship in an Age of Insecurity*, published by McGill-Queen's University Press, appeared in spring 2014. Some of her recent work has appeared in journals such as *Economic and Industrial Democracy*, *Industrial Relations Journal, Industrial Law Journal, Journal of Ethnic and Migration Studies* and *Journal of Industrial Relations*.

Tonia Warnecke is Associate Professor of Social Entrepreneurship and Business at Rollins College, USA. She is a development economist and has written and spoken extensively on development processes and policy, particularly related to gender. She has researched most world regions, but specializes in Asia. She has published more than 25 articles and chapters, characterized by interdisciplinary, policy-oriented research. She is a member of the Regulating for Decent Work (RDW) Network, has collaborated with the United Nations Research Institute for Social Development, and is a founding coach of the Ashoka U Commons programme for social innovation education. Her research specialities include international development, globalization, gender, social entrepreneurship and microfinance.

Preface

This book goes to print some ten years after the Financial Crisis and the onset of what in some parts of the world was considered a Great Recession. In the years immediately after the advent of the crisis, intense debate continued about the impact of labour regulation on labour market outcomes. This happened in particular because many countries pursued austerity policies that involved not only fiscal measures but also changes to labour market regulation. The recipe was generally the same as that promoted by some academic and institutional sources for some years before the onset of the crisis, and derived from orthodox economics.

The impact and the prevalence of arguments for deregulatory policies for labour markets were in large part the impetus for the establishment of the Regulating for Decent Work (RDW) Network. The Network brings together scholars from different disciplinary perspectives, and from all parts of the globe, to examine the effects and the nature of labour regulation. A central RDW concept is that labour regulation, and the social world that it seeks to shape, are assumed to be both complex and unpredictable, with no necessary direct or linear impacts, relationships or phenomena. The contributions in this volume are very much in keeping with the assumptions, goals and methods of the RDW project. The contributions shed important light on the conceptual ambiguity that besets key aspects of debate about labour market regulation and its impact, most especially the complexity of the notions of formality and informality. They call into question how accurately we measure key phenomena and whether we have the data necessary to devise effective policy, whatever its orientation. They draw attention to the heuristic devices and social practices that lead either to exclusion or inclusion, as well as to the challenges of largely linking effective social protection to the standard employment relationship. In the broad, the chapters remind us that while the impact of labour regulation in practice may not be precisely known in advance, there remains nevertheless an essential role for carefully calibrated state (and private) labour regulation. This is particularly true for the groups who feature in many chapters of the book, and who are regularly among those most excluded from labour markets and from effective protection: migrants, women and younger workers, for many of whom work is informal and/or in agriculture.

The publication of the volume has taken time, but we are nevertheless confident of the continuing originality and relevance of the research and the arguments presented. In this respect, it bears remarking that in recent years we are perhaps able to detect some important shifts in the positions of key global actors and institutions towards perspectives on labour regulation that might be considered more consistent with the approaches presented here. We as editors are deeply grateful to the whole group of contributors for their patience and persistence in the project.

The patience and ongoing support of the ILO Publishing unit were also essential to the finalization of this project. We thank Chris Edgar, Alison Irvine and Charlotte Beauchamp for this, and for their continual good humour. We also owe a particular debt of gratitude to our co-publisher, Edward Elgar. At the ILO, both Raymond Torres and Moussa Oumarou gave us (jointly and severally, and at different times) the space to pursue the work required to publish this book. Our final thanks go to our colleague in the Labour Law and Reform Unit, Tvisha Shroff. Her role in the final months was as significant as it was effective. Her collegial and conscientious administrative, editorial and research assistance were essential in getting this book published.

1. Labour market regulation and the imperative to stimulate job-rich growth*

Colin Fenwick and Valérie Van Goethem

This collection of chapters has its origins in the activities of the Regulating for Decent Work (RDW) Network. Founded in 2008, the RDW Network is a collaboration between researchers at the International Labour Organization (ILO), the Centre for Employment and Labour Relations Law at Melbourne Law School, and academic and policy institutions from across the world. The project is interdisciplinary, and involves researchers from a range of fields including economics, law, sociology and industrial relations.

The aim of the RDW Network project is to examine and, where possible, respond to the arguments against labour regulation that have dominated employment policy in many forums, and in many countries, in recent years. The project also aims to advance research and policy directions tailored towards making labour market regulation more effective. To this end, it questions whether the goal of improving working life can be advanced through legal regulation, and whether carefully designed labour regulation and enforcement mechanisms may be a more promising avenue for future social and economic progress than a simple retreat from labour regulation, whether public or private.

Section 1.1 of this introductory chapter briefly outlines the RDW Network project, and situates it in the context of wider literature that examines the operation and effect of labour regulation, although largely not from an economic perspective. Section 1.2 surveys developments at the global level, identifying an emerging consensus that labour regulation per se is neither negative nor positive for economic and social outcomes: balanced regulation is what is essential, and is what should be sought. Section

---

* The views expressed here are those of the authors, and do not represent the views of the International Labour Organization or the International Labour Office.

1

1.3 provides an overview of the contributions in this volume, and section 1.4 concludes.

1.1   REGULATING FOR DECENT WORK AND THE EVOLUTION OF THE UNDERSTANDING OF LABOUR REGULATION

The RDW Network was established, in large measure, as a way to stimulate analysis and research in response to the continuing influence of orthodox economic theory in policy debate over the effects of labour market regulation. It 'was established with the goal of nurturing efforts to fashion a coherent response to the deregulatory agenda in its contemporary guise' (Lee and McCann, 2011a: 4). In this sense, a key objective was 'to feature innovative ideas and approaches, new subjects and debates, and theoretical perspectives and methodologies that characterise contemporary research on labour market regulation' in order to propound 'an international and interdisciplinary response to the most influential account of the role and significance of labour market regulation, namely that derived from orthodox economic theory' (Lee and McCann, 2011a: 1). The project sought, among other things, to contest the rise of large-scale use of quantitative measures of the effects of labour market regulation. It did so because their increasing use had the effect of broadening the scope of the deregulatory narrative derived from orthodox – or neo-classical – economic theory (both in terms of topics and in terms of countries), while simultaneously reducing the efficacy of the analysis, and therefore the strength of the arguments built upon it (Lee and McCann, 2011a: 3). Paradoxically perhaps, the rise in the significance of quantitative measures has not always been matched by an equivalent increase in the robustness with which they are constructed (Cazes and Aleksynska, 2014).

A key pillar of Lee and McCann's argument was the proposition that a proper analysis of labour market regulation ought also to take into account its potential benefits. These might include: operating as a tool to pursue the public good of more and better jobs; building a platform for stable working relationships that can therefore be more functionally flexible and responsive to external shocks; and serving as an effective means to address economic coordination challenges (on the last of these compare, for example, Deakin, 2011). Moreover, a fair analysis of labour market regulation and its effects should take account of long traditions in other disciplines: some of these emphasise its significance as a conduit for social values; others point to the indeterminacy of regulation in practice, and the relative uncertainty that surrounds the question of how actors in the relevant 'regulatory space' (Morgan and Yeung, 2007: 59–68) interact with each other and with the regulatory scheme itself. In short: quantitative assessment alone of the purported economic effects of any regulatory measure is unlikely to address whether states have the capacity to implement effectively the regulation that they adopt.

Later, the project focused more specifically on the need for the analysis of labour regulation to do more to account for regulatory indeterminacy, that is, 'to elaborate with more precision the pressures that drive and underpin regulatory indeterminacy' (Lee and McCann, 2014: 6). That indeterminacy might derive from a number of possible sources, such as exclusion from legal frameworks, and the fragmentation that is characteristic of what David Weil christened the 'fissured' workplace (Weil, 2014a, 2014b). Again, a key goal was to draw on a range of disciplinary perspectives, in order to problematise the perceived dominance of understandings of the effects of labour market regulation based on orthodox economic theory. The addition – to economics – of traditions in social science and labour law (among others) served to bring into focus the constant evolution of business organisation, and the complexity of the legal notion of employment (Lee and McCann, 2014: 12). This in turn brought into focus not only the indeterminacy but also the dynamism of regulation in practice. Thus, for example, wage regulation could be seen to be externally dynamic in its impact on informal markets and practices not otherwise strictly caught. Labour regulation should also, however, be understood as exhibiting internal dynamism: that is, being characterised by unpredictable interactions. As Lee and McCann emphasise: institutional dynamism could be 'both a significant component of regulatory indeterminacy and a gateway to improved protective outcomes' (Lee and McCann, 2014: 13). Hence the value in considering the interaction of minimum wage regulation with poverty rates, and collective bargaining as a means of setting wages above a statutory minimum. This in turn highlights the need to take an institutional perspective: that is, to see minimum wage regulation (for example) as only one of a number of institutions in an industrial relations system, each of which interacts with others.

The RDW Network project also draws on the growing literature on how labour regulation is implemented in practice by state agencies; that is, how states operate within regulatory frameworks to promote compliance with regulatory requirements. For these purposes, the RDW Network 'situates research on enforcement and implementation of labour standards within the quest to clarify the components of regulatory indeterminacy' (Lee and McCann, 2014: 19). Among other things, this serves to draw attention to the interaction of public and private regulation, and/or of hybrid models of regulation (see, e.g., Dupper et al., 2016; Locke, 2013; Amengual, 2010;

Kolben, 2007), taking into account the growing consensus 'that hybrid initiatives support the implementation of legal standards' (Lee and McCann, 2014: 24).

Indeed the literature on the operation of regulation in practice – and particularly the literature on labour regulation in practice – is extensive, and spans a range of disciplines including regulation (and/or 'new governance') theory, industrial relations, political economy, political science, labour law and global labour studies. The literature examines many facets of the enterprise and the operation of labour regulation. It explores the drivers of non-compliance, including motivational factors (e.g., Kagan et al., 2011); the impact of structural, political, social and economic dynamics (e.g., Howe et al., 2014); the relative state of knowledge of regulatory requirements (e.g., Winter and May, 2001); and the relevance of firm and industry dynamics, size and structure (e.g., Wright et al., 2004). There are studies that consider the 'architecture' and day-to-day operation of regulation, including the design of regulatory frameworks, with particular consideration to the relative allocation of authority and responsibility for enforcement as between the state and private actors (e.g., Malmberg, 2009; Morgan and Yeung, 2007). Other studies address the goals, resources and internal organisation of regulatory agencies (e.g., Weil and Pyles, 2005). Some studies explore the management and work of front-line regulatory agents themselves. This literature explores the structure of regulatory mandates (e.g., Pires, 2008); the level of professionalisation of front-line regulatory agents and their scope to exercise individual discretion (e.g., Piore and Schrank, 2008); the use of record-keeping systems and the collection and management of data (e.g., Milena Galazka, 2015); and the way that regulatory agents themselves measure progress towards compliance by those subject to regulatory requirements (e.g., Weil, 2010).

A significant body of literature considers the ways in which regulatory agencies plan and target their compliance actions and sanctions. This literature explores the range of enforcement approaches and strategies, including whether regulators emphasise deterrence or compliance, and the extent to which they engage in strategic enforcement (e.g., Gunningham, 2011). The literature has developed new typologies to conceptualise different approaches to regulation in practice, including 'responsive regulation' (e.g., Bluff and Johnstone, 2003); 'smart regulation' (e.g., Gunningham and Grabosky, 1998); 'risk-based regulation' (e.g., Black, 2005: 512); and 'really responsive' regulation (e.g., Baldwin and Black, 2008). Some studies explore how agencies plan and target the detection of non-compliance, exploring the extent to which they emphasise response to complaints (e.g., Gellatly et al., 2011), compared with their use of proactive detection strategies (e.g., Howe et al., 2014). Still others examine the range and the use of different options for resolution and for sanctioning of regulatory non-compliance. These studies consider the relative merits, and the predilection of different agencies to use civil litigation and/or prosecution (e.g., Hardy et al., 2013); cooperative approaches to enforcement compared with the use of sanctions (e.g., Howe et al., 2014); the application of administrative sanctions (e.g., Vega and Robert, 2013); and the use of preventive measures and techniques to achieve voluntary resolution of non-compliance (e.g., Hardy and Howe, 2013).

1.2 LABOUR REGULATION AND THE GLOBAL FINANCIAL CRISIS: AN INTERNATIONAL PREOCCUPATION

As it happens, the RDW Network project was launched, and has continued, more or less in parallel with the global financial crisis of 2008–09 and its after-effects. Nearly ten years after the onset of the crisis, the world continues to experience rising unemployment, precarious work, inequality, and pressure on collective bargaining. All of these threaten economic and social stability in many parts of the world. Unease over the austerity agenda pursued in many countries is accompanied by a growing recognition that the post-crisis world should not return to 'business as usual'. Rather, more effective and balanced models should be adopted, which would integrate employment creation in growth policies and meet equally important objectives: equity, security and job quality.

While emerging and developing economies seem to have escaped the brunt of the recession, the debate continues on how to extend labour market institutions into the informal economy, with a focus on particularly vulnerable groups. The vast majority of the workers in the world are working at or beyond the margins of formal regulation. Workers in many cases are excluded from the formal scope of employment and labour regulation, either because they work in small enterprises that are exempt from application of the law, or because they are engaged in particular forms of work that are excluded, such as domestic work. Even when formally covered by employment and labour regulation, many workers can effectively be rendered informal because of the weaknesses of labour administration and inspection systems. In some societies, the capacity to exercise rights within labour regulation frameworks may depend on class, cultural norms, family structures and religion. At the same time, changes in the ways that workers are contractually engaged continue to lead to greater labour market segmentation, which is associated in turn with more workers being engaged in insecure work and, in some cases, informality.

Thus, both the initial shock and the continuing impact of the crisis continue to serve as the framework for much of the analysis of the purpose, role and effects of labour regulation, in both academic and policy-making circles. As noted, a particular preoccupation has been the desire and need to find ways to return to pre-crisis levels of economic growth, and with it, pre-crisis levels of job creation. Not surprisingly, international organisations have been active in trying to identify policy experience that can provide examples of how to address these manifold challenges. Quite naturally, the ILO has paid significant attention to these issues. The ILO has addressed the role of jobs in development (ILO, 2014), the 'jobs gap' – that is, the number of jobs that would have been created in the time since the crisis, had job creation continued at the same rate (ILO, 2015a) – and the spread of 'non-standard forms of employment' (ILO, 2016, 2015b). Similarly, the ILO has turned its attention to 'the changing nature of jobs', examining the relationships between jobs, incomes, poverty and social protection, and also the role of labour regulation in employment generation (ILO, 2015c).

During the same period, the World Bank has examined in depth the role of jobs in development. In this context, the Bank summarised its findings on the effects of labour market regulation in this way: 'Estimated effects prove to be relatively modest in most cases – certainly more modest than the intensity of the debate would suggest . . . Overall, labour policies and institutions are neither the major obstacle nor the magic bullet for creating good jobs for development in most countries' (World Bank, 2013: 258). More recently, the Bank has developed a policy advice manual on how to balance labour regulation with the importance of promoting job growth, in which it noted that labour regulation is essential for the protection of fundamental human rights, and also that it:

> can correct imperfections in labor markets resulting from inadequate informa-
> tion, uneven bargaining power, limited ability to enforce long-term commit-
> ments, or insufficient insurance mechanisms against employment related risks.
> Thus, labor regulations can, if well designed, avoid inefficient and inequitable
> labor market outcomes and have an important role to play in any country.
> (World Bank, 2015: vi)

Moving beyond jobs per se, the 2015 *World Development Report* exam-
ined the contribution of work to human development, taking a broad view of work so as to capture work beyond jobs, including for example care work and voluntary work. The report concluded that work can be positive for human development, 'when policies expand productive, remunerative and satisfying work opportunities, enhance workers' skills and potential and ensure their rights, safety and well-being' (UNDP, 2015: 1). From

a human development point of view, the report argued that '[l]egislation and regulation are critical for the protection of millions of workers who are engaged in activities that damage human development or who are involved in high-risk work' (UNDP, 2015: 161). In the same year, the ILO adopted its Transition from the Informal to the Formal Economy Recommendation (No. 204). Many of its paragraphs presume that regulation is necessary, and that its effects can be positive, provided an appropriate balance is drawn (ILO, 2015d).

As the *World Development Report* noted (UNDP, 2015: iv), it was published just after the United Nations adopted the Sustainable Development Goals for the period 2015 to 2030 which include, as Goal 8, a global commitment to 'Promote sustained, inclusive and sustainable economic growth, full and productive employment and decent work for all' (UN, 2015: 21). Within this Goal, Target 8.5 is to 'achieve full and productive employment and decent work for all women and men, including for young people and persons with disabilities, and equal pay for work of equal value' (UN, 2015: 22).

For its part, in recent years the Organisation for Economic Co-operation and Development (OECD) has developed a Jobs Quality Framework, which combines measures of earnings and inequality, security of employment, and the working environment (examined for these purposes from the perspective of working hours). Finding that higher job quality is correlated with higher employment rates (in better-performing economies), the OECD therefore argues that carefully chosen labour market and social protection policies – that is, labour regulation – 'should not be viewed as a necessary drag on job creation' (OECD, 2015: 18). The International Monetary Fund (IMF) has also cautiously acknowledged that reforms to labour market regulation may not necessarily achieve improved employment outcomes, and indeed may be counter-productive, especially if poorly sequenced relative to the prevailing economic cycle (IMF, 2016: 116–17). In the context of the debate on the causes and consequences of inequality, the IMF has also acknowledged both, that inequality may be harmful for economic growth in the long run, and that redistributive policies – that is, labour regulation – are generally not incompatible with economic growth (Ostry et al., 2014). This, in turn, is in keeping with broader literature on how and why inequality may harm countries' economic performance, and on the corresponding benefits of labour market institutions as means to address inequality (e.g., Berg, 2015).

1.3   REGULATING FOR EQUITABLE AND JOB-RICH GROWTH

This volume – *Regulating for Equitable and Job-Rich Growth* – builds on the debate and discussion that took place during the 2013 RDW Conference. As the title suggests, that conference centred on the role of labour market regulation as a policy tool to promote job creation. (Within the discipline of labour law, some scholars have addressed this issue over quite a period of time: Howe, 2008; Biagi, 2000.) The conference was organised around four themes: (1) comparing and evaluating labour regulation systems; (2) regulating informal work; (3) industrial and employment relations for inclusive growth; and (4) new patterns of labour market segmentation and new challenges for promoting inclusive labour markets. Based on a selection of papers from the conference, when taken together the chapters in this volume argue that effective and efficient labour market regulation can contribute to achieving the key policy goals of the formalisation of employment and inclusive labour markets, while also pursuing equitable distribution. In comparing the concerns, concepts and methodologies of various academic disciplines to the complexities of labour market regulation, the volume focuses on countries and regions of diverse socio-economic contexts and institutional traditions. The contributions to this volume confirm the importance of comparative international research, which lies at the heart of the RDW Network project.

Part I of this volume ('Introduction') is concerned with the ways in which the global financial crisis increased labour market segmentation. Access to stable employment has fallen, while at the same time the numbers of both the unemployed and those employed in new forms of less protected employment have grown. Against this background, this part of the book aims to articulate the broad goals of labour market regulation and its potential to contribute to inclusive development. It also considers the limits of some current developments in regulation and governance. It investigates new challenges for promoting inclusive rather than exclusive labour markets, focusing on the implications of changing patterns of labour market segmentation and polarisation for social cohesion and inclusive labour markets.

Chapter 2 (Jill Rubery: 'Reregulating for inclusive labour markets') builds on the assessment that the crisis, together with the austerity policies that were introduced in many countries, have increased labour market segmentation and inequality. Rubery argues that the expansion of non-standard forms of employment, the increasing exclusion of young people, and the pressure on those without wage work to accept poor working conditions, necessitates a complete reinvention and recasting of employment and social regulation. In Rubery's view, this evidence of a growing *precariat* (compare Standing, 2014, 2011) has drawn attention to growing inequalities, and at the same time given new life to insider/outsider debates. Rubery draws on a range of key contributions to the literature (Vosko, 2010; Freedland, 2013; Standing, 2011; Lee and McCann, 2014, 2011b) to develop her understanding of the insider/outsider debate and its influence. She draws as well on segmentation theory, gender analysis, and recent work on interactions between regulation and institutions. She then shows that the insider/outsider perspective is not limited to its traditional home in mainstream economics: it is also used by those calling for significant reforms to reduce inequalities. From this point of view, the main problem is the growth in dualism, that is, the result of the sharply decreasing number of workers covered by traditional employment regulation, and the social protection associated with the standard employment relationship (SER).

Subsequently, Rubery identifies four main issues that require reform and renewal of regulation of employment and social protection: first, the increasingly narrow scope of employment and social protection in many countries; second, the difficulty in identifying and effectively regulating the responsible employer (compare Prassl, 2015); third, the lack of value attached to unpaid care work; and fourth, the increasing deprivation of human rights for those working at the margins. Rubery calls for a large and coordinated approach to reform that is capable, both of devising stronger forms of protection for those in precarious jobs, and of developing policies likely to limit or reverse the trend to precarious employment. She argues for a wide agenda of reforms that would be incremental and evolutionary, to reflect myriad differences between countries, and to avoid feeding the impetus for deregulation. The argument here is that holding employers to account must be central to any reform agenda. In Rubery's view, rather than more flexible employment, policies are needed that would extend and reinforce the SER, together with new, higher legal minimum standards and mechanisms to reduce the penalties for not being on an SER-type contract. To this end, she presses not only for creating new rights but also for empowering workers and for promoting implementation and monitoring of rights and of regulation. Rubery suggests three key tracks for her proposed strategy: (1) disentanglement of social rights and protections from employment status; (2) extension of rights at work to non-standard and marginal workforce groups; and (3) promoting transparency in employment arrangements to facilitate monitoring and pressure for fair treatment.

Against this background, Rubery's case for a more nuanced and multifaceted approach to reform is developed in four stages. First, she starts with a review of current academic debates calling for reform from a wide range of disciplinary perspectives. Second, she singles out broad principles for reform along three lines of action, namely: reforming social policy, extending employer obligations, and strengthening enforcement and monitoring. Third, she lays out what a reform programme for inclusive labour markets might entail, while emphasising that a progressive reform agenda needs to be distinguished 'from the pervasive and potentially insidious insider/outsider rationale'. In her conclusion, she considers the contribution of these proposals to the long-term objective of providing the necessary political impetus for progressive regulatory reform. Here she also emphasises the need to pay attention to the potential of new compliance mechanisms such as transparency requirements, advocacy and raising public awareness on fundamental rights and minimum standards, and developing accountability and governance principles across supply chains.

Chapter 3 (Leah F. Vosko, John Grundy and Mark P. Thomas: 'Beyond new governance: Improving employment standards enforcement in liberal market economies') explores how the crisis in employment standards enforcement has provoked increased experimentation in liberal market economies with new instruments to improve workplace regulation. Vosko et al. consider in particular the impact of the influence of 'new governance' theory in regulatory practice. For them, this implies that a wide range of policy measures – from those aimed at preventing violations of workplace regulations, to complaint-handling processes and alternative dispute resolution mechanisms – are introduced at all stages of the enforcement process. The authors reflect on the long-run effects of changes in methods of production on how work is structured, particularly in common law jurisdictions. Taken together with legislative deregulation and declining rates of unionisation, the outcome is growing precarious employment. Against this background, the authors explore the operation of reforms in four distinct jurisdictions, and question whether the impact of 'regulatory new governance' (RNG) has been positive in practice. The authors focus on four high-income liberal jurisdictions – Australia, California, Ontario and the United Kingdom – that have historically been characterised by extensive employment regulation, and which are each confronted with similar issues in seeking to find a balance between fostering flexibilisation and maintaining a base of labour protection.

Vosko et al. observe that RNG is not 'a homogenous set of practices'. Rather, RNG covers a range of mechanisms and arrangements that are designed to advance more flexible regulatory regimes. The authors argue, however, that 'certain prominent RNG arrangements display an overreliance on "soft law" mechanisms'. In their view, such arrangements do not sufficiently acknowledge the role of state institutions and 'hard law' mechanisms, and therefore they fail to take adequate account of the power dynamics of the employment relationship. Thus, in practice they risk further undermining employment rights, particularly for precarious workers.

The argument has three main pillars. First, the authors outline the main principles that are inherent in RNG-based reforms in relation to employment standards enforcement. Here, they focus on two principles that have significant implications in terms of contributing to regulatory degradation, namely: (1) the plurality of enforcement mechanisms, particularly the use of 'soft law' and self-regulation; and (2) the involvement of multiple actors in RNG-based reforms and the related dispersion of authority. Second, they investigate the scope and significance of these two principles through a survey of enforcement mechanisms that demonstrate the influence of RNG on employment standards in the four selected common law jurisdictions. In each case, they consider three general stages of employment standards enforcement that are common to the four jurisdictions, namely: (1) pre-emptive measures to prevent violations; (2) complaint handling process; and (3) claims resolution. The authors argue that their examples show that RNG reforms, which de-centre state regulation and put the focus on voluntary, 'soft law' and 'multi-party regulatory strategies' may help to fuel the underlying crisis in enforcement of employment standards.

Vosko et al. advance three normative principles in order to better secure the regulatory protection of workers in precarious situations. In their view, these normative principles should help to balance traditional regulatory models with some of the more promising elements of RNG. The first principle is to maintain a prominent role for 'hard' enforcement mechanisms. The second is to augment workers' voices across all stages of the enforcement process. Finally, the third normative principle is concerned with the engagement to develop meaningful participatory structures. Thus, Vosko et al. point a way towards devising reforms that can be appropriately tailored to the context, but without the risk of abandoning the impact and the use of law as a means of regulation.

Part II of this volume ('Labour Market Regulation and Vulnerability') addresses the needs of key groups that often remain at the periphery of labour markets, and of labour market regulation: girls and young women workers, migrants and home care workers.

Chapter 4 (Maarten van Klaveren and Kea Tijdens: 'Assessing the scale of women's informal work: An industry outlook for 14 developing countries') considers the difficulty of assessing the scale of informal employment from a gender perspective, given the weaknesses in national studies and statistical data. Van Klaveren and Tijdens present evidence from a trade union project, Decisions for Life (DFL), aimed at empowering adolescent girls and young women in work in 14 countries. The study focuses on industries with a large share of women workers, in particular agriculture, wholesale and retail, and hotels, restaurants and catering (tourism). The study covers large states: Brazil, India and Indonesia; Commonwealth of Independent States (CIS) countries: Azerbaijan, Belarus, Kazakhstan and Ukraine; and southern African countries: Angola, Botswana, Malawi, Mozambique, South Africa, Zambia and Zimbabwe. The authors argue that an industry perspective is both necessary and useful, because labour allocation mechanisms are determined by industry structures. Moreover, employment prospects tend to vary greatly across industries, due to the diverse competitive structures, as well as to technological development at the industry level. Finally, the authors emphasise the extent to which working closely with workers' organisations was an important element in the DFL project. In addition, in most of the countries under consideration, trade unions were predominantly organised along industry lines. Drawing on ILO research showing the significant correlation between the incidence of informal employment and indicators of poor job quality (ILO, 2014), van Klaveren and Tijdens focus on the position of women workers in the shift from agriculture to services, and in particular to commerce. They observe that the large numbers of women working in the informal economies of the countries under scrutiny are largely or totally beyond the protection of some labour market institutions such as social dialogue and collective bargaining, minimum wage setting and labour inspection.

Van Klaveren and Tijdens argue that better employment data at country and industry levels is needed to clarify the prospects and problems of particular categories of workers, and that this would be especially useful if combined with industry-based evidence. In their view, socio-economic policies aimed at decent work and a decent living, inclusive of the interests of women, cannot plausibly be developed without adequate statistics that capture their large contribution to the informal economy. As a starting point, Van Klaveren and Tijdens use the work done by the International Conference of Labour Statisticians (ICLS) to untangle the difficulties of addressing the issue of the informal economy from a statistical perspective (ILO, 2012). They review the various attempts made in the past decade to define, and subsequently to measure, informal employment. Moreover, on the basis of extensive comparative statistical data for the countries under analysis, the authors question the exclusion by the ICLS of agriculture as a sector from the definition of the informal economy. They argue, by contrast to other authors such as Charmes (2012), that this kind of exclusion is likely to impede efforts to get a full picture of the situation for women in developing countries. Van Klaveren and Tijdens depict in detail the statistical consequences of excluding agriculture from employment data for the 14 countries under consideration, with a particular focus on women's employment. They conclude that the consolidated national statistics pertaining to labour forces contribute only partially to grasping the possibilities and constraints facing women in agriculture in their struggle to attain a decent living. Van Klaveren and Tijdens infer from this that better employment data at country and industry levels are required to clarify the issues and the prospects of specific worker categories.

Chapter 5 (Mark Freedland: 'Regulating informal work at the interface between labour law and migration law') reflects on the many points where migration law impacts on labour law's regulation of labour markets and of employment relations (compare, e.g., Crock and Friedman, 2006). Freedland's conceptual framework is grounded in the observation that the failure to observe certain kinds of regulation can contribute to the informality of work. Thus, informal work is the epi-phenomenon to 'formal' regulation. On this analysis, the failure to observe formal regulation in the area of migration law leads to the 'undocumented worker' or 'illegal immigrant' typology. To further illustrate the concept, Freedland identifies and considers two other examples: the failure to observe formal regulation in the field of labour law and collective bargaining leads to the 'sweatshop' typology, while the failure to observe formal regulation in the related fields of tax law and social security law leads to the 'black economy' typology.

Freedland develops three interconnected arguments about the regulation of informal work to show that the very notion of informal work is itself both 'analytically and normatively fragile'. The first is the 'imprecision argument'. Freedland argues that the application of migration law is deeply complex, and not at all clear-cut: it is simply not easy to determine whether a non-national may lawfully engage in work. This in turn illustrates how there is no precise line between formality and informality. The second is the 'normative ambiguity argument'. The starting point here is the simple observation that the policy goal of migration law is not protection of the migrant *qua* worker, but rather protection of the national labour market and of those workers who are lawfully entitled to participate in it. Thus, the migration law-generated model of work by 'undocumented workers' contains within it especially strong connotations of culpability on the part of these workers themselves. This in turn leads to uncertainty about whether regulatory protection should be extended to these workers: rather, they are constructed as less 'deserving' of regulatory protection, and in fact seen to be more justly susceptible to regulation which penalises them. In Freedland's view, this normative ambiguity stands in at least partial contrast to tax and social security law: in those fields, culpability for the informality of work would far more frequently be attributed to the employer or employing organisation. There is an even clearer contrast with labour law: here it would be counter-intuitive at best to treat the worker as primarily culpable for failure to observe labour standards.

Freedland's third argument, albeit one he advances far more tentatively, is the 'argument for inclusiveness'. As he makes clear in his concluding section, his starting point is 'a conviction that there are great dangers in allowing labour law's regulation to falter and fall short in the difficult or "informal" territory where it is in fact most needed'. For Freedland, a consideration of migration law and its interaction with labour regulation brings into focus both, the different roles, and the pervasive impact of the concept of criminality that is characteristic of the field. The migrant worker who works informally, the person or enterprise that engages them, and the person or enterprise that facilitated their entry to the jurisdiction: all may be criminally culpable. Freedland points to the decision of the Supreme Court of the United Kingdom in *Hounga v Allen*[1] as illustrative of how his argument for inclusiveness might be applied in practice. There the Supreme Court decided that an illegal immigrant could proceed with her claim for enforcement of basic labour rights. Rather than operating as a bar to bringing proceedings, as the Court of Appeal had held,[2] the claimant's immigration status was considered merely the 'context'[3] in which the abuses of which she complained had taken place. Here then, can be seen, in Freedland's view, an appropriate way of resolving a normative ambiguity between how labour law and migration law each regulate the sphere of informal work.

Freedland concludes by considering how the ambiguities and conceptual lacunae he has identified are evident in both the ILO Transition from the Informal to the Formal Economy Recommendation, 2015 (No. 204) and also a report of the EU Fundamental Rights Agency: *Severe Labour Exploitation: Workers Moving Within or Into the European Union* (FRA, 2015). He chooses these as two recent examples of supra-national articulation of regulatory policy, each concerned in some way with the regulation of informal work in the context of labour migration. He hastens to add that his purpose is not to 'denigrate' these efforts, or those who crafted them. Rather, he does so to illustrate further the inherent difficulties that face any effort to regulate effectively for the application of labour

---

[1]   [2014] UKSC 47.
[2]   [2012] EWCA Civ 609.
[3]   [2014] UKSC 47 [40].

standards in the informal economy, and especially where regulation of labour migration is also involved. His concern is rather to point to how, in part, the informal is constructed, and to the danger in overlooking how normalisation of the informal can also serve to normalise the existence of a sphere of work beyond labour regulation.

Chapter 6 (Sara Charlesworth: 'Partial protection? The regulation of home care workers' working conditions') examines the way in which the marginalisation of home care work is shaped by the regulatory context in which working conditions and wages of home care workers are defined. Charlesworth's chapter explores the Australian case, as an illustration of the national and international contexts that inform how home care work and employment regulation are constructed. Recalling that home care workers fall into the definition of 'domestic worker' set out in Article 1 of the ILO Domestic Workers Convention, 2011 (No. 189), Charlesworth explores two specific questions. The first relates to the historical and regulatory processes that gave rise to the current working conditions for home care workers (and their impact). The second question addresses the potential of employment and labour regulation to tackle the marginalisation of home care workers. Drawing on substantial literature (including Fudge, 2012; Freedland and Kountouris, 2013), Charlesworth starts by recalling that: '[i]n the world of paid employment, home care work is distinctive in that it trespasses not only the boundaries between the informal and formal economies but also those boundaries between market work and family work, and between public and private spaces'. Home care work therefore shows how the categories of formal/informal and regulated/unregulated, while often posed as static, are nothing of the sort. Only by moving beyond them can we properly understand how employment conditions for home care work are produced.

Charlesworth explores the historical and regulatory processes that have led to the prevailing working conditions for home care workers in Australia. To do so, she draws on a census and survey of aged care providers and aged care workers, including in community-based settings. She examines the federal Social, Community, Home Care and Disability Services (SCHCDS) Industry Award 2010 that provides sector-specific minima for the majority of home care workers. She also reviews the 2012 Equal Pay case, run under the SCHCDS Award, which showed how home care workers can easily be excluded from rights claims under the Award. Drawing on a number of sources (e.g., McCann and Murray, 2014), Charlesworth explores how in Australia – as elsewhere – government policy has promoted a market for home care work, while at the same time employment regulation has persisted in seeing this form of care work as exceptional. In her view, the situation is exacerbated by the type of work that home care workers do, by the difficulties in estimating the number of home care workers in the formal economy, and by the effective exclusion of home care workers from some labour regulation because so many of them are engaged as casual employees.

Charlesworth acknowledges the increased regulatory recognition of home care work as 'work' over time. However, in her view this recognition continues both to be partial, and to be shaped by shifts in both directions along the in/formalisation continuum. In particular, Charlesworth singles out three main shifts that, in her view, have 'contributed to the incomplete process of the regulatory recognition of home care work as "work" and, for many home care workers, a move backwards on the in/formalisation continuum'. These shifts include: (1) 'the increasing contracting out of home care services including requirements in some states for the compulsory tendering of local government services'; (2) 'the structural underfunding of social care'; and (3) 'the award modernisation process under the Fair Work Act 2006'. The last of these involved a rationalisation of more than 20 different sets of working conditions at state and national level into one federal minimum; in the process, a number of conditions that were particularly beneficial to home care workers were lost. These included, in some cases, the right to request full-time ongoing employment instead of casual employment. Charlesworth concludes by considering the extent to which there is potential in the Australian system of labour regulation to address the marginalisation of home care workers, and the prospects for change. In her view this would require an in-depth revision of employment regulation so that it can accommodate the specific nature of home care work, indeed so that employment regulation can properly value it as 'work'. She ends with a call for a strong and united commitment to this end by employers, unions and the Fair Work Commission itself, in the context of forthcoming revisions of minimum standards.

Part III of this volume ('Labour Market Regulation and Informality') looks at the challenge for labour market regulation posed by persistent informality; and conversely, at how labour market regulation can be tailored to contribute to the pursuit of key policy goals. It explores methodological issues while paying attention to developments in different regions of the world. Countries addressed in this part include Argentina, Colombia, Indonesia and the Republic of Korea.

Chapter 7 (Byung-Hee Lee: 'Informal work in the Republic of Korea: Non-regulation or non-compliance?') addresses the issue of the continued spread of informal employment in the Republic of Korea notwithstanding protective policy measures. The author identifies weaknesses in policy enforcement, in particular at the level of labour administration and labour inspection, as a key consideration. In Lee's view, the way in which labour market flexibility was fostered in the Republic of Korea after the 1997 financial crisis contributed to shifting the burden of flexibility to vulnerable groups of workers, thus expanding low-paid and non-standard work, and thereby intensifying the segmentation of the labour market. Drawing on various sources (e.g., Hwang and Lee, 2012), Lee explores the fact that despite a series of national policies to protect vulnerable groups in the Republic of Korea, a considerable number of workers engaged in informal work still remain unprotected by labour laws and social insurance. His argument is developed in five stages, drawing on data from the Supplementary Survey of the Economically Active Population Survey (Korea Statistical Office) and the Korea Labour and Income Panel Survey (Korea Labour Institute).

Lee begins with an explanation of the extent and the nature of informal work in the Republic of Korea, showing that while the share of informal work among employees has been falling over the past decade, about 40 per cent of employees still are not protected by labour law and social insurance. Second, he shows that in the decade 2001 to 2011, about 80 per cent of informal workers were excluded from more than two of three policies that should – in principle – be characterised by their universal application across all workplaces, namely: (1) the minimum wage; (2) the mandatory retirement allowance; and (3) the subscription to public pension plans. In the author's view, this overlapping trend of exclusion implies that measures to strengthen the effectiveness of any of these three protective policies may contribute to enhancing the compliance level of other policies. Lee then explores two key characteristics of informal work in the country: on the one hand, lack of regulation – that is, exclusion by law; and on the other hand, lack of compliance – that is, exclusion in practice. In Lee's view only four types of informal employment can be linked to non-regulation: independent contractors, domestic workers, workers with less than one year of tenure and part-time workers who work for less than 15 contractual hours per week. Lee argues that all other cases of informal employment should be linked to non-compliance; in total, some 80 per cent of all informal work in the Republic of Korea. Thus he concludes that the low level of policy enforcement is the crux of informal employment, and emphasises the need to reinforce the implementation of relevant regulation. In a fourth stage, Lee applies a logit regression analysis, setting 'informal employment' and 'informal employment due to employer non-compliance' as the two dependent variables, in order to explore the job characteristics of informal employment (for example, workplace size, employment type, industry, occupation and unions). This shows that informal work is more likely in smaller firms, and that informal employment due to non-compliance is strongly associated with work in construction, personal services and distribution services. It is also significantly more common for blue-collar workers and those in the services sector.

To conclude, Lee examines the issue of the persistence of informal work using a dynamic random effects probit model to analyse whether the persistence of informal work is linked to state dependence. He finds that being in informal work is a strong predictor of informal work in the future, and that genuine state dependence is closely related to the persistence of informal employment. One of the policy implications is the need to strengthen labour administration and labour inspection services as a deterrent, while also providing 'policy incentives for employers to comply with rules and policies and to formalize employment'. In other words, focusing on legislation to expand the scope of social protection coverage is not enough. Lee suggests promoting formal employment through 'a policy mix combining labour laws, labour policies, social insurance programmes and taxation policies'. He also advocates for policies that target vulnerable groups which present specific risks and probabilities of persistent informal employment.

Chapter 8 (Fabio Bertranou and Luis Casanova: 'Employment formalization in Argentina: Recurring and new challenges for public policies') analyses employment formalisation in Argentina during the 2000s, as well as the public policies associated with that process. Bertranou and Casanova note that more than 40 per cent of all employees in Argentina are affected in one way or another by informality. A large part of this informality is unregistered work; not surprisingly, this is the target of the most relevant public policy measures in Argentina. Bertranou and Casanova focus on the process of registered employment formalisation, and particularly the drop in non-registered salaried employment. In their view, the experience of Argentina demonstrates that a 'comprehensive strategy' is needed to drastically decrease informal employment. However, all the policy measures taken in this framework should be tailored as far as possible to the heterogeneity of productive structures.

Drawing on global ILO findings, Bertranou and Casanova single out several factors that tend to prevent public policies from being fully effective in the area of informality. In their view, these factors are: the persistence of informality, even during periods of economic growth and rising employment; the connection between the formal and informal sectors; the presence of informal employment within the formal economy; and the great variety of jobs affected by informality. With a view to developing a comprehensive policy approach, Bertranou and Casanova explore the impact on informality of the main characteristics of the critical segments of the job market and the issue of concentration of informal employment. The critical segments that are identified for this purpose include: domestic work, the textile industry, micro-enterprises in commerce and construction, self-employment and rural employment.

Bertranou and Casanova show that since 2003, the manner in which policy-makers have addressed informal employment in Argentina was by integrating and coordinating various programmes, as well as social and economic strategies linked with the factors that were likely to lead to informal work. Drawing on various authors (e.g., Beccaria, 2015), they focus their attention on the relationship between economic growth and the creation of salaried employment. Against this background, Bertranou and Casanova welcome the 2014 Law for the Promotion of Registered Employment and Labour Fraud Prevention, which was adopted in Argentina following a process of social dialogue on informality that was organised between the government and major actors from the world of work. This new law introduces a set of measures to create formal employment and to formalise informal employment in both the 'formal sector' and in the 'partly formal/partly informal sector'. Bertranou and Casanova consider that these new measures may give rise not only to an enhancement of working and employment conditions but also to productivity increases. However, in their view, the only way for these measures to have a real impact on employment formalisation is to ensure that they are accompanied by productive, fiscal, social and labour policies, along with a macroeconomic framework that fosters sustainable economic growth. The authors argue therefore that 'future strategies must take into account the heterogeneous nature of informality, seeking formal employment while fostering economic activity'. For this endeavour to succeed, not only is the role of the state essential, but the genuine involvement of workers' and employers' associations, and other relevant actors, is equally important.

Chapter 9 (Ana Maria Vargas-Falla: 'Formalizing street vendors: Regulating to improve well-being or to gain control?') investigates the impact of legal norms on the lives of informal vendors in developing economies. The chapter explores alternative forms of state regulation to promote voice and to upgrade vendors' circumstances in order to enhance their economic situation. The empirical basis for the analysis is drawn from four periods of ethnographic field research between 2011 and 2014 in Bogotá, Colombia. Bogotá provides rich material given that it experienced dramatic shifts in the regulation of street vending, moving from drastic prohibition and frequent evictions (1998 to 2003) to alternative forms of regulation that bolstered informal vendors (2004 to 2012). Vargas-Falla situates her work in the context of prior literature about formalisation and the regulation of urban vendors (e.g., Bhowmik, 2005; Donovan, 2008; Sen, 1999, 2013). She uses Sen's concept of well-being and his related capabilities approach to investigate the relation between formalisation of street vendors and the improvement of their working conditions. Vargas-Falla deconstructs the main assumptions in formalisation theory by shedding light on the ways in which formalisation can bring important outcomes for the human development of street vendors, especially their working conditions. Vargas-Falla recalls that a prevalent assumption in formalisation programmes for street vendors is that their legal status will help them in avoiding police evictions and harassment. It will also help them to improve their income and develop their businesses (as a result, notably, of access to formal credit). However, Vargas-Falla decides to focus not only on the economic impact of formalisation, but also on other aspects, such as working conditions and membership in organisations.

The question at the centre of the chapter is 'whether and how street vendors could improve their working conditions after formalisation'. The study shows two major improvements that followed formalisation: on the one hand, the ability of workers to work without fear of police eviction; and on the other hand, their protection from harsh weather conditions (since vendors benefit from tents and roofs in formalised vending zones). Vargas-Falla observes that both government and leaders of vendors' organisations were critical of formalisation; in her view, they did not understand the human development outcomes that helped vendors improve their working conditions. From the government's perspective, the situation was unsatisfactory and the formalisation programme was a failure because the transition from the informal to the formal economy had never occurred. However, in practice, many vendors were actually relatively satisfied, because their working conditions had improved. This led Vargas-Falla to conclude that formalisation of workers in the informal economy can have significant outcomes for the human development of vendors. Yet, formalisation is 'a venture that requires a bottom-up approach'. Against this background, and based on her extensive empirical work, Vargas-Falla considers that legal norms can become a tool for empowerment, voice and poverty reduction, provided that the law is used to improve the life of vulnerable groups, and not as a tool for control and coercion.

Chapter 10 (Alex de Ruyter, Muhammad Irfan Syaebani, Riani Rachmawati, David Bailey and Tonia Warnecke: 'Working conditions of urban vendors in Indonesia: Lessons for labour law enforcement') draws on the insights from field work in the Greater Jakarta region of Indonesia to investigate the labour market experiences of informal street vendors in Indonesia. De Ruyter et al. explore the consequences of their labour market vulnerability in terms of labour law enforcement. The chapter focuses on the interaction of vendors with 'customers', authorities, and with other labour market intermediaries trying to improve their welfare.

Drawing on various sources (e.g., Vosko, 2006; Folkerth and Warnecke, 2011) as well as ILO research (e.g., ILO, 2014), de Ruyter et al. begin by analysing the interaction between vulnerability and precariousness. In their view, the notion of vulnerability results from unequal social relations. Hence vulnerability encompasses class, gender and race dimensions. Therefore, for these authors, formalisation of the informal sector should be approached from the perspective of power relations, rather than in terms of legal regulation.

Building on Brata's (2010) typology (as adapted from Dabir-Alai, 2004), that seeks to develop an 'index of vulnerability' by exploring the working conditions of street vendors, de Ruyter et al. investigate the various types of working conditions to which vendors are exposed. Their results demonstrate that vulnerability is the result of a combination of economic and social factors, and that precarious work is aggravated by the unequal social relations faced by vendors. The vulnerability of street vendors is particularly sharp in terms of their low income, potential for harassment by authorities, lack of access to capital, and lack of access to affordable healthcare and education for some (in particular, for internal migrants). In the conceptual framework developed by de Ruyter et al., the factors shaping labour market vulnerability include: labour law, geography, earnings, representation, employment status, relations with creditors and suppliers, education, as well as gender, ethnicity and class. Against this background, they consider that a primary requirement should entail a move beyond a simple distinction between the 'formal' and 'informal' sector and an acknowledgement of 'a more nuanced gradation of vulnerability across the spectrum of employment arrangements' in both developing and emerging countries.

The policy recommendations that conclude their chapter include a number of measures aiming at reducing the vulnerability of urban vendors, and at contributing to a 'decent work' agenda. In particular, the findings suggest that greater efforts are needed to support the access of highly vulnerable workers, such as urban vendors, to adequate legal remedies and to fair and expeditious complaint procedures. The fight against corruption and unaccountable practices by officials with whom street vendors are to interact should also be more actively pursued. From a wider perspective, in the authors' view, supporting urban vendors to move out of poverty implies finding measures to extend social protection and welfare coverage to all vulnerable workers (for example, specific social security schemes that reach beyond the formal economy). The authors consider that such measures should be aligned with the recommendation of the World Trade Organization and the International Labour Organization (WTO and ILO, 2009) according to which a 'multidimensional approach' is needed to enhance formal employment and support those still in informal employment.

1.4   CONCLUSION

Notwithstanding the diverse range of countries and contexts addressed in the chapters of this book, a number of common arguments and themes can be identified. One is the need to account for the underlying causes of informality in attempting to regulate effectively to ameliorate its adverse consequences. A number of chapters point to the continuing fragmentation of forms of work, and to the role of supply chains in contributing to this phenomenon. Both de Ruyter et al. and Vargas-Falla identify the multiple and overlapping sources of vulnerability for those who work as informal street vendors, in Indonesia and Colombia (respectively). In Indonesia in particular, informal vendors experience the adverse effects of the combination of race, class and, for many, (internal) labour migrant status. Thus, de Ruyter et al. call for enforcement as a means of addressing the key underlying issue, which for them is the dynamics and reality of power relations. Vosko et al. also insist that we must not overlook the power dynamics of the employment relationship and how it has been changing, particularly by turning away from the state's role in implementing the law as it exists.

Several chapters emphasise that informality is not always or necessarily a consequence of legal exclusion from protective regulatory frameworks. Accordingly, and from their different perspectives Rubery, Lee and de Ruyter et al. each argue that there is a need for more and better enforcement of existing rules as one way of moving to address informality. For their part, Vosko et al. are not merely focused on enforcement, but are insistent on the importance of maintaining a role for hard law as well as, or perhaps in preference to, soft law. Interestingly, in light of the large literature on the operation of regulation in practice and the rise of (among others) 'new governance' theories of regulation (some of which is briefly touched on above), theirs can in some ways be considered a call not to overlook the 'traditional' goals and methods of regulatory enforcement.

Many authors identify the deep significance and pervasive impact of our differing conceptual frameworks for 'formality', 'work' and much else besides. Thus, Charlesworth points to the failure of regulatory frameworks – and indeed of key regulatory actors – to conceive properly of home care work as work at all. Without that being addressed, these workers seem in her view destined only to endure more of the same. For his part, Freedland's exploration of the interaction of the regulation of migration and the regulation of labour clearly illustrates the large area of conceptual uncertainty around the very idea of informality itself. Moreover, he carefully identifies the adverse, indeed pernicious, impact of the concept of criminality within the discourse of labour migration. Its influence can lead to the result that the worker who requires protection is considered culpable for not experiencing it and, to compound the injury, therefore not worthy of efforts to ensure the effectiveness of labour regulation for all who work. In this sense, his argument for an 'inclusive' approach to labour regulation is relevant well beyond the specific context of work by migrants: it is a call to ensure that labour regulation always, and in all ways, reaches all those who should benefit from it.

Van Klaveren and Tijdens are also deeply concerned with the conceptual framework within which we attempt to understand how work is structured, and how we can develop policies that will improve the lot of informal workers over time. In the end, theirs is a very clear and simple question: how will the situation improve if we simply exclude certain types of work – in this case, agricultural work – from our analysis, and if therefore we do not attempt to gather the data that could inform good policy-making? In this respect, their analysis has strong connections to Charlesworth's approach. In addition, both these chapters, together with those of de Ruyter et al., Lee, Vargas-Falla and Vosko et al., are all attuned to the gender implications of the operation of these underlying conceptual frameworks. In this way, the question from van Klaveren and Tijdens can be differently phrased: how will the situation improve for women?

In her opening, Rubery carefully unpacks the interrelationship of labour protection policy to the nature of the standard employment relationship (SER), and its continuing significance as the conceptual touchstone for how we establish frameworks of protective labour regulation (compare Deakin, 2013). Hence she calls for a conceptualisation of labour protection that is not so tied to the SER. Rubery's chapter is, naturally, alive to the very broad canvas on which she works: that is, of the very many interrelated economic and social phenomena that shape work relations, and thus the outcomes for workers, whether formal or informal. Likewise, Bertranou and Casanova argue for policy approaches to address informality that can take account of wider policy frameworks, while also being tailored to the specific characteristics exhibited by informality in any particular context. As does Lee in his analysis of the situation in the Republic of Korea, they emphasise how informality is frequently associated with particular industry structures and/or forms of work.

For her part, Vargas-Falla illustrates the significance of the conceptual framework in a different way: by framing her analysis in terms of Sen's conception of well-being, she is able to conclude that policy had a positive effect for street vendors. While they did not become fully formal, they reported that their working conditions had been improved in important ways, and in ways that might further enhance their capabilities. Here, then, Vargas-Falla is explicit about what is sometimes less directly said in other chapters: there is a positive role for states in devising and implementing labour regulation.

In different ways, and from their different perspectives, each of the chapters in this book makes that point. Whether because of the need to address the adverse effects of increasing labour market segmentation; to ensure that women workers are treated as equals; to tackle the underlying power relations that conspire to construct informality; or to promote development and improved economic outcomes, the authors agree that labour regulation is essential. It should be carefully designed. It should be effectively enforced. But it should be neither gainsaid, nor overlooked, in the continuing pursuit of decent work for all.

REFERENCES

Amengual, M. 2010. 'Complementary Labor Regulation: The Uncoordinated Combination of State and Private Regulators in the Dominican Republic', *World Development*, **38** (3), https://pdfs.semanticscholar.org/1b4e/fe654a7d44e 19cd839a6a980bb7c44712aea.pdf.

Baldwin, R. and Black, J. 2008. 'Really Responsive Regulation', *Modern Law Review*, **71** (1), 59–94.

Beccaria, L. 2015. 'Perspectiva de políticas de formalización de la economía informal', in Bertranou, F. and Casanova, L. (eds), *Caminos hacia la formalización laboral en Argentina* (Buenos Aires: ILO), pp. 185–206.

Berg, J. (ed.). 2015. *Labour Market, Institutions and Inequality – Building Just Societies in the 21st Century* (Cheltenham, UK and Northampton, MA, USA and Geneva, Switzerland: Edward Elgar Publishing and ILO).

Bhowmik, S.K. 2005. 'Street Vendors in Asia', *Economic and Political Weekly*, **40** (22–3), 2256–64.

Biagi, M. 2000. *Job Creation and Labour Law: From Protection to Pro-action* (The Hague: Kluwer Law International).

Black, J. 2005. 'The Emergence of Risk-Based Regulation and the New Public Risk Management in the UK', *Public Law*, Autumn, 510–46.

Bluff, E. and Johnstone, R. 2003. 'Infringement Notices: Stimulus for Prevention or Trivialising Offences?', *Journal of Occupational Health and Safety*, **19**, 337–46.

Brata, A. 2010. 'Vulnerability of Urban Informal Sector: Street Vendors in Yogyakarta, Indonesia', *Theoretical and Empirical Researches in Urban Management*, **5** (14), http://um.ase.ro/no14/4/pdf.

Cazes, S. and Aleksynska, M. 2014. 'Comparing Indicators of Labour Market Regulations across Databases: A Post Scriptum to the Employing Workers Debate', Conditions of Work and Employment Series No. 50 (Geneva: ILO).

Charmes, J. 2012. 'The Informal Economy Worldwide: Trends and Characteristics', *Margin – The Journal of Applied Economic Research*, **6** (2), 103–32.

Crock, M. and Friedman, L. 2006. 'Immigration Control and the Shaping of Australia's Labour Market: Conflicting Ideologies or Historical Imperatives?', in Arup, C., Gahan, P., Howe, J., Johnstone, R., Mitchell, R. and O'Donnell, A. (eds), *Law and Labour Market Regulation* (Sydney: Federation Press), pp. 322–43.

Dabir-Alai, P. 2004. 'The Economics of Street Vending: An Empirical Framework for Measuring Vulnerability in Delhi in the Late 1990s', paper presented at the EDGI and UNU-WIDER Conference, 17–18 September, Helsinki.

Deakin, S. 2011. 'The Contribution of Labour Law to Economic and Human Development', in Davidov, G. and Langille, B. (eds), *The Idea of Labour Law* (Oxford: Oxford University Press), pp. 156–73.

Deakin, S. 2013. 'Addressing Labour Market Segmentation: The Role of Labour Law', Working Paper No. 52, Governance and Tripartism Department (Geneva: ILO).

Donovan, M.G. 2008. 'Informal Cities and the Contestation of Public Space: The Case of Bogotá's Street Vendors, 1988–2003', *Urban Studies*, **45** (1), 29–51.

Dupper, O., Fenwick, C. and Hardy, T. 2016. 'The Interaction of Labour Inspection and Private Compliance Initiatives: A Case Study of Better Work Indonesia', paper presented at the 4th Regulating for Decent Work Conference, July, Geneva.

Folkerth, J. and Warnecke, T. 2011. 'Organizing Informal Labor in India and Indonesia', paper presented at the Global Labor University Conference, Johannesburg.

FRA. 2015. *Severe Labour Exploitation: Workers Moving Within or Into the European Union: States' Obligations and Victims' Rights*, European Union Agency for Fundamental Rights (Luxembourg: Publications Office of the European Union).

Freedland, M. 2013. 'Burying Caesar: What Was the Standard Employment Contract?', in Stone, K. and Arthurs, H. (eds), *Rethinking Workplace Regulation: Beyond the Standard Contract of Employment* (New York: Russell Sage Foundation), pp. 81–94.

Freedland, M. and Kountouris, N. 2013. *The Legal Construction of Personal Work Relations* (Oxford: Oxford University Press).

Fudge, J. 2012. 'Blurring Legal Boundaries: Regulating for Decent Work', in Fudge, J., McCrystal, S. and Sankaran, K. (eds), *Challenging the Legal Boundaries of Work Regulation* (Oxford: Hart Publishing), pp. 1–26.

Gellatly, M., Grundy, J., Mirchandani, K., Perry, J.A., Thomas, M.P. and Vosko, L.F. 2011. '"Modernising" Employment Standards?: Administrative Efficiency and the Production of the Illegitimate Claimant in Ontario, Canada', *Economic and Labour Relations Review*, **22** (2), 81–106.

Gunningham, N. 2011. 'Strategizing Compliance and Enforcement: Responsive Regulation and Beyond', in Parker, C. and Lehmann Neilsen, V. (eds), *Explaining Compliance: Business Responses to Regulation* (Cheltenham, UK and Northampton, MA, USA: Edward Elgar Publishing), pp. 199–221.

Gunningham, N. and Grabosky, P. 1998. *Designing Environmental Policy* (Oxford: Clarendon Press).

Hardy, T. and Howe, J. 2013. 'Too Soft or Too Severe? Enforceable Undertakings and the Regulatory Dilemma Facing the Fair Work Ombudsman', *Federal Law Review*, **41**, 1–33

Hardy, T., Howe, J. and Cooney, S. 2013. 'Less Energetic but More Enlightened?

Exploring the Fair Work Ombudsman's Use of Litigation in Regulatory Enforcement', *Sydney Law Review*, **35** (3), 565–97.

Howe, J. 2008. *Regulating for Job Creation* (Sydney: Federation Press).

Howe, J., Hardy, T. and Cooney, S. 2014. 'The Transformation of Enforcement of Employment Standards in Australia: A Review of the Fair Work Ombudsman's Activities from 2006–2012' (Melbourne: Centre for Employment and Labour Relations Law, Melbourne Law School, University of Melbourne).

Hwang, D. and Lee, B. 2012. 'Low Wages and Policy Options in the Republic of Korea: Are Policies Working?', *International Labour Review*, **151** (3), 243–59.

ILO. 2012. *Measuring Informality: A Statistical Manual on the Informal Sector and Informal Employment* (Geneva: ILO).

ILO. 2014. *World of Work Report 2014: Developing with Jobs* (Geneva: ILO).

ILO. 2015a. *World Employment and Social Outlook: Trends 2015* (Geneva: ILO).

ILO. 2015b. 'Non-Standard Forms of Employment', Report for discussion at the Meeting of Experts on Non-Standard Forms of Employment, MENSFE/2015 (Geneva: ILO).

ILO. 2015c. *World Employment and Social Outlook 2015: The Changing Nature of Jobs* (Geneva: ILO).

ILO. 2016. *Non-Standard Employment around the World: Understanding Challenges, Shaping Prospects* (Geneva: ILO).

IMF. 2016. *World Economic Outlook: Too Slow for Too Long* (Washington, DC: IMF).

Kagan, R., Gunningham, N. and Thornton, D. 2011. 'Fear, Duty and Regulatory Compliance: Lessons from Three Research Projects', in Parker, C. and Lehmann Nielsen, V. (eds), *Explaining Compliance: Business Responses to Regulation* (Cheltenham, UK and Northampton, MA, USA: Edward Elgar Publishing), pp. 37–58.

Kolben, K. 2007. 'Integrative Linkage: Combining Public and Private Regulatory Approaches in the Design of Trade and Labor Regimes', *Harvard International Law Journal*, **48** (1), https://www.academia.edu/3232855/Integrative_linkage_combining_public_and_private_regulatory_approaches_in_the_design_of_trade_and_labor_regimes?auto=download.

Lee, S. and McCann, D. 2011a. 'New Directions in Labour Regulation Research', in Lee, S. and McCann, D. (eds), *Regulating for Decent Work: New Directions in Labour Market Regulation* (Basingstoke, UK and Geneva, Switzerland: Palgrave Macmillan and ILO), pp. 1–27.

Lee, S. and McCann, D. (eds). 2011b. *Regulating for Decent Work: New Directions in Labour Market Regulation* (Basingstoke, UK and Geneva, Switzerland: Palgrave Macmillan and ILO).

Lee, S. and McCann, D. 2014. 'Regulatory Indeterminacy and Protection in Contemporary Labour Markets: Innovation in Research and Policy', in McCann, D., Lee, S., Belser, P., Fenwick, C., Howe, J. and Luebker, M. (eds), *Creative Labour Regulation: Indeterminacy and Protection in an Uncertain World* (Basingstoke, UK and Geneva, Switzerland: Palgrave Macmillan and ILO), pp. 3–28.

Locke, R. 2013. *The Promise and Limits of Private Power – Promoting Labor Standards in a Global Economy*, Cambridge Studies in Comparative Politics (New York: Cambridge University Press).

Malmberg, J. 2009. 'Enforcement of Labour Law', in Hepple, B. and Veneziani, B.

(eds), *The Transformation of Labour Law in Europe: A Comparative Study of 15 Countries 1945 to 2004* (Portland, OR: Hart Publishing), pp. 263–85.

McCann, D., Lee, S., Belser, P., Fenwick, C., Howe, J. and Luebker, M. (eds). 2014. *Creative Labour Regulation: Indeterminacy and Protection in an Uncertain World* (Basingstoke, UK and Geneva, Switzerland: Palgrave Macmillan and ILO).

McCann, D. and Murray, J. (2014). 'Prompting Formalisation Through Labour Market Regulation: A "Framed Flexibility" Model for Domestic Work', *Industrial Law Journal*, **43** (3), 319–48.

Milena Galazka, A. 2015. 'Report on the Global Survey into the Use of Information and Communication Technologies in National Labour Administration Systems', Working Paper, Governance and Tripartism Department (Geneva: ILO).

Morgan, B. and Yeung, K. 2007. *Law and Regulation: Text and Materials* (Cambridge: Cambridge University Press).

OECD. 2015. *Employment Outlook 2015* (Paris: OECD).

Ostry, J.D., Berg, A. and Tsangarides, C.G. 2014. 'Redistribution, Inequality, and Growth', IMF Staff Discussion Note, Research Department. SDN/14/02 (Washington, DC: IMF).

Piore, M. and Schrank, A. 2008. 'Toward Managed Flexibility: The Revival of Labour Inspection in the Latin World', *International Labour Review*, **147** (1), https://www.brown.edu/academics/sociology/sites/brown.edu.academics.sociology/files/uploads/PublishedILR-English.pdf.

Pires, R. 2008. 'Promoting Sustainable Compliance: Styles of Labour Inspection and Compliance Outcomes in Brazil', *International Labour Review*, **147**, 199–223.

Prassl, J. 2015. *The Concept of the Employer* (Oxford: Oxford University Press).

Sen, A. 1999. *Development as Freedom* (New York: Knopf).

Sen, A. 2000. 'Work and Rights', *International Labour Review*, **132**, 119–28.

Standing, G. 2011. *The Precariat: The New Dangerous Class* (London: Bloomsbury Academic).

Standing, G. 2014. *A Precariat Charter: From Denizens to Citizens* (London: Bloomsbury Academic).

UN. 2015. *Transforming our World: The 2030 Agenda for Sustainable Development*, Resolution adopted by the General Assembly on 25 September 2015 (A/RES/70/1).

UNDP. 2015. *Human Development Report 2015: Work for Human Development. Overview* (New York: UNDP).

Vega, M.L. and Robert, R. 2013. 'Labour Inspection Sanctions: Law and Practice of National Labour Inspection Systems', Working Document No. 26, Labour Administration and Inspection Programme (Geneva: ILO).

Vosko, L. 2006. 'Precarious Employment: Towards an Improved Understanding of Labour Market Insecurity', in Vosko, L. (ed.), *Precarious Employment: Understanding Labour Market Insecurity in Canada* (Montreal: McGill-Queens University Press), pp. 3–42.

Vosko, L. 2010. *Managing the Margins: Gender, Citizenship, and the International Regulation of Precarious Employment* (Oxford: Oxford University Press).

Weil, D. 2010. 'Improving Workplace Conditions Through Strategic Enforcement: A Report to the Wage and Hour Division', United States Department of Labor.

Weil, D. 2014a. 'Fissured Employment: Implications for Achieving Decent Work', in McCann, D., Lee, S., Belser, P., Fenwick, C., Howe, J. and Luebker, M. (eds), *Creative Labour Regulation: Indeterminacy and Protection in an Uncertain*

World (Basingstoke, UK and Geneva, Switzerland: Palgrave Macmillan and ILO), pp. 35–62.

Weil, D. 2014b. *The Fissured Workplace: Why Work Became So Bad for So Many, and What Can Be Done to Improve It* (Cambridge, MA: Harvard University Press).

Weil, D. and Pyles, A. 2005. 'Why Complain? Complaints, Compliance and the Problem of Enforcement in the US Workplace', *Comparative Labor Law and Policy Journal*, **27**, 59–92.

Winter, S.C. and May, P.J. 2001. 'Motivation for Compliance with Environmental Regulations', *Journal of Policy Analysis and Management*, **20** (4), 675–98.

World Bank. 2013. *World Development Report 2013: Jobs* (Washington, DC: World Bank).

World Bank. 2015. *Balancing Regulations to Promote Jobs: From Employment Contracts to Unemployment Benefits* (Washington, DC: World Bank).

Wright, M., Marsden, S. and Antonelli, A. 2004. 'Building an evidence base for the Health and Safety Commission Strategy to 2010 and beyond: A literature review of interventions to improve health and safety compliance', Research Report 198 (Reading: Health and Safety Executive).

WTO and ILO. 2009. *Globalization and Informal Jobs in Developing Countries* (Geneva: World Trade Organization and International Labour Organization).

PART I

Introduction

2. Reregulating for inclusive labour markets

Jill Rubery

Calls to change the approach to regulating labour markets have been on the rise. They have been coming from a wide range of sources, and not always from the usual suspects: that is, the mainstream economists who regard regulation as distorting the otherwise pure operation of markets. For some the problem is the narrowing of the segment of the population covered by traditional employment regulation and social protection (Stone and Arthurs, 2013; Vosko, 2010) associated with the standard employment relationship (SER), and the consequent growth in dualism (Palier and Thelen, 2010) conceptualised as an increase in 'working on the margins' (Vosko, 2010) or the rise of the precariat, an emergent class in itself (Standing, 2011). For these writers, as well as mainstream economists, regulation is said to be working for the insiders but not the outsiders, although their perspectives differ on whether regulation is simply ineffective or itself a cause of inequality. A common policy solution is said to be to move towards more comprehensive entitlements to social protection, not dependent on employment status (Vosko, 2010; Standing, 2011). This follows developments in developing economies where new social protection initiatives have increasingly been delinked from employment status and extended to the informal economy, often on a non-contributory basis (Barrientos, 2013; Martínez Franzoni and Sánchez-Ancochea, 2014).

The four main problems associated with current forms of regulation and protection can be identified as: the increasingly narrow scope of employment and social protection in many countries; the difficulty in identifying and effectively regulating the responsible employer; the lack of value attached to unpaid care work; and the increasing deprivation of human rights for those working at the margins. These are major and serious lacunae that need to be addressed. However, this chapter develops an argument that the current reform proposals that focus mainly on social policy are too narrowly specified. Although the debate is highlighting current deficiencies, it also misses the macroeconomic linkages between employment and social protection, as pointed out by Heintz and Lund (2012) and Martínez Franzoni and Sánchez-Ancochea (2013, 2014).

This approach reduces the function of employment regulation to that of social protection. But policies for greater social inclusion cannot be effective unless employers are willing to employ a wider range of people and provide more jobs that conform to the notion of decent work. Reducing employment regulation to its social protection function runs the risk of letting employers off the hook by giving up on direct attempts to change employer behaviour. It is true that employers may be incentivised to arrange employment in certain ways; by, for example, tax systems. They may be constrained in their employment choices by global competition or by global supply chains. But many employers continue to have the final say on the working conditions they provide for their own employees. Many also exercise indirect influence over conditions in their supplier organisations.

The case for a more nuanced and multifaceted approach to reform is developed in four stages. First, in section 2.1, I review the debates calling for reform from a variety of disciplinary perspectives. Second, in section 2.2, I identify some general principles for reform under three headings of: (1) reforming social policy; (2) extending employer obligations; and (3) strengthening enforcement and monitoring. The case for this three-pronged approach is based on the recognition that it is increasingly difficult to link social protection rights to employment status. This approach is most relevant for those in formal sector, continuous employment where employees are often earning above a minimum threshold. Jobs, however, are becoming more short term, informal and low paid. However, it is equally based on the premise that social policy is not a substitute for, but rather a complement to, employment regulation. On this analysis, strengthening and widening coverage of employment rights is also required. In developing this argument I identify eight separate functions of employment regulation. In section 2.3 I outline what a reform programme for inclusive labour markets might entail for each of these functions. The conclusion, section 2.4, considers the contribution of these proposals to the long-term project of generating political momentum for progressive regulatory reform.

2.1 EMPLOYMENT REGULATION AND THE INSIDER/OUTSIDER DIVIDE

The most influential and persistent argument against employment regulation stems from mainstream economics (Lee and McCann, 2011: 3).

The general premise underpinning the 1994 Organisation for Economic Co-operation and Development (OECD) Jobs Study (OECD, 1994) and the World Bank's *Doing Business* Index (Botero et al., 2004), is that the most efficient markets are free of institutional constraints.

Many studies (Howell, 2004; Howell et al., 2007; Berg and Kucera, 2008), including OECD analyses (OECD, 2006), find no direct correlation between regulation and macro employment performance and growth. In general, more regulated economies are found to have comparable overall performance to deregulated economies. Nevertheless, this debate has refused to die. Instead, the protagonists have changed the terms of the debate from performance to social justice issues, arguing that employment regulation is still harmful because it favours insiders over outsiders. Again, empirical evidence is lacking: the OECD was only able to produce quite a small number of studies (see Rubery, 2011 for a review), which often relied on inadequate policy specifications that fail to capture the design problems that may put groups at risk of exclusion.

Despite these theoretical and methodological critiques, recourse to insider/outsider discourse has still provided legitimacy for employment deregulation during the economic crisis and beyond. For example, the European Commission (2011: 7) called for reforms 'to reduce over-protection of workers with permanent contracts, and provide protection to those left outside or at the margins of the job market'. However, this rhetoric belies the fact that most of the actual changes are weakening protection for marginal groups by reducing protections for temporary contracts, lowering minimum wages, limiting the extension of collective agreements, and allowing firms to derogate from agreements (ETUI, 2014).

What is in fact striking is the lack of policies to make regulation more inclusive and to protect groups that are vulnerable to austerity measures. This is in contrast to developments during crises elsewhere: in Korea in the 1997 crisis (Lee and Yoo, 2008) unemployment protection was extended; and in the 2002 Argentinian currency crisis, Freeman (2009) found that strengthening employment and social protection assisted with adjustment to devaluation. In the absence of any positive policies for inclusivity, attention is better focused on contributions from law and other social sciences aimed at imagining more inclusive forms of employment and social protection.

Although Freedland (2013) has demonstrated the existence of major differences among legal regimes in the degree of SER regulation and in its influence on employment practices, the SER, in its various manifestations and meanings, has still provided the cornerstone of employment regulation in advanced countries and beyond. Two influential books have recently advocated seeking a new paradigm, rather than seeking to revive the SER.

The first, by Stone and Arthurs (2013), makes a primarily empirical case: the world has changed, fewer people are now covered by the SER, and there is little appetite for or possibility of its renewal. This work can be considered as the latest contribution to long-standing legal debates over how to overcome arbitrary divisions between standard and non-standard employment. Deakin (1986), for example, provided an early critique of the role of employment continuity criteria in United Kingdom (UK) employment law in creating workforce divisions. Collins (1990) identified the complexities in contract law that stem from the disintegration of the vertically integrated organisation. Supiot (2001) proposed extending social rights to encompass care work, and extending regulation of employee status to reduce the scope for narrowing the coverage. McCann (2012) has explored the potential for extending employment regulation to domestic workers, while Freedland and Kountouris (2011) have advocated the concept of 'personal employment relations' to extend regulation to cover many who are currently treated as self-employed. However, Stone and Arthurs (2013) appear to have gone further in rejecting the SER as a core framework of rights upon which to build. Their work in this respect can be contrasted with Bosch's (2004) proposal to extend the SER into a flexible and more inclusive concept, more open to diversity of contracts and life-course patterns.

The second book, by Vosko (2010), a political economist, also rejects what she describes as the SER-centric regulatory approach to resolve the problems of increasing segmentation between standard and non-standard work. (She observes that the approach is also adopted by the International Labour Organization and the European Union.) Vosko takes a more idealist stance against the SER and its capacity to create divisions between those in standard and non-standard work, and between those in paid work and unpaid care work. Efforts to rescue the SER, by extending it to forms of non-standard work or by integrating opportunities for care, only provide protection for those groups closest to the SER, thereby recreating new divisions and hierarchies. This analysis finds parallels in more directly legal scholarship, such as the work of Fredman (2004: 301) who advocates 'a shift away from the employment relationship to free-standing social rights'.

For Vosko (2010) and Fredman (2004), the SER is both a structural cause of inequality, and an anachronistic form. For them, the solution is to grant equality of status to all forms of work, to ensure equal treatment across the whole workforce. Vosko regards Supiot's proposal on care work, and Bosch's (2004) on extending SER coverage, to be promising but only partial solutions. For Vosko, setting a standard against which to measure deviation inevitably sets up a hierarchy. However, the other functions of a standard ought not to be ignored, in particular a standard's role in imposing obligations on an employer to provide regular and sufficient paid work. To place all forms of employment into one category might allow employers increasingly to slough off their customary obligations of maintaining employment contracts over periods of slack or down time (Supiot, 2001). While Stone and Arthurs (2013) make the case that these trends are in already in train and non-reversible, for Vosko and Fredman, the privileging of continuity in the employment relationship is in itself discriminatory and divisory.

The approach to policy renewal is also very different between the two volumes: Stone and Arthurs (2013) offer no grand scheme for re-regulation, only examples of mainly micro-level experiments in new forms of regulation, due to their focus on the 'plausible' in a context of political reluctance to re-regulate. Vosko, in contrast, provides 'alternative imaginaries' of a world that has addressed all the three main divisions: between precarious and standard wage work; between paid work and unpaid care work; and between citizens and non-citizens, through the development of transnational global citizenship. Neither approach fits the objectives here: the plausibility emphasis in Stone and Arthurs prevents recent experiments being evaluated against a set of principles for reform; in contrast, the imaginaries in Vosko's work take us beyond the immediately plausible. The discussion is of principles, but without specification of either the concrete possibilities for action or the key actors. The state is implicitly relied on to deliver more universal rights, but in Vosko's transnational citizenship imaginary, the nation-state loses power and legitimacy, with action implicitly dependent on transnational state action.

The debate on the sustainability of the SER at the core of employment regulation runs in parallel, and overlaps with some other social science perspectives on the development or intensification of insider/outsider divides, also associated with the term 'dualism'. These debates include political science analysis of insider/outsider divisions on engagement in politics (associated with Rueda, 2005 and colleagues); interdisciplinary debates on transitional labour markets to reduce the impact of life stages and other causes of outsider status on life chances (Schmid and Gazier, 2002); debates in industrial relations and social policy on emerging and reinforced dualism (associated with Palier and Thelen, 2010; Emmenegger, 2009; Hassel, 2014; amongst others); and feminist debates on the inequality in gender relations embedded in current forms of employment and social protection (associated with Vosko, 2010; Fredman, 2004; Wajcman, 1991).

Within this broad field, although difficult to classify by discipline, perhaps the best-known contribution is Standing's (2011) analysis of the rise of the precariat. This also provides the strongest condemnation of existing approaches to employment and social protection, labelling them 'labourist' (implying a critique of any protection attached to employment status); hierarchical (where anti-discrimination policies are critiqued as limited to 'mainly women with positional advantages'; Standing, 2011: 60); and coercive (for example where increased conditionality attached to social protection coerces the unemployed and inactive into poor-quality jobs). Standing's solution is to reverse the growing obligation to work by providing all with a basic income, to free citizens to make their own decisions. According to Standing, employers would then have to persuade people to work. By highlighting the erosion of rights to resist pressure to work, and by imagining an alternative world in which employers have to entice people to work, Standing provides some fresh and significant critiques of the current 'work first' mantra, and undermines the notion of the Scandinavian adult worker model as a utopia.

Two key criticisms can be made of both the analysis and policy solutions, beyond that of failing Stone and Arthurs's plausibility test. The first is that the long-term social, economic and political conditions for guaranteeing a basic income adequate to protect living standards are not specified. A progressive government could bring in a reasonably generous basic income but this could still be eroded in the future, as demonstrated by the speed of cutbacks in social protection under austerity in some European countries. The second is Standing's proposal to leave all regulation of employment to the market: by calling for full commodification of jobs, all issues of unfair practices and power relations between employees and managers are apparently resolved without the need for labourist protections, as work would be voluntary. As with Vosko, the function of protection is only that of social protection and solidarity among citizens, not the need to hold employers to account. Organisations, however, are complex political institutions. It is implausible that the threat of labour market quits would be sufficient to ensure fair treatment without any detailed 'labourist' regulations.

Standing is also concerned with the risk of political instability if the precariat becomes increasingly excluded from social rights and disengaged from mainstream politics. This chimes with the work of Rueda (2005) and colleagues whose starting premise is that governments tend to protect the median voter, often at the expense of the outsider, giving rise to exclusion and radical political movements, often on the right. These exclusionary policies are found in social democratic as well as more conservative or neoliberal regimes. Moreover, King and Rueda (2008) argue that there is an inherent tendency for capital to seek cheap labour; if labour market systems set minimum floors too high, the cheap labour will be found in the more informal or non-standard sector. Thus, all societies have their functional equivalents. This position is very close to that of mainstream economics when it argues that efforts to protect those on the margins may be counterproductive, harming those whom they are intended to help. Their claims are, however, based on shaky data: for example a high proportion of non-standard work in Sweden (King and Rueda, 2008: 292 and Table 7) is used to justify the argument. However, the fact that, for example, part-time work in Sweden is relatively more regulated, skilled and higher paid is not discussed. Rueda's approach contrasts with the earlier transitional labour market analysis provided by Schmid and Gazier (2002) (amongst others) who argued that smart policy innovations could provide a win–win outcome, allowing insiders to be less trapped by requirements for continuous and long hours of employment by offering them flexibility over the life cycle in return for opportunities for outsiders to gain work experience. This more positive approach allows for some alignment of interests between insiders and outsiders, a position also taken by Emmenegger (2009, 2010) in a critique of Rueda, who questions whether outsiders are less in favour of employment protection than insiders.

Palier and Thelen (2010) provide an alternative account of increasing dualism, in countries such as France and Germany. They see these trends as the outcome of a complementary and reinforcing process of change in closely coupled industrial relations, labour market and social protection systems. Instead of institutional complementarities promoting stability and inclusivity, as hypothesised under the varieties of capitalism perspective, these interdependencies have created the momentum towards dualism as trade unions, employers and the state have protected the core at the expense of the periphery (see also Hassel, 2014). This work neglects the changing labour force – towards, for example, more women and more migrants – such that the growth of dualism may reflect in part the integration of previously excluded groups, particularly women in Germany. However, these analyses do link the growth of non-standard and flexible employment to growing divides in access to social protection. This demonstrates the pivotal role played by employment in interconnecting core institutional fields in any social model including social protection, care services, family system, education systems, production and trade, and so on (Rubery, 2010). These interconnections mean that any change to social protection systems also needs to be compatible with and sustained by employment systems (Heintz and Lund, 2012). Policies to change employment and social protection thus need to consider the connections between the different spheres which are likely to be specific to the architecture of each social model (Bosch et al., 2007, 2009).

This focus on interconnecting spheres has resonances with the final perspective on the insider/outsider debate reviewed here: that is, feminist scholarship. For feminists the problem is that the SER is often mistakenly considered only as a function of labour market institutions, ignoring the institutional arrangements in the family and social reproduction sphere upon which the SER rests (Vosko, 2010; Fredman, 2004; Wajcman, 1991). Women's provision of care work enables men to participate in the SER, and employers to demand continuity of employment and long working hours. This analysis not only questions the desirability of retaining the SER concept but also calls for an integrated approach to reform in order to deliver more social protection to the hidden outsiders: those who care in the domestic economy.

2.2   BEYOND THE INSIDER/OUTSIDER FOCUS

These divergent debates have highlighted many shortcomings in the current system of regulation, most of which have always been present, although they may be increasing in importance. To recap, the four main issues identified that require reform and renewal of regulation of employment and social protection include:

1. the increasingly narrow scope of employment and social protection in many countries;
2. the difficulty in identifying and effectively regulating the responsible employer;
3. the lack of value attached to unpaid care work; and
4. the increasing deprivation of human rights for those working at the margins.

These four problems provide ample motivation for seeking a comprehensive reform of employment and social regulation in favour of greater inclusivity. But a progressive reform agenda needs to be separated from the pervasive and potentially insidious insider/outsider rationale. We need to invent a new language for reform to avoid contributing, even if inadvertently, to what Hirschman (1991: 11) labelled the rhetoric of perversity, a tactic used against progressive policies. Supporters of progressive regulation, here employment protection, are represented as either misguided or fraudulent because the regulation supports relatively privileged employees to the detriment of the excluded. The wider inequalities, for example between capital and labour, may thereby be overlooked. Austerity policy measures are indeed promoted by a rhetoric of reducing protection for the overprivileged, even though the changes are more likely to harm the more vulnerable (ETUI, 2014). Counter-arguments can be made that increasing competition for all jobs may be to the disadvantage of outsiders. They are more likely to belong to groups which face difficulty in accessing employment due to discrimination and stereotyping such that, as Emmenegger (2010) argues, preferences for employment security reflect differential risks of discrimination. Outsiders such as the unemployed, women and older workers may favour job security even if unlikely personally to achieve job security. Furthermore, arguments against current protections risk promoting deconstruction of institutionalised protections, but without an evident political will to reconstruct security on a more inclusive basis.

A broader approach to reform is needed which includes developing not only better forms of protection for those in precarious jobs, but also policies that seek to halt or reverse the trend to precarious employment. To address only the former is effectively to ignore employers' responsibility as the core agents that decide on the terms of employment engagement, even in a globalised world. In segmentation theory it is employers' selection, investment and retention decisions that create segmented or divided labour markets (Osterman, 1984, 1994; Rubery, 1978, 2007). These divisions may be influenced by various forms of social stratification, but it is employer actions that reinforce and reproduce these divisions by, for example, restricting employment opportunities for those who do not conform to the ideal-type underpinning the SER concept of an independent and fully fit adult. The increased slipperiness of the concept of the employer (see Weil, 2012; Marchington et al., 2005; Prassl, 2015) is also not a reason to reduce efforts to control and shape employers' influence over employment arrangements. Instead, there may be a need for more joint employer responsibility across a supply chain or franchise network (Weil, 2012; Marchington et al., 2005). The more employment is controlled by multinational companies operating outside the national jurisdiction, the more difficult it is to use national regulations to promote decent work conditions. But this argument should be used to further strengthen international efforts at regulation. These are not addressed in detail within this chapter, but the notion of limited scope for national action by employers may also be exaggerated, particularly in the developed world where both highly regulated and deregulated economies continue to compete in global markets. Moreover, studies of more deregulated liberal market economies suggests that the outcome is not to create uniform low-level employment conditions but to increase the dispersion of employment conditions and rewards, indicating the exercise of employer discretion in the distribution of quasi rents (Simón, 2010).

This argument suggests that a reform agenda needs to include not only social policy enacted mainly by the state, but also obligations on employers. These obligations may be enacted by the state or through collective bargaining or both. Whatever the mechanism – in the UK context, for example, it would have to be largely state-enacted, at least initially – ways need to be found not only of developing new rights, but also of promoting voice, enforcement and monitoring of rights and regulation. This three-pronged approach is represented in Figure 2.1.

Three key themes run through this proposed strategy: first, disentanglement of social rights and protections from employment status; second, extension of rights at work to non-standard and marginal workforce groups; and third, promoting transparency in employment arrangements to facilitate monitoring, and pressure for fair treatment. The first two themes can be considered to be general principles reinforcing the notion that proposals for new forms of social protection as alternatives to employment relations, as found for example in Standing's and Vosko's work, only address part of the needs for reform. In particular, they take employers out of the picture when it is their strategies and actions that are the prime motors of dualism and insecurity. Furthermore, by separating out social policy proposals from new obligations on employers, the potential both for extending SER-type employment and for reducing the penalties for those not in an SER-type relationship are made clearer. This moves the approach beyond Stone and Arthurs's search for incremental and small-scale changes that may include both types of developments. The focus on transparency as the third theme is partly a response to the absence of obvious opportunities to promote more collective responses. The European Union, for example, has recently stressed the importance of transparency in providing the knowledge base upon which equal pay claims can be pursued. Increasing awareness of inequalities can stimulate new collective responses to unfair pay, such as the strikes of fast-food workers and other low-income works in the United States (US) in the wake of the debates on inequality after the Occupy movement (Milkman, 2013). It is, in fact, hard to imagine how inclusive labour markets can develop without greater transparency, and the use of that knowledge to hold employers more publically to account.

A key rationale for this three-pronged approach is that employment plays a pivotal role in the economic and social system, such that the function of employment protection includes, but is by no means confined to, the provision of social protection. Employment not only shapes the everyday experience of many citizens, but it also acts as the interface between production and social reproduction (Rubery, 2010). It is the very combination of the centrality of employment and its multifaceted nature that demands a more multifaceted reform agenda. Indeed

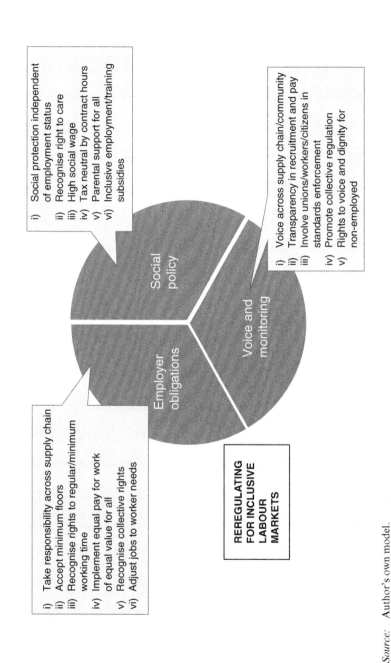

i) Social protection independent of employment status
ii) Recognise right to care
iii) High social wage
iv) Tax neutral by contract hours
v) Parental support for all
vi) Inclusive employment/training subsidies

i) Voice across supply chain/community
ii) Transparency in recruitment and pay
iii) Involve unions/workers/citizens in standards enforcement
iv) Promote collective regulation
v) Rights to voice and dignity for non-employed

Social policy

Voice and monitoring

Employer obligations

i) Take responsibility across supply chain
ii) Accept minimum floors
iii) Recognise rights to regular/minimum working time
iv) Implement equal pay for work of equal value for all
v) Recognise collective rights
vi) Adjust jobs to worker needs

REREGULATING FOR INCLUSIVE LABOUR MARKETS

Source: Author's own model.

Figure 2.1 A policy framework for inclusive labour markets

41

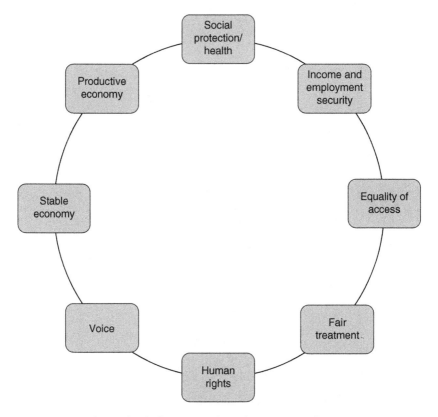

Figure 2.2   The multiple functions of employment regulation

there are at least eight different functions for employment regulation which should be addressed in any reform agenda. These are shown in Figure 2.2.

The first function is to shape access to social protection for employees during periods of non-employment. It is this interface which generates many of the exclusionary effects of the SER (Vosko, 2010; Standing, 2011). A major issue is thus to develop more universal social protection, and so more widespread decommodification. However, as recent contributions have identified (Heintz and Lund, 2012; Martínez Franzoni and Sánchez-Ancochea, 2013), formal employment also provides the fiscal base upon which welfare states are built. Universal protection may not be sustainable where employment arrangements become primarily based on informal employment outside the tax system. The problem of social protection therefore cannot be solved without employment reform; these two-way interactions between employment and social protection need to be recognised.

A second function of employment regulation, still within its role in social reproduction, is to provide for income security. Again there may be strong divides between standard employment with guaranteed hours and more insecure, non-standard jobs subject to variable hours. Social protection may offer some guarantees through, for example, in-work benefits, but the costs of these benefits to the state depends again upon employer actions.

Rights of access to employment is a third function as labour market exclusion may be considered the outcome of employers' selective hiring policies. Rights to non-discrimination, for example, can provide important protection against exclusion and marginalisation.

A fourth function is to secure fair treatment throughout the employment hierarchy; that is, both fair conditions and fair processes. Current insiders benefit directly, but it is outsiders who may be most at risk of unfair conditions and arbitrary management, even if they are able to find employment. Reforms need to focus on how to extend fair treatment to currently marginalised and non-standard workers, and how to rethink regulation to adjust to employment under interorganisational networks or partnerships, and fissured employer responsibilities (Weil, 2012; Marchington et al., 2005).

A fifth function is to ensure respect for human rights, including rights to non-discrimination and to dignity (Sayer, 2007). A more inclusionary regulatory systems might need to guarantee human rights to those outside of employment, who may be subject to undue pressure and coercion from state agents when claiming benefits (Chan and Bowpitt, 2005). A sixth function for regulation is to ensure rights to voice and representation. But a reform agenda needs to focus on making these rights more inclusive in workplaces and beyond.

The final two functions for employment regulation relate to the macro-economy through its role in promoting economic stability and long-term productivity growth. These stability and productivity growth objectives may been seen as reinforcing the position of insiders, as it is they, for example, who are able to benefit from work-sharing during recessions, and to contribute through their tacit knowledge and skills to productivity growth. The issue for reform is to identify how far these benefits can be extended and generalised, but without rejecting the overall objectives of stability and high productivity.

A reform agenda thus needs to address the exclusionary problems associated with the standard employment relationship. But it also needs to be more ambitious. The continuing centrality of both employers and employment arrangements to the social model requires policies to hold employers more to account, and to promote more inclusive employment arrangements, as well as providing more universal social protection.

2.3   APPLYING THE FRAMEWORK

To develop these arguments further, Table 2.1 provides an overview of a reform agenda across all eight functions of employment regulation. For each specific function the current deficiencies with respect to inclusion are first identified. The other three columns set out possible social policy reforms, possible extensions to employer obligations, and possible ways of improving compliance and monitoring of regulation. This latter point is important given the decline in union presence in workplaces, and evidence that the impact of regulation is not only indeterminate (McCann et al., 2014), but also likely to be reinterpreted though a managerial lens when implemented without checks and balances (Deakin et al., 2011). New strategies to promote enforcement of rights may also need to draw on support from some of the new social movements that extend outside of the workplace, such as living wage campaigns, where the aim is to increase the general control on employers of low-wage labour.

The purpose is to provide a template for reform based on general principles, not detailed proposals, as feasible reforms depend on the specific national context. The objective is to identify potential directions for reform towards more inclusive employment and social systems, based on arguments concerning the current deficiencies of existing regulation with respect to inclusivity. Many of the proposed reforms have not been tried and tested, so that this review may be regarded as speculative. However, this is also the case with other sets of proposals within the insider/outsider debates, whether these are the efficiency benefits of deregulated labour markets – for mainstream economists – or the social benefits of promoting social protection over employment protection. In outlining these possible directions for policy development, some examples of specific regulatory measures or approaches that follow the lines of reform suggested are, nevertheless, discussed.

Access to Social Protection and Health

The origins of the intertwining of employment status and social protection vary across countries. For example, the regularisation of employment in the UK has been linked to employers' need to comply with social protection regulation (Deakin and Wilkinson, 2005). Where social protection follows insurance principles these links are strongest, and the potential

Table 2.1 A reform agenda for inclusive labour markets across eight dimensions to employment regulation

	Insider/outsider problem	Social policy reforms	Extending the SER	Improving voice, enforcement and monitoring
Social protection/ health	Exclusion of non-standard workers and carers	Disconnect access and contributions from employment status	Consider taxing wage bill so contributions not linked to employment status or earnings	Universal benefits increase take-up, awareness
Individual income and employment security at work	Evasion through non-standard work	In-work benefits to be coupled with high minimum wage, guaranteed hours provisions	High minimum wage plus rights to guaranteed hours, across supply chain Protection against arbitrary dismissal for all	Publicity re universal minimum standards plus collective community action
Access to employment	Discrimination against non-linear careers and those needing workplace adjustments Lack of support for care and carers	Support for disabled in getting to work and at workplace Accreditation of training for unemployed and returners Support for care through childcare, paid leave, etc.; also for non-employed	Enforcement of non-discrimination in recruitment including age-related Adjustment to schedules, etc. for carers at point of recruitment not linked to tenure Adjustments for partially disabled, etc.	Reinforce opportunities to challenge failures to adjust to worker needs and discrimination on grounds of age

Table 2.1 (continued)

	Insider/outsider problem	Social policy reforms	Extending the SER	Improving voice, enforcement and monitoring
Fair employment conditions	Variation of conditions by contract and employer Exclusion from grievance procedures Increased inequality in rewards	Remove benefit sanctions for those who quit due to unfair conditions	High minimum standards across supply chain Co-employer responsibility for standards in networked organisations Non-standard workers included in grievance systems at workplace General rights to regular/minimum working hours and to equal pay for equal value	High minima lower incentives to fragmentation Increase transparency in pay and working time to facilitate monitoring Allow for claims against co-employers Community-based living wage campaigns to promote high minimum standards
Rights to non-discrimination and dignity at work	More disadvantaged – benefit recipients, migrants, etc. – subject to discrimination, lack of respect	Policies to reduce harassment and coercion of benefit recipients Good-quality care a precondition for carers being expected to seek wage work	Protect those raising grievances or quitting jobs against penalties (e.g. tied labour due to visa rules)	Reduce costs (financial, employment) of making complaints Independent complaints system for benefit recipients
Rights to voice and	Workers and subcontractors	Opportunities for voice among non-employed	Information and consultation rights,	Transparency and high minimum standards

representation	excluded Non-employed lack voice	carers and benefit recipients	stakeholder rights for all workers in workplace, across companies and supply chains	to empower citizens and worker groups Institutions for voice for the non-employed and marginally employed
Stabilise employment	Protection for those in work and often in permanent full-time work, not for others	Social policy subsidies for all at workplace. In-work benefit systems should not allow employers to pass on costs of demand fluctuations	Extend work sharing to all contract types to receive subsidies	
Promote productivity growth	Exclusion of non-standard workers from training and high-productivity work systems	Training subsidies for all including non-employed	Promote higher productivity workplaces and extend higher-quality employment relationships, training opportunities to wider range of workplaces and workers Extend leave arrangements, rights to employee-oriented flexibility, to reinforce employment relationship for more workers	Enforcement of rights to leave, flexibility and training

for gaps in coverage and/or inequalities between social insurance benefits and social assistance the largest. The linkages to employment records may extend to duration, continuity, working time and employment contract status (Leschke, 2007a, 2007b), with outcomes reflecting country-specific eligibility criteria and employment patterns. For example, in a four-country study Leschke (2007a) found wide variations in the shares of the unemployed entitled to social benefits. Some countries link benefits to citizenship, for example for pensions in Denmark and the Netherlands (Ginn, 2004), although the citizenship pension in overall social provision has declined. Universality of social benefits may be improved by limited contribution requirements, or by credits for time spent as primary carer for children. The latter applies to the state pension in the UK, but only gives access to a low, flat-rate pension.

The precise gaps in protection for non-standard workers or those providing unpaid care work vary significantly across countries. Nevertheless, three common reform principles for generating greater inclusivity are suggested. First, state-mandated social benefits should be high, to avoid inegalitarian top-ups to state benefits (for example, maternity pay or pensions) by selective employers. Some earnings-related element to state-based benefits might be less inegalitarian than flat-rate benefits and market top-ups. Second, eligibility should be independent of employment status; a key example here is the UK's National Health Service. Insurance-based health services may also grant access to those without employment status, as is common in Europe, though this may maintain, for example, women's dependency on a male breadwinner. Disentangling social protection from employment status should raise the status attached to care work, but this is more likely to be effective through individual, not family entitlements. The third principle is that reforms should maintain and even improve employer contributions to welfare funding. An example where universal social protection systems have been jeopardised by labour market trends is Costa Rica; employers only paid towards the welfare system for formal employees, so that the fiscal base to support social protection was eroded (Martínez Franzoni and Sánchez-Ancochea, 2013). In the UK, exemptions to contributions for those employing workers on low wages may also be encouraging the growth of short-hours, low-paid employment, as well as limiting fiscal support for the welfare state. It may be better to consider taxing the employer on their wage bill rather than linking contributions directly to individuals and employment contracts.[1]

---

[1]   In Germany, low-income jobs known as 'mini-jobs' also provide workers and employers with subsidies. As the income is exempt from tax, the workers do

Income and Employment Security

Income security depends on both employment security and social protection. Outsiders or marginal workers are often denied sufficient wage income, so that high social benefits are important for income protection. So too, however, are wage levels and guaranteed work hours, an issue thrown into debate in the UK due to the rise of zero-hours contracts (Resolution Foundation, 2013). The unemployed have difficulties taking zero-hours jobs as income may be insufficient and variable, and quitting the job may lead to benefit penalties. Although employees can enjoy some income protection through in-work benefits, the risk is that employers may pass responsibility for guaranteeing adequate income onto the state, either by paying a low wage or by varying hours to fit demand (Grimshaw et al., 2016). Extending rights to guaranteed hours – possibly averaged over more than a week – could protect both employees and the state, while still providing for scheduling flexibility where needed.

Job security regulation underpins income protection in many countries, although mainly for the so-called insiders. Resistance to reduced job protection will be stronger where social protection is weak and benefits low. Employment protection guards against arbitrary and unfair treatment of individuals and helps to share the costs of cyclical downturns or restructuring. Protection against the former could well be extended to all workers regardless of contract or length of employment, as already happens, for example, in the UK for sex or racial discrimination. The issue over whether job loss compensation should be linked to employment duration is more complex. The individual with longer tenure has invested more in that particular job than someone who has just joined. The question of rights in a job and in a workplace thus extends beyond the question of fairness in selecting between a tenured and a newly arrived worker. Moreover a long-tenured person may face more risk of non-employment (Tinsley, 2012). On the other hand, the recently hired employee may have waited a long time for this opportunity, had little time to benefit from it, and may be a more productive worker. These considerations point to a mixture of protections, ranging from high social benefits, improved access to employment (in line with the flexicurity debate in Europe), but still some higher compensation for those with longer tenure.

---

not have to pay social contributions, and the employer has been able to set a low hourly wage, at least until the introduction of the national minimum wage in 2015. However, unlike the UK, employers have to pay a higher rate of social contributions for these workers, thereby maintaining the fiscal base for the welfare state and reducing the subsidy.

Equality of Access to Employment

Employers are the gatekeepers to employment: their hiring, selection and retention strategies determine access to employment. Interrupted employment due to unemployment, care work or even part-time work can often result in long-term scarring effects (Gangl, 2006; Olsen and Walby, 2004). Moreover, training or qualifications undertaken at non-standard times may be insufficient to secure new careers. Indeed the key barrier to re-entry often lies in employer attitudes towards those following non-linear careers. This contrasts, for example, with the European flexicurity debate, which regards motivating employees to retrain as the main issue.

Most current constraints on employer hiring are non-discrimination laws; in Europe now covering gender, ethnicity, religion, sexual orientation and age. Changing age norms in recruitment is vital to enable non-linear careers, but requires active interventions to change social norms with respect to age. Accreditation of retraining programmes might improve signals to employers, but in the UK, for example, employers appear to pay limited attention to vocational training (UKCES, 2011). Labour market structures need to be more flexible to adjust to stages of the life-course, and more open to those displaced from employment. The current concern is with employability and workers fitting the market, but markets also need to fit the workers (Schmid, 2010). That is, employment needs to adapt to the circumstances of the individual (Deakin, 2009: 28), if the objective of more involvement of carers, older workers and the partially disabled in employment is to be achieved (Deakin, 2009).

Additional social support may be needed for the partially disabled and for those providing care. For carers, there is a need for alternative care provision, and for leave provisions to enable interruptions without loss of employment position (Supiot, 2001). These kinds of support are particularly important for women, although Standing has argued that this support is currently available only for women with 'positional advantages', by which he means simply having a formal sector job. However, the alternative to such support is to reinforce gender difference by forcing women into fragmented careers due to childbirth. There are nevertheless strong arguments for some paid leave for childbirth being provided to all, as those not in employment should not be under pressure to seek employment for a period following childbirth. As Blofield and Martínez Franzoni (2015) found, where paid leave is given to non-employees, this has particularly progressive consequences in countries with high shares of informal and self-employed workers. There are also strong arguments for extending rights to leave to men as well as to women, in order to improve work–life balance, reduce gender stereotyping by employers, and encourage sharing of care work. However the leave may need to be only for the men to take: sharing is unlikely to work while men earn higher wages and payment for leave is low.

Fair Treatment

Fairness has both a distributive and a process dimension. Non-standard or marginalised workers face problems on both counts. Inclusive labour markets require a high minimum wage floor applicable to all contract types. Where wage differentials between organisations for low-skilled jobs are low, incentives to outsource are also reduced (Grimshaw et al., 2015). The informal economy is outside the direct impact of regulation, but recent research has found a strong lighthouse effect with legal minimum wages influencing pay in the informal economy, although mainly for higher-paid informal workers (Boeri et al., 2011; Ham, 2013).

Fairness can relate to pay relativities or to income needs. Movements in several countries have promoted standards based on living wages rather than minimum wages (Reich et al., 2014). Living standards provide a basis for connecting standards in employment to social protection standards for those outside employment. However, the issue of how to reward for additional responsibilities, skill or effort still has to be resolved at the workplace.

Minimum standards are also needed to regulate flexible work (Grimshaw et al., 2016). These could include rights to minimum work periods, to prior notice of changes to schedules, and so on. The trend away from the SER can only be reversed by actions to control employers' use of the flexible employment form or by changing the incentives for flexible working, for example by requiring premiums to be paid for flexible labour to compensate for lack of security. This could be said to apply in the Australian practice of setting a higher minimum wage for casual workers, but this is mainly compensation for lack of other benefits such as paid leave and vacations. This may, however, be more effective than the situation in the UK, where casual workers are legally entitled to paid holidays but are often unaware of their rights (CIPD, 2013). However, there is also a case for a premium simply to reflect flexibility in scheduling and hours, rather than merely to compensate for lack of other benefits.

Problems of fair treatment at work extend throughout the employment hierarchy, not only at the bottom. With respect to fair pay, the main legal regulation is the principle of equal pay for work of equal value, but this at present applies only between men and women, and is not a general principle applied at the workplace. It is, however, true that the European temporary agency work directive provides for equality in pay with directly employed workers after 12 weeks working at a client's establishment. There may be a case for extending this right to all within a workplace, organisation or even supply chain in order to develop a wide constituency to benefit from fair pay principles. The need for regulations to promote proportionate and fair pay between types of jobs and workers has grown with the trend towards individualised pay, which has not only provided employers with more discretion, but has also reduced knowledge of pay differences, thereby making it more difficult to monitor for fair treatment. Regulation requiring pay transparency may lead to employers exercising more constraint when setting individualised pay. This is suggested by the experience in Sweden, where more individualised pay bargaining has not led to widening income inequality, possibly because of greater pay transparency and gender pay audits (Anxo and Ericson, 2012). Extending the principle of equal pay for work of equal value could promote a more general commitment to fair pay, but measures to increase fairness within organisations still need to be combined with high minimum floors to reduce disparities across firms and sectors.

In complex networked organisations it may be unclear where responsibility for fair process actually lies (Marchington et al., 2005). Workers of all contract statuses, except the genuinely self-employed, need to be covered by workplace grievance procedures to protect agency workers against unfair treatment by a client. Co-responsibility for employees across collaborating employing organisations, as applies for example in the US (Earnshaw et al., 2002; Weil, 2012), may be preferable to treating subcontracted staff as the sole responsibility of the subcontractor. The US does have a concept of joint employment; interestingly the new German national minimum wage regulation puts the onus on the client for compliance across the supply chain.

Human Rights

In principle some human rights, such as the right not to suffer discrimination, often apply to all in employment and with immediate effect; that is, without qualifying periods or employment status requirements. However, many countries lack effective enforcement of these rights. Improving enforcement may require measures to reduce complaint costs, not only through better grievance procedures without fees, but also protecting against job loss and exclusion through poor references. Another group perhaps even more vulnerable to lack of dignity and respect is those in receipt of benefits. Requirements on public officials to treat claimants with respect could be a necessary partial corrective to the increasing pressure on claimants to behave in particular ways determined by the state and imposed by 'street-level' bureaucrats (Lipsky, 1980). Independent complaint systems need to be established or reinforced, but will only be effective with a change if the rhetoric around 'welfare scroungers' can be changed. Those responsible for care should also be protected from coercion to take employment, if the quality and availability of care is in doubt. Research suggests that in the UK not enough attention is paid to the matching of jobs to available care arrangements for lone parents (Whitworth, 2013).

Voice

Rights to voice and representation for marginalised workers are both a mechanism for enforcing rights, and also rights in themselves. Marginalised workers may face three types of representation gaps: there may be no institutional provision for voice at the workplace; they may be ineligible to participate if employed by another organisation (a temporary work agency, for example); or they may face barriers to participating due to part-time or unsocial hours or to language problems (for example if they are migrants). Each gap requires different reform strategies. Extending information and consultation rights to all in the workplace is straightforward enough, but where there are stakeholder rights in corporate governance, defining stakeholders and their interests is more complex. The need to extend rights beyond those on SER-type contracts is clear, but the extension could include all those working at a common workplace, or even those working along the supply chain.

To fill institutional gaps, new mechanisms may be needed not only inside the workplace, but also outside the workplace; that is, across communities or supply chains, as for example in the case of the US Justice for Janitors campaign (Erickson et al., 2002). Other examples include the living wage campaigns in the UK (ACAS, 2013) and the US (Reich et al., 2014). These external voice and representation mechanisms may focus on issues of fair conditions for community groups, or they may seek to establish standards for an occupation, that is, setting external standards for employers to follow. Vosko and Thomas (2014) found that the involvement of unions and other workforce groups was important in enforcing minimum employment standards in non-unionised workplaces in Ontario.

The most difficult issue is to provide voice and representation for the unemployed and others outside wage work, such as carers. Organisations for the non-employed can emerge or be supported, while retaining links with occupational or professional associations, or trade unions, to facilitate re-entry to work through support for updating skills and maintaining social contacts.

Stable Economy

Employment regulation may assist in stabilising the economy over the business cycle by reducing incentives to employers to lay off workers and by encouraging work-sharing, thereby reducing the downward multiplier as people are laid off and consumption falls. Although these policies favour insiders, the alternative of more rapid employment adjustment may simply intensify the downturn in demand, as found over the recent financial crisis when the degree of employment change was highly variable across countries depending in part on regulation (Messenger and Ghosheh, 2013). Thus, practices which directly benefit insiders may protect overall employment, and limit the downturn. Nevertheless, work-sharing mechanisms could be extended to those in non-standard jobs or outside employment at the point when the downturn starts. Furthermore, if the downturn is associated with particular sectors, measures to stabilise the economy should not be used to postpone indefinitely necessary sectoral adjustments to changed conditions. Employment regulation may also underpin macro-institutional arrangements. For example, regulation theory (Boyer, 1979) has emphasised the role of collective wage-setting institutions in securing regular rising real wages in the post-Second World War period, and thereby underpinning the mass consumption market in the Fordist period (Boyer, 1979). The SER system likewise reduced the costs of welfare state development by ensuring that employers paid for labour even when demand for labour decreased (Supiot, 2001). Thus the issue of equity across individuals or groups is not the only issue for social justice; the stability of the employment and social welfare system also affects the volume of jobs available, and the capacity of the state to provide social assistance.

Some proposals to unify protection across employment statuses may risk further commodification of labour. Thus, in seeking to improve conditions for flexible workers it is important not to inadvertently spread flexibility through the whole employment system, indirectly increasing welfare state costs as well as individual insecurity. The UK's proposed universal credit system falls into this category. Employers could rethink their offers of guaranteed hours to any groups of low-paid staff (Grimshaw et al., 2016), as the new system will allow them to pass more of the costs of variable demand on to the state. Their employees may be eligible for state-funded top-ups if the volume of paid work hours decreased, and employers may be able to pass more of their employment obligations on to the state.

Productive Economy

Arrangements which promote investment in the workforce on the one hand, and commitment by the employed workforce on the other, can be expected to foster long-term productivity growth. Marsden (1999) sees these as mutual benefits of the SER, thereby underpinning its widespread usage and long-term survival. Insider employees not only develop the appropriate skills, but also the tacit knowledge that provide them with an edge over less-expensive outsiders in any implied or actual competition for their jobs. Long-term employees can also be considered to develop a form of property stake in their company and their profession, as they have invested time and effort in the company, and derive much of their social identity from that investment.

A key issue is whether there is scope for extending the share of jobs where there can be mutual benefits from insider-type employment relationships. In other words, whether the trend to more commodified employment relationships is irreversible, or whether employers might rediscover longer-term employment relationships and develop employee capacities to enhance productivity instead of cost-cutting at current productivity levels, if exposed to more 'beneficial constraints' (Streeck, 1997) in the form of employment regulation. This approach sees regulation as a means to extend regular or better-paid employment to stimulate higher productivity in a wider range of jobs and organisations. This contrasts with the pessimistic mainstream perspective (Lindbeck and Snower, 2002), where efforts to extend insider status to jobs where this is not market led will lead to job destruction, increasing unemployment or informal employment. The optimistic perspective assumes that encouragements to employers to invest in employees – perhaps through more ambitious individualised learning accounts schemes and employer-training levies than those found so far in Europe (CEDEFOP, 2009) – would extend quality employment, provided however that these initiatives were not limited to those in SER-type status. For example, long-term employment relations can be extended to more women by providing rights to paid leave and to flexible working to allow retention of their employment position, ensuring continued opportunities to utilise skills and develop potential. Where women workers are forced to leave the labour market or change employers, this frequently results in occupational downgrading (Connelly and Gregory, 2008), or longer than necessary economic inactivity.

The role of quality employment relationships in underpinning long-term productivity enhancement provides workers with one of their main sources of leverage in the employment relationship, outside of collective action. This leverage, based on the dependence of employers on specific employees and their knowledge and commitment, also generates segmentation between those in an employment relationship and those outside the organisation. To the extent that the principle of disposable labour spreads through the employment system and replaces the notion of mutual dependency, the outcome is likely to be lower overall productivity and national income, although profits may still rise. Employment regulation which provides a platform for the development of mutual dependency (Marsden, 1999) thus also feeds into more macro struggles over the declining wage share and living standards.

2.4 CONCLUSION

The growing international claims that current employment regulation is not fit for purpose and needs reforming appear compelling. There are clear needs to address issues of narrow coverage, especially in developing countries; in relation to women's work; to extend coverage to those on non-standard contracts; and to find ways to provide rights under more complex employment relationships that span organisational boundaries. More disadvantaged social groups are facing increasing pressure to engage in work, regardless of job quality, and without adjusting job tasks and scheduling to meet the person's needs. However, these valid critiques of current practices do not warrant the abandonment of SER-type regulation, understood here as regulation to constrain the actions of employers and require them to provide some guarantees of continuity, hours and income, and some mechanisms for employee fair treatment and voice. The argument made here is that holding employers to account must be central to any reform agenda. Otherwise, not only may the conditions of work deteriorate, but more of the costs of the decommodification of labour may be passed to the state or to families.

Instead of more flexible employment, policies are needed to extend and reinforce SER-type relationships, alongside new higher legal minimum standards, and mechanisms to reduce the penalties for not being on an SER-type contract. Indeed SER-type relationships are still dominant, at least in their weak forms in OECD countries, and more needs to be done to reinforce and to renew the guarantees associated with these contracts. This can reduce the scope for employers to pass labour costs on to the state. In a world of weak unions and increased employer power it is important to find new ways for workers and citizens to exercise control. Here, I have stressed new regulation requiring transparency in relation to employment practices, on the grounds that this provides citizens with important knowledge. Moreover, if transparency became embedded as a social norm it may be more difficult to reverse than other progressive policy actions.

The argument is also made that this reform agenda can be pursued without subscribing to the insider/outsider rhetoric. Indeed, moves towards a deinstitutionalised and competitive labour market might reduce mutual dependency between employers and workers. As this interdependency provides the basis for long-term productivity growth, short-term profits and shareholder values may be prioritised over long-term developments and the interests of wider stakeholders. There is thus a need to preserve, develop and extend the benefits to society that stem from this mutual dependency within the employment relationship, while at the same time providing more universal rights and support to those in need of work and income.

Figure 2.1 provides an overview of the three-pronged approach to reform, across social policy, employment policy, and mechanisms for voice and monitoring. The need to act on both developing employment relationships and disentangling social protection from employment status is more evident once the functions of employment regulation are recognised as multifaceted, involving macroeconomic, social reproduction and fairness-at-work objectives. Efforts to embed fairness in workplace practices should not be abandoned simply because employers have become more hidden from view. Likewise, where social protection is tied to employment status, opportunities should be found either to disentangle these rights or to offer the non-employed similar rights. The role of other actors also needs to be addressed. Putting forward a progressive reform agenda is undoubtedly dependent on a progressive state, but the complexion of the state may change or may be forced to change by international pressures. These problems beset any progressive reform policies. But to increase the likelihood of effective implementation, attention needs to be paid to new enforcement mechanisms and practices such as transparency requirements, promoting public awareness of universal rights and minimum standards, and establishing principles of accountability across the supply chain.

REFERENCES

ACAS (2013) 'What is the living wage?', http://www.acas.org.uk/index.aspx?art icleid=4157.

Anxo, D. and Ericson, T. (2012) 'The effects of pay reforms and procurement strategies on wage and employment inequalities in the Swedish public sector', Report For EU Social Dialogue Unit, European Work and Employment

Research Centre, https://research.mbs.ac.uk/european-employment/Portals/0/docs/Sweden-national%20report.pdf.

Barrientos, A. (2013) *Social Assistance in Developing Countries*, Cambridge: Cambridge University Press.

Berg, J. and Kucera, D. (eds) (2008) *In Defence of Labour Market Institutions: Cultivating Justice in the Developing World*, Basingstoke, UK and Geneva: Palgrave Macmillan and ILO.

Blofield, M. and Martínez Franzoni, J. (2015) 'Maternalism, co-responsibility and social equity: a typology of work–family policies', *Social Politics* **22** (1): 38–59.

Boeri, T., Garibaldi, P. and Ribeiro, M. (2011) 'The lighthouse effect and beyond', *Review of Income and Wealth Series* **57** (May), Special Issue, S54–S78.

Bosch, G. (2004) 'Towards a new standard employment relationship in Western Europe', *British Journal of Industrial Relations* **42**: 617–36.

Bosch, G., Lehndorff, S. and Rubery, J. (eds) (2009) *European Employment Models in Flux: A Comparison of. Institutional Change in Nine European Countries*, Basingstoke: Palgrave.

Bosch, G., Rubery, J. and Lehndorff, S. (2007) 'European employment models under pressure to change', *International Labour Review* **146** (3/4): 253–77.

Botero, J., Djankov, S., La Porta, R., Lopez-de-Silanes, F. and Shleifer, A. (2004) 'The regulation of labor', *Quarterly Journal of Economics*, November, 1339–82.

Boyer, R. (1979) 'Wage formation in historical perspective: the French experience', *Cambridge Journal of Economics* **3** (2): 99–118.

CEDEFOP (2009) 'Panorama: Individual Learning Accounts', http://www.cedefop.europa.eu/EN/Files/5192_en.pdf.

Chan, C.K. and Bowpitt, G. (2005) *Human Dignity and Welfare Systems*, Bristol: Policy Press.

CIPD (2013), 'Zero hours contracts: myth and reality', available at http://www.cipd.co.uk/hr-resources/research/zero-hours-contracts-myth-reality.aspx.

Collins, H. (1990) 'Independent contractors and the challenge of vertical disintegration to employment protection laws', *Oxford Journal of Legal Studies* **10** (3): 353–80.

Connolly, S. and Gregory, M. (2008) 'Moving down: women's part-time work and occupational change in Britain 1991–2001', *Economic Journal* **118** (526): F52–F76.

Deakin, S. (1986) 'Labour law and the developing employment relationship in the UK', *Cambridge Journal of Economics* **10**, 225–46.

Deakin, S. (2009) 'Capacitas: contract law and the institutional preconditions of a market economy', in Deakin, S. and Supiot, A. (eds), *Labour and Employment Law and Economics*, Oxford: Hart Publishing.

Deakin, S., McLaughlin, C. and Chai, D. (2011) 'Gender inequality and reflexive law: the potential of different regulatory mechanisms for making employment rights effective', Centre for Business Research, University of Cambridge, Working Paper No. 426.

Deakin, S. and Wilkinson, F. (2005) *The Law of the Labour Market: Industrialization, Employment, and Legal Evolution*, Oxford: Oxford University Press.

Earnshaw, J., Rubery, J. and Cooke, F. (2002) *Who is the Employer?*, Liverpool: Institute of Employment Rights.

Emmenegger, P. (2009) 'Barriers to entry: insider/outsider politics and the political determinants of job security regulations', *Journal of European Social Policy* **19** (2): 131–46.

Emmenegger, P. (2010) 'Gendering insiders and outsiders: labour market status and preferences for job security', REC-WP 02/2010 Working Papers on the Reconciliation of Work and Welfare in Europe, RECWOWE Publication, Dissemination and Dialogue Centre, Edinburgh.

Erickson, C., Fisk, C., Milkman, R., Mitchell, D. and Wong, K. (2002) 'Justice for Janitors in Los Angeles: lessons from three rounds of negotiations', *British Journal of Industrial Relations* **40**: 543–67.

ETUI (2014) *Benchmarking Working Europe 2014*, Brussels: ETUI.

EU Commission (2011) *Annual Growth Survey: Advancing the EU's Comprehensive Response to the Crisis*, COM(2011) 11 final.

Fredman, S. (2004) 'Women at work: the broken promise of flexicurity', *Industrial Law Journal* **33** (4): 299–319.

Freedland, M. (2013) 'Burying Caesar: what was the standard employment contract?', in Stone, K. and Arthurs, H. (eds), *Rethinking Workplace Regulation: Beyond the Standard Contract of Employment*, New York: Russell Sage Foundation.

Freedland, M. and Kountouris, N. (2011) *The Legal Construction of Personal Work Relations*, Oxford: Oxford University Press.

Freeman, R. (2009) 'Labor regulations, unions, and social protection in developing countries: market distortions or efficient institutions?', NBER Working Papers 14789, National Bureau of Economic Research.

Gangl, M. (2006) 'Scar effects of unemployment: an assessment of institutional complementarities', *American Sociological Review* **71** (December): 986–1013.

Ginn, J. (2004) 'Actuarial fairness or social justice? A gender perspective on redistribution in pension systems', CeRP Working Paper No. 37/04 http://cerp.unito.it/english/publications/cerp_wp.htm#2004.

Grimshaw, D., Johnson, M., Rubery, J. and Kaizer, A. (2016) 'Reducing precarious work: protective gaps and the role of social dialogue', http://www.research.mbs.ac.uk/ewerc/Portals/0/Documents/Comparative-Report-Reducing-Precarious-Work-v2.pdf.

Grimshaw, D., Rubery, J., Anxo, D. et al. (2015) 'Outsourcing of public services in Europe and segmentation effects: the influence of labour market factors', *European Journal of Industrial Relations* **21** (4): 295–313.

Ham, A. (2013) 'Revisiting the effects of minimum wages in developing countries: evidence from a particular policy change in Honduras', http://ssrn.com/abstract=2217835 or http://dx.doi.org/10.2139/ssrn.2217835.

Hassel, A. (2014) 'The paradox of liberalization – understanding dualism and the recovery of the German political economy', *British Journal of Industrial Relations* **52** (1): 57–81.

Heintz, James and Lund, Francie (2012) 'Welfare regimes and social policy: a review of the role of labour and employment', UNRISD Research Paper No. 2012-4.

Hirschman, A. (1991). *The Rhetoric of Reaction: Perversity, Futility, Jeopardy*, Cambridge, MA: Harvard University Press.

Howell, D. (2004) *Fighting Unemployment: The Limits of Free Market Orthodoxy*, Oxford: Oxford University Press.

Howell, D., Baker, D., Glyn, A. and Schmitt, J. (2007) 'Are protective labor market institutions at the root of unemployment? A critical review of the evidence', *Capitalism and Society* **2** (1): 1–71.

King, D. and Rueda, D. (2008) 'Cheap labor: the new politics of "bread and roses" in industrial democracies', *Perspectives on Politics* **6** (June): 279–97.

Lee, B.-H. and Yoo, B.-S. (2008) 'The Republic of Korea: from flexibility to segmentation', in Lee, S. and Eyraud, F. (eds), *Globalization, Flexiblization and Working Conditions in Asia and the Pacific*, Geneva: ILO.

Lee, S. and McCann, D. (2011) *Regulating for Decent Work: New Directions in Labour Market Regulation*, Basingstoke, UK and Geneva: Palgrave Macmillan and ILO.

Lee, S., McCann, D. and Torm, N. (2008) 'The World Bank's "Employing Workers" index: findings and critiques – a review of recent evidence', *International Labour Review* 147 (4): 416–32.

Leschke, J. (2007a) 'Gender differences in unemployment insurance coverage – a comparative analysis', Discussion Paper, Berlin: WZB.

Leschke J. (2007b) 'Are unemployment insurance systems in Europe adapting to new risks arising from non-standard employment?', DULBEA Working Paper, Research Series, No. 07-05.RS, Brussels: Université Libre de Bruxelles.

Lindbeck, A. and Snower, D. (2002), 'The insider–outsider theory: a survey', Discussion Paper 534, IZA, Bonn.

Lipsky, M. (1980) *Street Level Bureaucracy*, New York: Russell Sage Foundation.

Marchington, M P., Grimshaw, D., Rubery, J. and Willmott, H. (2005) *Fragmenting Work: Blurring Organisational Boundaries and Disordering Hierarchies*, Oxford: Oxford University Press.

Marsden, D. (1999) *A Theory of Employment Systems Micro-Foundations of Societal Diversity*, Oxford: Oxford University Press.

Martínez Franzoni, J. and Sánchez-Ancochea, D. (2013) 'Can Latin American production regimes complement universalistic welfare regimes?: Implications from the Costa Rican case', *Latin American Research Review* **48** (2): 148–73.

Martínez Franzoni, J. and Sánchez-Ancochea, D. (2014) 'The double challenge of market and social incorporation progress and bottlenecks in Latin America', *Development Policy Review* **32** (3): 275–98.

McCann, D. (2012) 'New frontiers of regulation: domestic work, working conditions, and the holistic assessment of nonstandard work norms', *Comparative Labor Law and Policy Journal* **34** (1): 167–92.

McCann, D., Lee, S., Belser, P., Fenwick, C., Howe, J. and Luebker, M. (eds) (2014) *Creative Labour Regulation Indeterminacy and Protection in an Uncertain World*, Basingstoke, UK and Geneva: Palgrave Macmillan and ILO.

Messenger, J. and Ghosheh, N. (2013) *Work Sharing During the Great Recession*, Cheltenham, UK and Geneva: Edward Elgar Publishing and ILO.

Milkman, R. (2013) 'Back to the future? US labour in the new gilded age', *British Journal of Industrial Relations* **51** (4): 645–65.

OECD (1994) *The Jobs Study*, Paris: OECD.

OECD (2006) *Employment Outlook*, Paris: OECD.

Olsen, W. and Walby, S. (2004) 'Modelling gender pay gaps', EOC Working Paper Series 17, Manchester: Equal Opportunities Commission.

Osterman, P. (1984) *Internal Labour Markets*, Boston, MA: MIT Press.

Osterman, P. (1994) 'Internal labour markets: theory and change', in Kerr, C. and P.D. Staudohar (eds), *Labour Economics and Industrial Relations: Markets and Institutions*, Cambridge, MA: Harvard University Press.

Palier, B. and Thelen, K. (2010) 'Institutionalizing dualism: complementarities and change in France and Germany', *Politics and Society* **38** (1): 119–48.

Prassl, J. (2015) *The Concept of the Employer*, Oxford: Oxford University Press.

Reich, M., Jacobs, K. and Dietz, M. (2014) *When Mandates Work*, Berkeley, CA: University of California Press.

Resolution Foundation (2013), 'A matter of time: the rise of zero hours contracts', http://www.resolutionfoundation.org/media/media/downloads/A_Matter_of_Time_-_The_rise_of_zero-hours_contracts_final_1.pdf.

Rubery, J. (1978) 'Structured labour markets, worker organisation and low pay', *Cambridge Journal of Economics* **2** (1): 17–36.

Rubery, J. (2007) 'Developing segmentation theory: a thirty year perspective', *Économies et Sociétés* **28** (6): 941–64.

Rubery, J. (2010) 'Institutionalizing the employment relationship', in Morgan, G., Campbell, J., Crouch, C., Pedersen, O. and Whitley, R. (eds), *The Oxford Handbook of Comparative Institutional Analysis*, Oxford: Oxford University Press.

Rueda, D. (2005) 'Insider–outsider politics in industrialized democracies: the challenge to social democratic parties', *American Political Science Review* **99** (February): 61–74.

Rubery, J. (2011) 'Towards a gendering of the labour market regulation debate', *Cambridge Journal of Economics* **35** (6): 1103–26.

Sayer, A. (2007) 'Dignity at work: broadening the agenda', *Organization* **14** (4): 565–81.

Schmid, G. (2010) 'Beyond flexicurity: active securities for flexible employment relationships', Alternatives to Flexicurity conference, Madrid, http://www.guentherschmid.eu/pdf/2010/Madrid_Schmid_TLM-2.pdf.

Schmid, G. and Gazier, B. (2002) *The Dynamics of Full Employment. Social Integration through Transitional Labour Markets*, Cheltenham, UK and Northampton, MA, USA: Edward Elgar Publishing.

Simón, H. (2010) 'International differences in wage inequality: a new glance with European matched employer–employee data', *British Journal of Industrial Relations* **48** (2): 310–46.

Standing, G. (2011) *The Precariat: The New Dangerous Class*, London, UK and New York, USA: Bloomsbury Academic.

Stone, K. and Arthurs, H. (eds) (2013) *Rethinking Workplace Regulation: Beyond the Standard Contract of Employment*, New York: Russell Sage Foundation.

Streeck, W. (1997) 'Beneficial constraints: on the economic limits of rational voluntarism', in Hollingsworth, J.R. and Boyer, R. (eds), *Contemporary Capitalism: The Embeddedness of Institutions*, Cambridge: Cambridge University Press.

Supiot, A. (ed.) (2001) *Beyond Employment: Changes in Work and the Future of Labour Law in Europe*, Oxford: Oxford University Press.

Tinsley, M. (2012) 'Too much to lose: understanding and supporting Britain's older workers', Policy Exchange, http://www.policyexchange.org.uk/publications/category/item/too-much-to-lose-understanding-and-supporting-britain-s-older-workers.

UKCES (2011) 'Employers and the recruitment of unemployed people: an evidence review', Briefing Paper.

Vosko, L. (2010) *Managing the Margins Gender, Citizenship, and the International Regulation of Precarious Employment*, Oxford: Oxford University Press.

Vosko, L. and Thomas, M. (2014) 'Confronting the employment standards enforcement gap: exploring the potential for union engagement with employment law in Ontario, Canada', *Journal of Industrial Relations* **56** (5): 631–52.

Wajcman, J. (1991) 'Patriarchy, technology, and conceptions of skill', *Work and Occupations* **18** (1): 29–45.

Weil, D. (2012) 'Examining the underpinnings of labor standards compliance in low wage industries', New York: Report for Russell Sage Foundation.

Whitworth, A. (2013) 'Tailor-made? Single parents' experiences of employment support from Jobcentre Plus and the Work Programme', London: Gingerbread, https://www.shef.ac.uk/polopoly_fs/1.284059!/file/Tailor-made-Full-report-12mar2013.PDF.

3. Beyond new governance: Improving employment standards enforcement in liberal market economies*

Leah F. Vosko, John Grundy and Mark P. Thomas

In the liberal market economies of Australia, Canada, the United Kingdom and the United States, long-standing patterns of economic restructuring are changing the way work is organized. Coupled with legislative deregulation and declining rates of unionization, these changes are contributing to the growth of precarious employment. Employment standards (ES) legislating minimum conditions in areas such as wages, working time, vacations and leave, and termination and severance, are increasingly the only source of workplace protection, alongside health and safety, for a mounting number of workers. Yet there is growing evidence that non-compliance with ES is becoming a key strategy of labour cost reduction for employers, particularly at the lower end of the labour market (see, e.g., Bernhardt et al., 2008; Howe et al., 2013; Vosko et al., 2011; Weil, 2010).

Facing conditions of limited resources, as well as more complex, fissuring employment relations (Weil, 2010), many agencies charged with ES enforcement, particularly through the handling of individual complaints, are struggling to manage their expanding workload. Their activities have been compromised by processes of neo-liberal re-regulation, which have simultaneously augmented the individualization of enforcement practices and reduced funding for regulatory bodies, exacerbating longer-standing weaknesses of state-based enforcement agencies (see Ayres and

* The research conducted for this chapter grew out of a partnership grant, titled 'Closing the Enforcement Gap: Improving Protections for People in Precarious Jobs', funded by the Social Sciences and Humanities Research Council of Canada. The authors are grateful to this granting agency for its support as well as to members of the larger research team for their comments on an earlier version of this text.

Braithwaite, 1992; Estlund, 2005; Fine, 2013). As resources devoted to enforcement decline, inspectorates are increasingly less able or likely to identify violations and apply formal legal penalties, thus contributing to regulatory degradation (Tombs and Whyte, 2010). Such deficiencies of ES enforcement are particularly detrimental for those in precarious forms of work, whose precarious status is exacerbated by individualized complaints systems and the paucity of proactive mechanisms.

A range of new ES enforcement approaches is emerging as part of an attempt to manage deepening regulatory challenges amid mounting pressure for more efficient and cost-effective regulation. Responding to a variety of internal and external factors, including pressure from civil society groups, governments are undertaking reforms to all stages of the enforcement process – from measures that aim to prevent violations before they occur, to shifts in complaints-handling processes, to new methods of dispute resolution – many of which bear evidence of the increasing influence of regulatory new governance (RNG) (Lobel, 2012). According to the RNG paradigm, the growing complexity of regulatory problems challenges the efficacy of traditional, centralized modes of public authority exercised through hierarchical, bureaucratic public institutions. Although its strands vary, RNG casts the proper task of the state as one of steering rather than rowing; that is, pursuing regulatory objectives by facilitating networks of actors that span public/private and state/civil society divides. Its proponents call for participatory arrangements in which regulatory responsibility is dispersed among the state, employers, employees and civil society actors, and thus at least partially privatized.

Focusing on reforms to enforcement under way in four liberal market economies, and building on scholarly critiques (Davidov, 2010; Tombs and Whyte, 2010; Tucker, 2013), this inquiry raises serious concerns around the current enthusiasm for RNG-styled enforcement mechanisms. Recognizing that RNG is not a homogenous set of practices, but rather takes a variety of forms aiming to foster more flexible regimes of regulation, we argue that certain prominent RNG arrangements display an over-reliance on 'soft law' mechanisms. Such arrangements run the risk of exacerbating, rather than mitigating, poor ES enforcement. Specifically, while the enforcement models envisioned by RNG proponents aim to extend social protections to workers, we argue that those failing to retain a sufficient role for state institutions and 'hard law' mechanisms fail to adequately account for the power dynamics of the employment relationship, and thereby threaten to further undermine employment rights, particularly for those in precarious forms of work.

We develop this argument in three sections. First, in section 3.1, we outline the central principles underpinning RNG-based reforms in relation to ES enforcement, focusing on two that have significant implications in terms of contributing to regulatory degradation. These principles relate to: (1) the plurality of enforcement mechanisms that reforms envision, particularly the use of 'soft law' and self-regulation; and (2) the involvement of multiple actors and the related dispersion of authority that reforms encourage.

Section 3.2 then explores the implications of these two principles through a survey of enforcement mechanisms that exemplify the influence of RNG on ES in four jurisdictions. The mechanisms analysed are: enforceable undertakings and the National Franchise Program undertaken at the federal level in Australia; the Citizens Advice Bureaux operating nationally in the United Kingdom (UK); inspector deputization programmes based in Los Angeles, California, USA; and self-help mechanisms introduced in the administration of the Employment Standards Act, 2000 of Ontario, Canada. These are four high-income states, characterized historically by extensive employment regulation, but facing similar dilemmas in attempting to foster flexibilization, while also seeking to maintain a floor of labour protection. These examples are therefore selected because they illustrate core aspects of RNG principles, and with the aim of exploring developments at various levels of government (federal, national, state or provincial, and municipal). They are examined in relation to three general stages of ES enforcement common to liberal jurisdictions, schematized for the purpose of our analysis as: pre-emptive measures to prevent violations; the complaints-handling process; and claims resolution. We demonstrate that although elements of several reforms in the complaints-handling and complaints-resolution processes privilege a more proactive orientation to enforcement, they show tendencies to downplay workplace power asymmetries and may undermine the effective exercise of employee voice.

Based on this assessment, in section 3.3 we argue that those alternative ES enforcement mechanisms that are most successful in achieving the objective of minimum workplace standards include a central role for state institutions, for example through the administration of 'hard law' measures such as legal sanctions when necessary. Recognizing that 'hard law' and 'soft law' mechanisms are not mutually exclusive or incompatible, we conclude by advancing three normative principles for ES enforcement that aim simultaneously to address the limitations of both outmoded traditional modes of public regulation and strategies grounded in RNG.

3.1   REGULATORY NEW GOVERNANCE: UNDERLYING PRINCIPLES WITH IMPLICATIONS FOR ES ENFORCEMENT

A brief sketch of the central tenets of governance theory is warranted before critically interrogating its increasing influence across spheres of regulation. In the fields of political science, law and sociology, a distinction is now made between the concepts of 'government' and 'governance'. 'Government' refers to the exercise of power through the formal legal and administrative apparatus of the state. 'Governance', in contrast, emphasizes the collaboration of institutions and actors drawn both from and beyond the state in pursuit of social and economic goals. In place of the traditional hierarchical and centralized organization of public authority, governance emphasizes mutual dependence and shared interests among actors from government, business, the third sector and advocacy organizations. Its privileged organizational form is the self-governing, horizontal network. According to governance theory, such networks are well equipped to handle rapid change and the complexity of public problems (Stoker, 1998).

Notions of RNG are increasingly influential in proposals that aim to modernize public regulation. They appeal to policy-makers as a solution to the deficiencies of traditional public regulation, often deemed 'command and control' (CC), and characterized by the imposition of standards by a public regulatory agency backed by the threat of legal punishment (Baldwin, 1997: 65; Mascini, 2013). Proponents of RNG typically cast public regulation as inflexible and encumbered by unnecessarily complex regulations that thwart innovation and competition. In this view, the adversarial logic of detecting and punishing wrongdoing represents an ineffective use of scarce resources, fails to distinguish between good and bad actors, and exacerbates antagonisms between regulators and the regulated (Lobel, 2005: 1089). While the validity of this account is subject to debate (Malloy, 2010; Short, 2012), the effectiveness of public regulation across a range of jurisdictions and policy fields is clearly undermined by government austerity measures implemented alongside expanding responsibilities. In the field of ES enforcement, resources allocated to enforcement agencies are not keeping pace with the growing number of workplaces and workers covered by ES (Vosko et al., 2011; Weil, 2010).

RNG rose to prominence not only as a solution to problems associated with public regulation, but in response to the increasingly evident adverse effects of neo-liberal deregulation. Regulatory lapses in fields such as financial governance, public health, the environment, ES, and occupational health and safety, and the public harms flowing from them, have fuelled public unease with deregulation and posed challenges to the legitimacy of governments (Prudham, 2004; Strauss, 2009). RNG purports to offer a 'third way' for rebuilding regulation that eschews both the bureaucratic deficiencies of CC and deregulation. It advances new practical arrangements that seek to reconcile the regulatory mandate of governments with a greater sensitivity to administrative burdens and the competitive market realities that regulated parties face (Lobel, 2012).

Models of RNG take a variety of forms, most of which entail a greater role for self or third-party regulation. They nonetheless also generally involve some degree of public regulation, thus constituting hybrid or what Crouch (2005) aptly labels 'recombinant' modes of regulation, rather than a dichotomous break with traditional public regulation (which, in practice, has itself often assumed hybrid forms). By far the most influential is Ayres and Braithwaite's (1992) formula of 'responsive regulation', now the basis for regulatory reform initiatives across a range of policy fields and jurisdictions. The central idea is that regulators must use different strategies depending on a given firm's compliance track record. It is based on a pyramidal enforcement system under which regulators proceed from light-touch, self-regulatory measures at the bottom, escalate to moderate penalties in the face of evidence of non-compliance, and reserve the most severe sanctions for the most problematic offenders. Gunningham and Grabosky's (1998) model of smart regulation builds on the idea of the enforcement pyramid, but calls for the dispersion of regulatory responsibility among a broader array of actors including not only the state and firms, but also industry and professional associations, and civil society groups, among others (Baldwin et al., 2011; Gunningham, 2010). Smart regulation also entails a greater diversity of enforcement instruments including voluntary codes of conduct, information-sharing on best practices, market and peer pressure, performance measurement and associated forms of 'naming, faming and shaming'. A third model of reflexive or meta-regulation is gaining influence, where the central role of government envisioned is to facilitate and monitor the use of self-governance systems (Gunningham, 2010).

Labour and employment regulation has long been an important field for the elaboration of RNG (Lobel, 2012). Many developments associated with RNG in this field, such as participatory regulation, precede the emergence of new governance discourse and are obscured in simplistic dichotomies of 'old' and 'new' governance (de Burca and Scott, 2006: 3; see also Colling, 2012; Tucker, 2013). While recognizing that many elements of RNG are by no means entirely new, the ensuing analysis focuses on two key principles that are prominent features of ES enforcement reform agendas in liberal market economies: the use of a plurality of enforcement strategies and mechanisms; and multi-stakeholder participation in the regulatory process. Both principles entail substantial risks of further weakening workplace regulation.

Multiple Enforcement Strategies: Prioritizing 'Soft' and Self-Regulation

Models of RNG in ES enforcement envision a smaller role for public regulation and the veritable threat of legal punishment, as a means of mediating employer–employee conflict flowing from inequitable power relations. RNG strategies expand the range of policy instruments beyond those associated with 'hard law', particularly in those jurisdictions where 'hard law' has played a primary role in ES regulation (for example, federal and provincial or state jurisdictions in Canada and Australia). They aim to secure compliance through techniques such as persuasion and negotiation, codes of conduct, information-sharing on industry best practices, and non-governmental monitoring. The oft-stated rationale for this diversification of enforcement strategies is the need to make regulation more flexible and responsive. For proponents of these measures, the uniform application of universal standards is a strategy ill-suited to rapidly shifting production methods, such as increasingly complex supply chains and subcontracted employment, which, when coupled with the twin problems of the expanding mandate of public regulators and declining state financial resources, make effective public regulation unlikely. Advocates of RNG also claim that the diversification of enforcement strategies is more apt to gain the support of the regulated firms.

The growing preference among policy-makers for the use of 'soft law' enforcement implies various degrees of self-regulation. As Estlund (2005: 325–6) notes: 'the locus of enforcement is moving inside the workplace and away from direct public monitoring'. While traditional forms of regulation have long imposed prescriptive regulation that assumes the internal regulatory capacities of firms, with developments such as subcontracting and vertical disintegration more broadly, RNG strategies seek to further harness firms' increasingly elaborate internal control systems in areas of quality assurance, human resources and dispute resolution to monitor ES.

Some models of RNG retain a revised role for public enforcement. Reflecting the notion that states should steer rather than row, Estlund's (2005) proposal of monitored self-regulation entails employers signing up to a code of conduct that guarantees their compliance with both ES and the external monitoring process. According to this model, the role of public authority is to oversee self-enforcement systems devised by firms themselves.

Enforcement of self-regulation is carried out by independent monitors accountable to workers in the monitored workplace and the broader public domain. Communication between workers and external monitors is fostered through anti-reprisal provisions and whistleblower protection. The entrance of firms into monitored self-regulation is not totally voluntary. Firms can be pushed into it or face more intensive penalties and sanctions from public enforcement agencies, or private litigation. In this sense, Estlund's model remains a hybrid model of enforcement rather than one that is wholly privatized or oriented towards 'soft law'.

Other influential models dispense entirely with 'hard law' public enforcement. For example, at the heart of Sabel et al.'s (2000) conception of ratcheting labour standards is an 'information regime' that aims to mobilize social and market pressures in the public interest. In this model, firms would self-regulate their workplaces, and report their efforts to certified monitors: competitive public or private agencies with high degrees of expertise and credibility. In turn, the monitors compare and rank employers and make the information publicly available. In this model, soft pressures of brand diminishment and loss of market share substitute entirely for hard mechanisms. This model derives standards from the input of industry leaders, and the ratcheting mechanism refers to the continual elaboration and emulation of best practice.

Considered from the perspective of countering precariousness, numerous weaknesses are evident in proposals for 'soft' and self-regulation. First, they often downplay social antagonisms and inequities, much less the specific power dynamics of capitalist production that undermine incentives for cooperation on the part of employers and firms (Tucker, 2013). Despite evidence that non-compliance with labour standards is a strategy of labour cost reduction for a growing number of employers (Bernhardt et al., 2013), a process exacerbated by shifts in the balance of workplace power towards employers, given declining unionization rates and deregulation through legislative reform (Bernhardt et al., 2008; Pollert, 2009; Thomas, 2009; Vosko, 2006), models of RNG are based on the assumption that most employers seek to abide by the law but need education and incentives to do so. In taking as a starting point the goodwill of employers, and the related need to minimize use of adversarial mechanisms, RNG can facilitate rather than mitigate the deepening asymmetries of power fuelling regulatory crises in the first place. Under these conditions, well-intended projects of self-regulation are likely to collapse into market regulation, and undermine the ability of workers to access their rights (Davidov, 2010; Seidman, 2009; Tombs and Whyte, 2010; Tucker, 2013). Arguably, such risks are heightened in small firms that often lack the internal regulatory systems that RNG models seek to work through.

The question of whether and how an expanded array of 'soft' and self-enforcement mechanisms can impose concrete costs for non-compliance is therefore critical in assessing their vulnerability to regulatory degradation. The central dilemma with proposals such as Estlund's, which advances self-regulation as a solution to collapsing public enforcement capacity, is that they require the existence of strong public oversight that can be mobilized when self-regulatory efforts fail. The model of ratcheting labour standards entails other potential weaknesses. For it to have regulatory teeth, companies must be concerned with their 'social performance' reputation, and a sufficiently large segment of the general public must be willing to engage in socially conscious consumption. In short, without the establishment of effective procedures through which soft and self-regulation strategies can trigger 'hard' sanctions, RNG mechanisms can entrench rather than mitigate regulatory degradation. Moreover, given the inadequacy at addressing the fundamental question of power relations in the workplace, these regulatory approaches can exacerbate tendencies that impede workers in precarious jobs from exercising workplace rights.

Participatory Enforcement

Another central principle of RNG in the field of ES is that of stakeholder participation. A brief sketch of this principle is necessary before pointing to its potential to exacerbate regulatory degradation. Whereas ES enforcement under public regulation has traditionally been conceived as a relation between public regulators and employers, models of RNG purportedly offer opportunities for a wider range of actors to participate in enforcement. New in this participatory enforcement principle is not the involvement of a plurality of actors, but rather the respective standing of labour, business and the state, as well as greater variety of actors. One prominent proposal is greater use of firm-level works councils, envisioned as a mechanism of employee representation especially in contexts of low union density such as the United States (Estlund, 2012: 11). Other proposals, which emanate from labour struggles, assign new regulatory roles to professional and industry associations, community groups and certified monitors (see, especially, Fine and Gordon, 2010; Hardy, 2011). This pluralization of actors finds theoretical justification in governance theory's repudiation of 'the capacity and desirability of state control in a complex society' (Pierre, 2012: 6). Proponents of participatory enforcement point to the difficulties labour inspectorates have in keeping up with shifting employer practices, and suggest that regulatory efforts suffer unless they draw on the expertise of relevant individuals and groups throughout the regulatory process (Lobel, 2012).

Efforts to incorporate different actors into the enforcement process have the potential to reinvigorate regulatory efforts and expand the reach of enforcement bodies (Fine and Gordon, 2010). Yet the capacity of proposed systems of employee representation to exercise employee voice effectively is questionable. In non-unionized environments where there is a risk of co-optation and intimidation, and in the absence of strong public enforcement, toothless employee committees may do little more than to shore up various pro-business initiatives such as privatization (Estlund, 2005: 403; Seidman, 2009). Many individual workers in precarious employment who rely on the minimum protections afforded through ES are not in a position to speak out and play the role of the workplace protagonist in ES enforcement (see, especially, Tucker, 2013; see also Thomas, 2009; Vosko, 2013). Research on recent third-party engagement initiatives in non-unionized environments raises additional concerns about the voice of worker advocates in these arrangements, as well as their ability to participate given the limited capacity of workers' organizations (Hardy, 2011; Vosko, 2006).

To evaluate the extent to which participatory enforcement systems are susceptible to regulatory degradation, it is necessary to consider what measures are in place to give these arrangements force, and to compensate for the asymmetries of power in the workplace often exacerbated by structural inequities of race, gender, citizenship and class, as well as new forms of work organization that enhance precariousness. As Fine and Gordon (2010: 561) point out, voices representing the interests of workers in multi-stakeholder regulatory arrangements must be given equal weight as those representing employers, and the relations must be formalized, sustained and vigorous. Short of this, the adoption of multi-stakeholder enforcement arrangements in a context of deepening workplace power imbalances may offer poor protections to workers and even provide cover for ongoing violations.

3.2 REGULATORY NEW GOVERNANCE MECHANISMS IN ES ENFORCEMENT IN LIBERAL MARKET JURISDICTIONS

Since the late twentieth century, deficiencies in ES enforcement have spawned a number of approaches offering new and renewed mechanisms seeking to improve workplace regulation. These approaches operate at different scales (for example, city, region and nation) reflecting variations in the organization of labour regulation. They also cut across the three central stages of the enforcement process – prevention, complaints and dispute resolution – and, hence, we select a mixture of mechanisms reflecting these stages for illustration and analysis.

Preventing Problems at Work

The pre-complaint stage encompasses pre-emptive measures. It covers enforcement activities that seek to prevent problems before they arise, specifically, to stem problems that could lead to violations and/or formal complaints. Pre-emptive measures range from random and proactive inspections to smaller-scale initiatives related to employer and worker education surrounding workers' rights. Each of the RNG principles described above, and in particular the critique developed therein, is pertinent to the evaluation of measures adopted at this stage: without channels for recourse that ultimately make those responsible face concrete costs of non-compliance, there would be few incentives for adherence to minimum standards. It is equally important that pre-emptive mechanisms compensate for the unequal distribution of power in the workplace. ES-dependent workers are already vulnerable and thereby require forward-looking or offensive mechanisms. Similarly, given that they are normally devoid of traditional channels of representation, there is certainly a role for multiple parties in the enforcement process, especially in the face of limited resourcing to state officials. However, the roles of various parties will likely not be meaningful if authority is distributed in ways that do not acknowledge and compensate for power imbalances between employers and employees.

One programme recently developed by Australia's Fair Work Ombudsman (FWO), the agency that enforces the Fair Work Act 2009, exemplifies RNG's emphasis on collaborative forms of regulation that leverage the internal regulatory capacity of firms to prevent ES violations. The National Franchise Program (NFP) was established in 2012, building on a former initiative, the National Employer Program (NEP), which involved collaboration between FWO officials and large employers in the development of compliance strategies. Along similar lines, the objective of the NFP is to support the work of franchisors aiming to ensure their franchisees' observance of ES. According to the FWO, the programme 'offers franchisors an opportunity to protect their brand by proactively working with us to support fair and compliant workplaces in their franchise business[es]' (FWO, 2013a). The NFP uses the surveillance capacity that franchisors already have over franchisees' standards and procedures to protect their brand equity as a pressure point for increasing compliance among small franchisees (Hardy, 2011: 132). Under this programme, a dedicated Fair Work Advisor from the Federal Government's Fair Work Ombudsman office collaborates with a franchisor to develop a compliance strategy based on the particular needs and structure of the franchise operation. The programme aims to provide the franchisor with strategies to improve the visibility of problems in franchisee workplaces as well as their prevention. In 2012–13, the NFP involved 14 franchisors covering more than 48 000 employees (FWO, 2013b: 19). The NFP reflects a number of elements of RNG, including emphasizing compliance primarily through information-sharing and self-regulation in firms. As Hardy (2011: 132) notes, a chief benefit of such programmes is that they facilitate relations and shared expectations between FWO officials and key 'gatekeeper' figures in firms. Unlike many proposals for monitored self-regulation, however, the NFP does not substitute more adversarial, 'hard' sanctions. Firms do not derive a formal legal advantage in the form of limited exposure to further enforcement measures by participating. The NFP is one among a range of other 'soft' and 'hard' enforcement instruments available to the FWO.

With respect to the degree to which the NFP makes room for the participation of workers and/or their representatives, more potential exists for regulatory degradation. The key actors under the NFP (and its NEP predecessor) are FWO representatives and firm managers. While greater collaboration between managers and FWO officials can improve compliance, the NFP lacks the formalized employee participation that is a necessary ingredient of effective strategies of RNG in the field of ES (Estlund, 2012: 10). Additionally, while the NFP was devised as part of the FWO's efforts to maximize its regulatory reach, it is arguable that franchisors operating in the low end of the labour market, and perhaps less concerned with managing brand visibility, have little incentive to volunteer for the programme. Voluntary regulatory mechanisms such as the NFP run the risk of securing compliance where it is most easily achieved rather than where such efforts are most needed.

The dispersion of responsibility under RNG enforcement is exemplified in programmes run by the Los Angeles Unified School District (LAUSD) and the Los Angeles Board of Public Works (LABPW), which deputize representatives from local building trade unions to enforce workplace standards on school district and public works projects. These programmes emerged following an amendment to California's Labour Code in 1989, prompted by public pressure for change and the threat of industrial relations disputes, which allowed for the establishment of labour compliance programmes for prevailing wage rates (Fine and Gordon, 2010). In 1996, the LAUSD developed its programme through an arrangement whereby building trade unions agreed not to strike if the LAUSD established an internal department to ensure compliance with prevailing wage rates on district projects. The LABPW launched a similar programme in 2004 covering standards related to hours, wages, job classification and official duties. Taking on the role of labour inspectors, union representatives are authorized to enter project sites in order to conduct inspections, interview workers about workplace standards, and fill out complaint forms in cases where violations are perceived to have occurred. They then provide workplace data to city inspectors, who prepare cases and determine violations and penalties. These programmes accord union labour inspectors with a form of institutional legitimacy that establishes employer acceptance of the programme and facilitates access to work sites and workers (Fine and Gordon, 2010).

Deputization programmes are rooted in an enforcement system based on public law, which includes formal sanctions in the form of fines, withholding of payments, and loss of eligibility for future public contracts. The connection to 'hard' law enforcement provides a threat of consequences not present in RNG models where 'soft law' approaches are predominant. In this way, they bolster public enforcement. The programmes nonetheless display elements of RNG through their involvement of third-party representatives, in this case unions, in place of city labour inspectors in the investigation and documentation of workplace practices. The involvement of union representatives is a key strength of the model, given the intimate knowledge these individuals have of the work sites and labour conditions, and in their clear alignment with the interests of workers. The union-based labour inspectors also provide the means to enhance worker voice, in that the business agents are present on a regular basis to assist in both identifying violations and submitting documentation to city inspectors (Vosko, 2013), thereby reducing the individualization of workplace rights enforcement that so often acts as a method of marginalizing those in precarious jobs. The programmes limit the role of the union representatives, however: instituted as a means of solving existing or potential industrial relations disputes, and thereby representing a compromise measure, unions are involved exclusively in the initial phases of inspection, not in later stages in advocating for workers or assessing and enforcing penalties. Furthermore, the programmes preclude the use of strike action to seek redress for violations, which the construction unions initially conceded in exchange for the creation of an internal compliance department by the school district enabling union representatives to conduct compliance visits. Nevertheless, they provide for public accountability mechanisms through both the integration of volunteers into the work structure and the relationship with the regulatory agency, which formalizes the deputization process. These particular processes can act as counters to regulatory degradation, but only if teamed with other mechanisms fostering greater public accountability in following up on complaints, and only insofar as they are adapted to enable volunteers and inspectors to act as advocates for workers throughout the process, rather than simply in the detection of violations.

The Complaints Process

Encompassing mechanisms for the intake and processing of formal claims, the individually oriented complaints process is at the heart of most countries' contemporary ES enforcement efforts. Relying disproportionately on workers to register their grievances, the majority of public resources are devoted to this stage. Yet in a range of jurisdictions, the complaints process is a source of mounting frustration. Complaints take long periods to pursue and settle, and there are significant backlogs in the jurisdictions under study, resulting in what for many is a form of bureaucratic disentitlement (see Gellatly et al., 2011; US Government Accountability Office, 2009). For this reason, across jurisdictions, complaints handling practices are subject to a number of RNG-styled reforms. Testing the efficacy of collaborative enforcement is thus vital to the evaluation of such reforms, since lodging complaints is often the only avenue open to workers seeking redress. It is critical to assess how new governance influenced reforms to ES configure 'hard' and 'soft' mechanisms. Because ES-dependent workers are often not in a position to complain, especially while they remain on the job, the degree to which multi-stakeholder enforcement and the dispersion of regulatory authority buffer employer retaliation must be considered.

The UK-based Citizens Advice Bureaux (CABs) provide an example of the RNG emphasis on self-help and shared (third-party) responsibility for problem-solving in the complaints-resolution process. The CABs stand in a mixed relationship with RNG as, established in Britain in 1939, they long predate new governance. Nevertheless, we include CABs as an illustrative case here as their involvement in providing assistance to non-unionized workers confronting ES violations both indicates a potential model for RNG-styled intervention in the complaints process, and offers insight into some potential limitations of this model.

CABs are volunteer-led organizations that offer free advice to citizens of the UK on a range of issues including employment rights (CA, 2013). Initially established by volunteers to deal with civilian problems during the Second World War, Citizens Advice grew in the following decades, particularly as successive Conservative governments of the 1980s and 1990s, as well as New Labour, promoted the voluntary (third) sector as both a cost-efficient alternative to state services and a means to promote 'active citizenship' (Jones, 2010; Tailby et al., 2011). Thus, while the CABs date to the era of CC regulation, as the voluntary sector shifts from

providing 'supplementary and complementary' forms of support to taking
on a much more central role in service provision (Tailby et al., 2011: 276)
the CABs are clearly implicated in the shift towards RNG approaches
to ES enforcement. More specifically, in this context, the CABs have
become a primary avenue of recourse for non-unionized workers seeking
support in addressing ES violations. In addition, the CABs have engaged
in legislatively oriented campaigns to pressure for improvements to the
employment tribunals system and, in particular, the lack of enforcement
of tribunal awards to workers (CA, 2012).

CAB advisors aim to empower workers experiencing employment
problems by providing information and legal advice, assistance with
writing letters, advice on self-representation at employment tribunals, and
referrals to more qualified experts when appropriate. If a worker is unionized, they will be referred back to their union (but will be helped if union
assistance has been inadequate). CABs also monitor employment problems and provide monthly reports to the Citizens Advice central office.
Though approximately 75 per cent of CAB workers are trained volunteers,
some CABs have employment specialists who are able to offer more direct
support and representation. Currently, there is a strong demand for CABs
due to both the declining rate of unionization and the growing precariousness of employment in the UK (Pollert, 2006). In 2012–13, CABs provided
assistance to more than 274 000 clients with more than 480 000 employment problems, the most prevalent problems being in the areas of pay and
entitlements, dismissal, and terms and conditions of employment (CA,
2014a, 2014b).

The CABs act in conjunction with the existing system of 'hard' law
in that they aim to provide assistance for workers who file complaints
through the traditional CC process. As such, CABs do not constitute a
new form or layer of ES regulation, but rather aim to create a mechanism
through which workers are better equipped to navigate the existing legislatively based system. A central aim of the CABs is to enhance worker
voice through providing both information and advice in order to assist
workers in representing themselves in the complaints process. In this way,
the CABs identify knowledge and education as the solution to power differentials in the complaints process. Thus, while CABs amount to a third-
party organization involved in the complaints process, with a primary
role in providing advice, they do not constitute a new form of worker
representation within that process. Moreover, they do not hold a formal
role in the broader process of enforcement outside complaints, as they
neither participate in investigations to determine violations, nor engage in
determining and enforcing sanctions. They thus reflect the RNG emphasis
on individualized self-representation, while at the same time acting to

bolster established complaints procedures by providing rights education and awareness in a system of public enforcement.

While aiming to create a mechanism for worker empowerment through enhancing capacities for self-representation, CABs clearly operate in the context of a broader process of regulatory degradation, with implications for their capacities to protect employment rights. For example, limited resources is a major factor in constraining the capacity of CABs, as funding cuts to the voluntary sector have had a significant impact on their ability to provide employee assistance (Pollert, 2008). Stable sources of funding are increasingly scarce and the CAB are inadequately staffed to meet the demand for their services. Moreover, CAB volunteers are general advisors, rather than employment specialists. And while they deal with large numbers of racialized and immigrant workers, very few CABs have immigration specialists. Surveys of workers who accessed CAB services have found dissatisfaction due to delays in obtaining advice, poor communication of case information from advisors, and a lack of continuity between advisors (Holgate et al., 2012; Pollert, 2006). Moreover, surveys of employment advisors within the CABs themselves document concern about insufficient numbers of employment specialists (Tailby et al., 2011). Thus, while aiming to empower workers who do not have collective representation, CABs do not amount to an alternative form of worker representation in the face of union decline (Holgate et al., 2012). With a primarily passive role in the complaints process, they are largely unable to effectively counter employer power and worker isolation.

Moreover, the limitations of the CABs illuminate additional concerns with respect to the RNG tendencies towards individual self-reliance and third-party responsibility for ES enforcement. If third parties are inadequately resourced, as in the case of CABs, their capacities to provide even limited services will be compromised. Further, without the presence of effective mechanisms of ES enforcement, the actions of third parties to assist workers in securing redress for ES violations will also be insufficient. Adopting a third-party model without accounting for these factors may in fact exacerbate both the individualized nature of the complaints process and tendencies towards regulatory degradation.

Claims Resolution

Representing the final stage in reactively oriented ES enforcement regimes, claims resolution entails the processes that workers and/or their representatives, often together with employers and state officials, are required to follow in order to determine, allocate and provide remedies after violations have occurred. Evaluating the degree to which RNG principles are at work, as well as their effects, is thus critical at this stage. Effective recourse to 'hard' law mechanisms, which provide for procedural as well as substantive fairness, is especially pertinent in dispute resolution, since this is the stage at which the parties tend to be most at odds with each other and the stakes are high for aggrieved workers. The extent to which the plurality of instruments supports public enforcement must thereby be evaluated. Giving voice to those with unequal stakes in the enforcement process is also essential here, as workers, in particular, will likely already have absorbed the risks involved in making a formal complaint. Many workers will have left their jobs by the time a dispute is resolved (and may thereby be in particular need of – especially pecuniary – recourse). And others may remain on the job under difficult conditions (for example, a retaliatory environment).

Changes to ES enforcement in Ontario, Canada exemplify how self-regulation and less adversarial dispute resolution processes can undermine workers' access to their legal entitlements, and further entrench regulatory degradation. The province's ES enforcement regime had long been criticized by business organizations as a main source of 'red tape'. Reforms to ES enforcement were therefore a feature of the provincial government's Open for Business Act (OBA) adopted in 2010. The OBA included more than 100 amendments to provincial regulations, the aim of which were to 'modernize' business–government interactions and reduce the regulatory burden faced by firms (Gellatly et al., 2011). With regard to ES, the legislation introduced a mandatory self-resolution step in the complaints process that extends greater responsibility to claimants to manage their own ES claims. The government in power made it mandatory for most workers[1] to first seek compliance from their employers before they are permitted to file an ES claim. The provincial government also produced a Self-Help Kit designed to assist workers in navigating this process (for example, in learning about their entitlements, determining which ES had been violated, and calculating the amount of unpaid wages owing in cases of violations) (Open for Business Act, s 96 (1) (3)(a) and (c)).

Alongside the self-resolution process, Ontario expanded the use of settlements in the claims-resolution process. Circumventing the need for an investigation, an assessment of complainant entitlement, or the use of an enforcement measure such as an order to pay, settlements involve

---

[1]   The exceptions are young workers, live-in care-givers, people with language barriers or a disability, workers who are afraid to contact the employer, workers with non-monetary complaints, workers approaching the six-month time limit, or workers whose employer has closed or gone bankrupt.

a monetary agreement between a complainant and their employer, and the withdrawal of the complaint without an admission of wrongdoing. Whereas the Ministry of Labour had long accepted settlements established between the employer and employee, the OBA assigned new powers to officials to act as settlement facilitators, essentially increasing their involvement in the settlement process. Along with the mandatory self-resolution step introduced in 2010, the increased use of both non-facilitated and facilitated settlements was intended to clear a backlog of 14 000 complaints which had amassed due largely to the under-resourcing of the complaints system in previous years.

Ontario's 2010 changes to ES enforcement exemplify how the greater use of self-regulation and non-adversarial negotiations can attenuate workers' access to legislative protections. The requirement that workers confronting ES violations first approach their employers, consistent with RNG calls for more self-regulation, fails to recognize power imbalances between workers and employers in workplaces, overlooking the original rationale for CC-oriented regulation. It exacerbates the risk that employees seeking to voice grievances will face reprisal from their employers, or be pressured to abandon their claim. To this end, administrative data indicate a marked reduction in the number of claims received following the implementation of the OBA's self-help reforms. In 2009–10, 20 365 new claims were filed with the Ministry. The following year that figure fell to 15 598 (Ontario MOL, 2011: 09). In 2012–13, 15 016 claims were received (Ontario MOL, 2013). Furthermore, the downward trend in claims receipt after 2010, when the self-resolution requirement was implemented, occurred as the absolute number of non-unionized employees in Ontario continued to increase. Consequently, a smaller proportion of the labour force is filing complaints. The self-regulation requirement is thus acting as a deterrent to claimants, especially for workers in precarious employment at risk of employer reprisal.

The increased use of settlements entails additional drawbacks. Settlements allow for a contracting-out of employment standards, and turn a question of law enforcement into a matter of dispute resolution (Vosko et al., 2011). They can also be marked by the same power imbalances of the employment relationship, whereby employees are subject to pressure to 'agree' to substandard terms from employers, many of which have legal and human resources representation throughout the settlement process (Fairey, 2005). The introduction of facilitated settlements thus further draws the MOL into the contracting-out of ES, a practice that runs directly counter to the conception of ES as a minimum floor of rights. Ultimately, settlements can incentivize non-compliance because they send a message to employers that, in the event of being caught in violation, a settlement can be reached so that less than the minimum will be paid. In short, the bid to further embed self-regulation and non-adversarial techniques in Ontario's ES complaint system is furthering regulatory degradation, and compromises the goal of protecting workplace rights.

Another innovation formalized recently in Australia and meriting analysis here is enforceable undertakings (EUs). Consistent with RNG's emphasis on the use of extra-legal, more flexible enforcement instruments, EUs are 'promises enforceable in court "offered" by an individual or [normally a] firm that has allegedly breached the law, and accepted by a regulator', to remedy disputes efficiently (Johnstone and Parker, 2010). The FWO may use this measure if 'he reasonably believes the person has contravened a civil remedy provision of the FW Act; it is in the public interest and appropriate in all the circumstances to resolve the matter through a formal enforcement outcome; and the contravention is admitted and the employer is willing to cooperate with the FWO' (FWO, 2011: 4). EUs were introduced in S. 87B of the federal Trade Practices Act (1974) in 1994, based on practices long undertaken informally by the Australian Competition and Consumer Commission (ACCC). Reflecting what Hardy and Howe (2009) call 'responsive regulation', EUs provide regulators with flexibility when determining a breach and the appropriate regulatory response or path to restorative justice (Goodwin and Maconachie, 2012: 3). They can achieve outcomes rarely accomplished in court or via administrative sanctions because of a limited array of sanctions available to courts and administrative bodies; in other words, EUs can be creative. The ACCC originally undertook EUs to avoid excessive costs of disputes. However, since their formal adoption in 1993, they have been taken up in occupational health and safety and environmental protection, as well as by several federal agencies responsible for labour standards enforcement, in an effort to respond to deficiencies in complaints systems, such as large backlogs of complaints.

EUs have been used for addressing non-compliance with minimum labour standards since the July 2009 introduction of Australia's Office of the FWO, which accepts them as mechanisms for formalizing voluntary rectification of breaches (that is, the alleged wrongdoer must take the initiative to rectify breaches) following an investigation (see, especially, Goodwin and Maconachie, 2012). The FWO's Enforceable Undertakings Policy stipulates what the employer must include in an enforceable undertaking. They must:

> admit the contravention, which must be described in detail in the Enforceable Undertaking; agree to remedy the contravention(s) in the manner specified (for example, through payment(s) to rectify underpayment) and identify the timeframe within which the contravention will be remedied (unless the contravention(s) have already been rectified); and specify any other actions

which the employer agrees to undertake and the timeframe within which those actions will be taken. (FWO, 2011: 5)

EUs can also stipulate that, should the wrongdoer fail to comply with the voluntary EU, the FWO may make an application to the court for orders against that person. EUs may contain commitments for improving compliance in the future, which may include, but are not limited to, participation in FWO educational programmes, the training of managers and staff, and the completion of audits and compliance plans as well as the adaptation of work organization systems. Furthermore, the wrongdoer is to publish a public notice declaring the contraventions and remedial actions to take place (FWO, 2011: 5–6).

The parameters for EUs under the FWO are weaker than the more established measures in the ACCC. For example, taking heed of the potential pitfall of effectively letting non-compliant employers off the hook, as well as the potential to weaken public accountability in a manner similar to other processes of mediation (Hardy and Howe, 2013: 7), the ACCC takes greater care in ascertaining whether an EU is a more appropriate first step than litigation. The ACCC considers the seriousness of the conduct and its impact on the public, the compliance history of the firm or individuals involved as well as the industry in which it is situated, and the degree of good faith of the ostensible wrongdoer. By contrast, FWO guidelines only make reference to taking into account the public interest, leading to the risk that EUs will be used in inappropriate circumstances, that is, where it may be difficult to achieve the three stages of sustained compliance envisioned (Goodwin and Maconachie, 2012: 4; see also Hardy and Howe, 2013: 24). FWO guidelines for investigative processes are similarly underdeveloped (FWO, 2010). Furthermore, EUs established between the FWO and an employer do not set binding precedents for regulators in relation to future EUs. In this way, they fail to institutionalize good practice and, hence, fall short on consistency and thereby on providing for accountability across administrative agencies and courts over time, one of the potential dangers of the dispersal of authority. At the same time, since the FWO can apply to the relevant court for orders against the wrongdoer if a voluntary EU fails, 'hard law' back-ups are available. Hardy (2011: 131) also demonstrates that the FWO recognizes the importance of facilitating non-unionized workers' collective voice in that 'it provides indirect support and assistance to community groups through funding grants and by encouraging firms to commit to paying a specific sum to community legal centres in enforceable undertakings', although engagement between the FWO and such groups in devising EUs is limited in part because they are negotiated privately. Enabled by the flexible character of EUs, such examples also highlight the potential of EUs to support worker voice, especially since workers facing violations also have recourse to external public enforcement systems when EUs fail, and given the requirement that the wrongdoer publicize the wrongdoing.

3.3   BEYOND REGULATORY NEW GOVERNANCE

Given the deepening challenges in ES enforcement, the need for reforms to traditional enforcement mechanisms is paramount. However, RNG reforms that decentre state regulation with a greater emphasis on voluntary, 'soft law', and multi-party regulatory strategies hold the risk of exacerbating the already-present regulatory crisis in ES enforcement. Indeed, most recent reforms in liberal market jurisdictions overestimate the promise of voluntary arrangements, and overlook the reasons behind ensuring compliance through active state intervention including, if necessary, sanctions. The foregoing analysis indicates that enhancements to ES regulation should build upon the strongest elements of public enforcement and draw selectively on those aspects of RNG that are particularly responsive to shifting actors in labour markets and 'fissured' (Weil, 2010) employment relationships. As scholarship on RNG suggests, the dichotomy between free markets and CC regulation fails to capture the full range of options that lie between the polar extremes of absolute employer discretion and total governmental control. In practice, RNG encompasses a much broader array of pressures and mechanisms deployed by a variety of actors, both governmental and non-governmental, to shape the behaviour of firms, and thereby address market failures and other public problems. On the basis of this more nuanced view of the range of regulatory models present in various jurisdictions, and recognizing that 'hard law' and 'soft law' mechanisms are not mutually exclusive or incompatible, we advance three normative principles that simultaneously address the limitations of both CC modes of public regulation and new governance. The intention is that these principles should buttress a regulatory governance toolkit aimed at preventing the further degradation of ES.

The first principle entails maintaining a prominent role for 'hard' enforcement mechanisms: effective ES enforcement must include a clear role for 'hard law' sanctions. Penalties backed by legislation are needed as a means to promote compliance with legislated standards. The existence of such penalties does not rule out 'soft law' strategies, particularly pertinent in early stages of the enforcement process, such as 'naming and shaming'. However, these measures should supplement rather than replace formal sanctions. EUs operating at the federal level in Australia, through the work of the country's FWO, represent a relatively successful mix of such strategies in that they institutionalize 'soft law'-oriented strategies of public disclosure of wrongdoing alongside 'harder' remedial measures to compensate aggrieved parties, while leaving open the possibility for greater resort to definitively 'hard' sanctions. They thereby recognize deficiencies of enforcement, rooted partly in the under-resourcing of labour inspectorates, without eliminating the roles of different public institutions founded in recognition of unequal power relations in the workplace.

The second principle entails augmenting worker voice across all stages of the enforcement process: ES enforcement must provide the means for the articulation of effective worker voice in prevention, complaints and dispute resolution activities. At the preventative stage, translating this principle into practice amounts to creating opportunities to identify violations in ways that do not put employees at risk of employer retribution. The LA Deputization programme, where a union representative works with employees to identify problems in working conditions, provides one such model which could inform the development of other models that take into account the challenges facing employees in non-unionized workplaces. At the complaints stage, worker voice can be enhanced through strategies that again act to mitigate the power imbalance of the workplace by shielding an employee with a complaint from the potential for employer retribution. Voice could be achieved at this level through a system of anonymous complaints or third-party representation. It could also be augmented by making use of complaints as a vital source of information on the nature of workplace violations in different sectors. Critical here is Weil's (2010) recommendation that regulators develop protocols for devoting more resources to complaints that emerge from economic sectors known for exploitative practices and low complaint levels. At the dispute resolution stage, worker representatives could aid in the negotiation of settlements. Elsewhere we canvass successful examples of anonymous and confidential complaints (Vosko, 2013). Through our critique of the LA Deputization programmes, here we also highlight the problems with limiting third-party involvement to investigative processes and preventing workers' representatives from playing advocacy roles down the line.

Our third normative principle, which involves a commitment to the creation of meaningful participatory structures, is intimately related to realizing the worker voice principle. In calling for meaningful participatory structures, we seek to address the need for expanded opportunities for public input into ES enforcement in contexts characterized at once by declining rates of unionization and long-standing enforcement systems that are highly individualized. Here, third parties, particularly those representing the interests of ES-dependent workers, such as unions and workers' centres, which are knowledgeable about specific industries and sectors, have a key role to play in identifying violations, enhancing worker voice and ensuring higher levels of accountability in the regulation of legislated standards. In advancing this principle, we follow Fine and Gordon's (2010) proposal for third-party workers' representatives across the different stages of enforcement. This requires relations that are formalized with the responsibilities of participants clearly specified, sustained rather than limited to specific short-lived campaigns or blitzes, vigorous rather than symbolic, and adequately resourced (Fine and Gordon, 2010: 61).

These normative principles by no means represent a panacea. Rather, they aim to point the way towards developing reforms suitable for implementation at different regulatory scales and that avert the threat of regulatory degradation that is heightened under some forms of RNG. At the same time, they aim to recognize that certain aspects of traditional modes of public regulation are out of sync with the proliferation of precariousness in contemporary labour markets.

REFERENCES

Ayres, I. and Braithwaite, J. (1992) *Responsive Regulation: Transcending the Deregulation Debate.* Oxford: Oxford University Press.

Baldwin, R. (1997) Regulation after command and control. In: Hawkins, K. (ed.), *The Human Face of Law: Essays in Honour of Donald Harris.* Oxford: Clarendon, pp. 65–84.

Baldwin, R., Cave, M. and Lodge, M. (2011) *Understanding Regulation: Theory, Strategy, and Practice.* Oxford: Oxford University Press.

Bernhardt, A., Boushey, H., Dresser, L. and Tilly, C. (eds) (2008) *The Gloves off Economy: Problems and Possibilities at the Bottom of America's Labor Market.* Ithaca, NY: Cornell University Press.

Bernhardt, A., Spiller, M. and Polson, D. (2013) All work and no pay: Violations of employment and labor laws in Chicago, Los Angeles and New York City. *Social Forces* **91**(3): 725–46.

Citizens Advice (CA) (2012) Social impact policy report 2011/12. London: Citizens Advice.

Citizens Advice (CA) (2013) Introduction to the service. London: Citizens Advice.

Citizens Advice (CA) (2014a) Making the case: the value to society of the Citizens Advice service. London: Citizens Advice.

Citizens Advice (CA) (2014b) The impact of employment advice. London: Citizens Advice.

Colling, T. (2012) Trade union roles in making employment rights effective. In: Dickens, L. (ed.), *Making Employment Rights Effective.* Oxford: Hart, pp. 183–204.

Crouch, C. (2005) *Capitalist Diversity and Change: Recombinant Governance and Institutional Entrepreneurs.* Oxford: Oxford University Press.

Davidov, G. (2010) The enforcement crisis in labour law and the fallacy of voluntarist solutions. *International Journal of Comparative Labour Law and Industrial Relations* **26**(1): 61–82.

de Burca, G. and Scott, J. (2006) Introduction: New governance, law and constitutionalism. In: de Burca, G. and Scott, J. (eds), *Law and New Governance in the EU and the US*. Oxford: Hart Publishing, pp. 1–14.

Estlund, C. (2005) Rebuilding the law of the workplace in an era of self-regulation. *Columbia Law Review* **105**(2): 319–404.

Estlund, C. (2012) A return to governance in the law of the workplace. In: Levi-Faur, D. (ed.), *The Oxford Handbook of Governance*. Oxford: Oxford University Press, pp. 540–53.

Fair Work Ombudsman (FWO) (2010) Guidance note 8: Investigative process of the Office. Available at: http://www.fairwork.gov.au/fwoguidancenotes/GN-8-FWO-Investigative-Process.pdf (accessed 4 January 2013).

Fair Work Ombudsman (FWO) (2011) Guidance note 4: FWO Enforceable Undertakings policy. Available at: http://www.fairwork.gov.au/fwoguidancenotes/GN-4-FWO-Enforceable-Undertakings-Policy.pdf (accessed 29 March 2013).

Fair Work Ombudsman (FWO) (2013a) National Franchise Program. Available at: http://www.fairwork.gov.au/about-us/franchise-assistance/pages/national-franchise-program (accessed 3 June 2014).

Fair Work Ombudsman (FWO) (2013b) Fair Work Ombudsman annual report 2012–2013. Available at: www.fairwork.gov.au/Publications/Annual%20report/Fair-Work-Ombudsman-Annual-Report-2012-13.pdf (accessed 16 November 2013).

Fairey, D. (2005) *Eroding Worker Protections: British Columbia's New 'Flexible' Employment Standards*. Vancouver, BC: Canadian Centre for Policy Alternatives.

Fine, J. (2013) Solving the problem from hell: Tripartism as a strategy for addressing labour standards non-compliance in the United States. *Osgoode Hall Law Journal* **50**: 813–43.

Fine, J. and Gordon, J. (2010) Strengthening labor standards enforcement through partnerships with workers' organizations. *Politics and Society* **38**: 552–85.

Gellatly, M., Grundy, J., Mirchandani, K. et al. (2011) 'Modernizing' employment standards? Administrative efficiency and the production of the illegitimate claimant in Ontario, Canada. *Economic and Labour Relations Review* **22**(2): 81–106.

Goodwin, M. and Maconachie, G. (2012) Enforceable Undertakings: A new mechanism for minimum labour standards enforcement. Paper presented at the AIRAANZ Conference 2012: Re-organizing Work, 8–10 February, Surfers Paradise, Australia. Available at: http://eprints.qut.edu.au/48730/ (accessed 5 December 2012).

Gunningham, N. (2010) Enforcement and compliance strategies. In: Baldwin, R., Cave, M. and Lodge, M. (eds), *The Oxford Handbook of Regulation*. Oxford: Oxford University Press, pp. 120–45.

Gunningham, N. and Grabosky, P. (1998) *Smart Regulation: Designing Environmental Policy*. Oxford: Oxford University Press.

Hardy, T. (2011) Enrolling non-state actors to improve compliance with minimum employment standards. *Economic and Labour Relations Review* **22**(3): 117–40.

Hardy, T. and Howe, J. (2009) Partners in enforcement? The new balance between government and trade union enforcement of employment standards in Australia. *Australian Journal of Labour Law* **23**(3): 306–36.

Hardy, T. and Howe, J. (2013) Too soft or too severe? Enforceable Undertakings and the regulatory dilemma facing the Fair Work Ombudsman. *Federal Law Review* **41**: 1–33.

Holgate, J., Pollert, A., Keles, J. and Kumarappan, L. (2012) De-collectivization and employment problems: The experiences of minority ethnic workers seeking help through Citizens Advice. *Work, Employment and Society* **26**(5): 772–88.

Howe, J., Hardy, T. and Cooney, S. (2013) Mandate, discretion, and professionalisation in an employment standards enforcement agency: An Antipodean experience. *Law and Policy* **34**(1/2): 81–108.

Johnstone, R. and Parker, C. (2010) Enforceable Undertakings in action: Report of a roundtable discussion with Australian regulators. University of Melbourne Legal Studies Research Paper no. 464. Available at: http://papers.ssrn.com/sol3/papers.cfm?abstract_id=1551627 (accessed 25 November 2012).

Jones, R. (2010) Learning beyond the state: The pedagogical spaces of the CAB service. *Citizenship Studies* **14**(6): 725–38.

Lobel, O. (2005) Interlocking regulatory and industrial relations: The governance of workplace safety. *Administrative Law Review* **57**(4): 1071–152.

Lobel, O. (2012) New governance as regulatory governance. In: Levi-Faur D. (ed.), *The Oxford Handbook of Governance*. Oxford: Oxford University Press, pp. 65–82.

Malloy, T. (2010) The social construction of regulation: Lessons from the war against command and control. *Buffalo Law Review* **58**(2): 267–355.

Mascini, P. (2013) Why was the enforcement pyramid so influential? And what price was paid? *Regulation and Governance* **7**: 48–60.

Ontario Ministry of Labour (MOL) (2011) Results-Based Plan 2011–2012. Available at: http://www.labour.gov.on.ca/english/about/pdf/rbp_11-12.pdf (accessed 10 March 2013).

Ontario Ministry of Labour (MOL) (2013) Results-Based Plan 2013–2014. Available at: http://www.labour.gov.on.ca/english/about/pubs/rbp/2013/index.php.

Pierre, J. (2012) Governance and institutional flexibility. In: Levi-Faur, D. (ed.), *The Oxford Handbook of Governance*. Oxford: Oxford University Press, pp. 187–200.

Pollert, A. (2006) The unorganized worker: Problems at work and routes to resolution with the Citizens Advice Bureau. Working Paper 6. Bristol: Centre for Employment Studies Research.

Pollert, A. (2008) Under-funded, overstretched and overwhelmed: The experience of Citizens Advice Bureaux and Law Centre Advisors in supporting vulnerable workers. Bristol: Centre for Employment Studies Research.

Pollert, A. (2009) Injustice at work: How Britain's low-paid non-unionised employees experience workplace problems. *Journal of Workplace Rights* **13**(3): 223–44.

Prudham, S. (2004) Poisoning the well: Neoliberalism and the contamination of municipal water in Walkerton, Ontario. *Geoforum* **35**(3): 343–59.

Sabel, C., O'Rourke, D. and Fung, A. (2000) Ratcheting labor standards: Regulation for continuous improvement in the global workplace. Available at: http://www.archonfung.net/papers/rls21.pdf (accessed 3 July 2011).

Seidman, G. (2009) Labouring under an illusion? Lesotho's 'sweat-free' label. *Third World Quarterly* **30**(3): 581–98.

Short, J. (2012) The paranoid style in regulatory reform. *Hastings Law Journal* **63**(3): 633–94.

Stoker, G. (1998) Governance as theory: Five propositions. *International Social Science Journal* **50**(155): 17–28.

Strauss, K. (2009) Challenging hegemonic deregulation? The UK Gangmaster Licensing Authority as a model for the regulation of casual work. Working Papers in Employment, Work and Finance. Oxford: School of Geography and the Environment, University of Oxford.

Tailby, S., Pollert, A., Warren, S., Danford, A. and Wilton, N. (2011) Underfunded and overwhelmed: The voluntary sector as worker representation in Britain's individualized industrial relations system. *Industrial Relations Journal* **42**(3): 273–92.

Thomas, M. (2009) *Regulating Flexibility: The Political Economy of Employment Standards.* Montreal and Kingston: McGill-Queen's University Press.

Tombs, S. and Whyte, D. (2010) A deadly consensus: Worker safety and regulatory degradation under New Labour. *British Journal of Criminology* **50**(1): 46–65.

Tucker, E. (2013) Old lessons for new governance: Safety or profit and the new conventional wisdom. In: Nichols, T. and Walters, D. (eds), *Safety Or Profit? International Studies in Governance Change and the Work Environment.* New York: Baywood Press, pp. 71–96.

United States Government Accountability Office (2009) Wage and Hour Division needs improved investigative processes and ability to suspend Statute of Limitations to better protect workers against wage theft. Report to the Committee on Education and Labor, House of Representatives. Available at: http://www.gao.gov/assets/300/291496.pdf (accessed 3 June 2012).

Vosko, L.F. (2006) Precarious employment: Towards an improved understanding of labour market insecurity. In: Vosko, L.F. (ed.), *Precarious Employment: Understanding Labour Market Insecurity in Canada.* Montreal and Kingston: McGill-Queen's University Press, pp. 1–39.

Vosko, L.F. (2013) 'Rights without remedies': enforcing employment standards in Ontario by maximizing voice among workers in precarious jobs. *Osgoode Hall Law Journal* **50**(4): 845–73.

Vosko, L.F., Tucker, E., Thomas, M. and Gellatly, M. (2011) New approaches to enforcement and compliance with labour regulatory standards: The case of Ontario, Canada. Available at: http://papers.ssrn.com/sol3/papers.cfm?abstract_id=1975867 (accessed 23 November 2012).

Weil, D. (2010) Improving workplace conditions through strategic enforcement: A report to the Wage and Hour Division. Available at: http://www.dol.gov/whd/resources/strategicEnforcement.pdf (accessed 2 February 2013).

PART II

Labour Market Regulation and Vulnerability

4. Assessing the scale of women's informal work: An industry outlook for 14 developing countries*

Maarten van Klaveren and Kea Tijdens

4.1 INTRODUCTION

This chapter examines the difficulty of assessing the scale of informal employment from a gender perspective: as we show, the widespread paucity of adequate data of sufficient quality is a major obstacle. This, in turn, has significant implications for effective policy-making for the informal economy generally, and from a gender perspective in particular. We focus on industries where large shares of women workers may be assumed, in particular agriculture; wholesale and retail; and hotels, restaurants and catering. Evidence is presented from 14 countries covered in the 2008–11 Decisions for Life (DFL) project, a major trade union project aiming at empowering adolescent girls and young women in work in which the authors were involved as researchers. This project covered the large countries Brazil, India and Indonesia, the Commonwealth of Independent States (CIS) countries Azerbaijan, Belarus, Kazakhstan and Ukraine, and the sub-Saharan African countries Angola, Botswana, Malawi, Mozambique, South Africa, Zambia and Zimbabwe.[1] Very many of those who work in the informal economies of these countries are largely or

* This chapter is based on research conducted as part of the Decisions For Life project. The project has received funding from the Ministry of Foreign Affairs in the Netherlands as part of its MDG3 programme (grant no. BE/285-2008). An earlier version was presented at the ILO's 3rd Regulating Decent Work conference (3–5 July 2013, Geneva). The authors wish to thank participants of this conference for comments on that paper.

[1] These countries were chosen by our project partners, the International Trade Union Confederation (ITUC), the UNI Global Union and the WageIndicator Foundation (WIF). See, for DFL project information, http://www.ituc-csi.org/ decisions-for-life?lang=en and http://dfl.wageindicator.org/home. The Amsterdam Institute for Advanced labour Studies (AIAS) was responsible for drafting a gender

totally beyond the protection of such labour market institutions as social dialogue and collective bargaining, minimum wage setting and labour inspection. According to recent International Labour Organization (ILO) analysis (ILO, 2014a: 39), there is a significant correlation between the incidence of informal employment and indicators of poor job quality.

Against this backdrop, the authors have elsewhere extensively analysed outcomes of the DFL project, in the context of challenges and barriers to empowering young women in work in developing countries (Van Klaveren and Tijdens, 2012). In this chapter we concentrate on the challenge of assessing accurately the scale of women's informal work in the 14 countries scrutinized, for the industries mentioned above. As we will show, our understanding of the scale of women's informal work is constrained by the fact that the relevant Labour Force Surveys do not fully capture the concept of informal work and, moreover, vary significantly across industries, countries and years. The chapter builds on a previous industry outlook (Van Klaveren and Tijdens, 2012: 89–94, 116–28), seeking a better understanding of the economic dynamics influencing informality, including its interplay with social, cultural and political forces, as well as with legal frameworks.

There are several reasons for considering the issues from the point of view of different industries. Cooperation with trade unions was important in the DFL project, and in most countries, including those scrutinized, unions are mainly organised along industry lines. Moreover, early in the DFL project a particular question concerning agriculture came to the fore, that ran as follows: can young women living in urban areas and trying to make a career there, rely on a 'fall-back scenario' in which they can reasonably expect to go back to their families who depend on agriculture, without placing a heavy burden on those families? In our effort to answer that question, we devoted special attention to the difficulties of measuring informal work in agriculture in the countries at stake, in particular as much statistical reporting concerning informal work tends to exclude agriculture. More generally, mechanisms that allocate labour basically follow industry divisions: employment prospects tend to differ largely across industries as they are interconnected with competitive structures and struggles, as well as with technological change at industry level.

This chapter is structured as follows. Section 4.2 reviews the available literature on defining and measuring informal employment, thereby exploring different measurement concepts and issues. Section 4.3 aims to

---

analysis of work and employment for the 14 countries involved, serving the campaigns and websites of the project.

analyse the statistical consequences of including or excluding agriculture in employment data for the 14 countries scrutinized, while focusing on female employment. Section 4.4 aims to assess the incidence of informal employment by gender in particular in agriculture and commerce, in a subsample of eight of 14 countries. Section 4.5 presents our findings in relation to harmonized labour force statistics. As a statistical background, the Appendix provides information on labour force participation rates in the 14 countries explored here (Table 4A.1), as well as a detailed table containing information on commerce sector employment in these countries (Table 4A.2).

4.2 LITERATURE REVIEW: INFORMAL EMPLOYMENT DEFINED AND MEASURED

In recent decades the informal economy has attracted considerable interest from researchers and international organizations aiming to estimate and explain its size, particularly in developing countries. Defining and subsequently measuring the informal economy has proven to be complicated. The International Conference of Labour Statisticians (ICLS) has attempted to harmonize the various definitional concepts used across countries. It distinguishes between the informal sector, referring to informal enterprises, and informal employment, referring to informal jobs of individuals. Employment in the informal economy can be understood as the sum of employment in the informal sector and informal employment found outside the informal sector (ILO, 2013b). The 1993 ICLS defined the informal sector as private unincorporated enterprises that are unregistered or small in terms of the number of employed persons. An enterprise is left out if it is not constituted as a separate legal entity independently of its owner(s) and does not maintain a complete set of accounts. Units engaged in the production of goods or services exclusively for own final use by the household are excluded as well, as are enterprises engaged in agriculture, hunting, forestry and fishing. Thus, agriculture as a sector has been excluded here, except for small-scale farmers not running legally settled enterprises though at least partly producing for the market (ICLS, 1993).

The 2003 ICLS defined informal employment as a job-based concept. It adopted guidelines for defining informal employment as comprising all jobs carried out in informal enterprises as well as in formal enterprises by workers, especially employees, 'whose employment relationship is, in law or in practice, not subject to national labour legislation, income taxation, social protection or entitlement to certain employment benefits' (ICLS,

2003: para 3(5)). Thus, the concept encompassed: (1) own-account workers and employers employed in their own informal enterprises; (2) members of informal producers' co-operatives; (3) own-account workers producing goods exclusively for own final use by their household; (4) contributing (unpaid) family workers; and (5) employees holding informal jobs in formal enterprises, informal enterprises or as paid domestic workers employed by households (ICLS, 2003: para 3(2)). Although with some variation in the precise wording, these concepts were subsequently used in the definitions in the ILO Transition from the Informal to the Formal Economy Recommendation, 2015 (No. 204).

In 2009 a joint overview study explored the views on informality of the ILO and the World Trade Organization (WTO) (Bacchetta et al., 2009). Summarizing the ILO's point of view, the informal economy is defined by its exclusion from the benefits and rights incorporated in labour laws and social security systems. From the WTO's point of view, the main distinction between the formal and the informal economy is that the latter is not subject to tax regulations and is excluded from administrative rules covering property relationships, financial credit systems and commercial licensing. We note that for its part the World Bank strongly emphasizes the risks of undermining the rule of law and governance that accompany a high level of informality. While recognizing that informal employment may provide a cushion for workers who cannot find a job in the formal sector, the World Bank argues repeatedly that 'it entails a loss in budget revenues by reducing taxes and social security contributions paid and therefore the availability of funds to improve infrastructure and other public goods and services. It invariably leads to a high tax burden on registered labour' (World Bank, 2011: 5; cf. ILO, 2013c: 9–10).

In 2002, the ILO's International Labour Conference at its 90th Session adopted a resolution on 'Decent Work and the Informal Economy'. It called upon the ILO to 'assist member States to collect, analyse and disseminate consistent, disaggregated statistics on the size, composition and contribution of the informal economy that will help enable identification of specific groups of workers and economic units and their problems in the informal economy' (ILO, 2002: para 37(n)). As far as we can see, this aim has been made operational along two lines of statistical efforts initiated by the ILO. First, in the course of the 2000s a major effort was undertaken by National Statistical Offices (NSOs), supported by ILO technical staff, to introduce the new statistical measures in national surveys. Based on this effort the ILO Department of Statistics, jointly with the research policy network known as Women in Informal Employment Globalizing and Organizing (WIEGO), has presented statistical updates on the various forms of informal employment as defined by the 2003 ICLS

(ILO LABORSTA, n.d.; ILO, 2013b). Second, in particular in the ILO's yearly *Global Employment Trends* reports,[2] the concept of vulnerable employment has been central. In this series, 'vulnerable employment' refers to the sum of own-account workers and unpaid family workers, thus encompassing three of the five categories that make up informal employment. Only members of informal producers' co-operatives, in most countries a negligible category, and employees holding informal jobs in formal enterprises have been excluded here. The ILO argues that workers in vulnerable employment are less likely to have formal work arrangements, and that they are therefore more likely to lack elements associated with decent employment such as adequate social security and recourse to effective social dialogue mechanisms. Vulnerable employment is often characterized by inadequate earnings, low productivity and difficult conditions of work that undermine workers' fundamental rights.[3]

In a *Statistical Manual* on measuring informality, the ILO Department of Statistics has tried to disentangle the complexity of the actual conceptual framework by treating the related data collection methods according to the chosen sampling unit. The study distinguishes surveys of establishments, households and individuals. Informality measured at the level of economic units usually defines the informal economy according to their registration status, access to social coverage, or size. Informality measured at the level of households focuses predominantly on the degree of self-provision; whereas informality measured at the level of individual workers focuses on the degree to which they are subject to labour regulation and social security (ILO, 2012a). Along these lines, a growing body of empirical research has emerged using job-based concepts by taking workers as the unit of analysis, and extending those concepts by including social security criteria while using an establishment-based sampling strategy. Entitlement and contribution to social security (or other employment benefits), as well as the existence of a written employment contract, have been applied here as main dimensions, resulting in positions on a scale of (in)formality (Luebker, 2008; Tijdens et al., 2015). In the countries

---

[2]   The series was replaced by the *World Employment and Social Outlook: Trends* reports from January 2015.

[3]   Though admitting that some limitations of the vulnerable employment indicator should be borne in mind: (a) wage and salary employment is not synonymous with decent work; (b) the unemployed are not included in the indicator, though they are vulnerable; and (c) a worker may be classified in one of the two vulnerable status groups but still not carry a high economic risk, especially in developed economies (ILO, 2010: 18).

scrutinized here, more specific rules apply, with mostly one or two of these dimensions as point(s) of reference.

4.3   MEASURES OF INFORMAL EMPLOYMENT WITH OR WITHOUT AGRICULTURE

The 2013 ILO–WIEGO statistical update comprises a compilation of statistics by sex on employment in the informal economy from 47 medium- and low-income countries. These statistics only present data concerning the non-agricultural sector. In Table 4.1 we select the figures for the seven countries out of the 14 DFL countries for which these data are available

Table 4.1   Employment in the informal economy in non-agricultural employment, by country and gender, x 1000 and in % of non-agricultural employment, latest year available

	Persons in informal employment (A + B – C)		Persons employed in the informal sector (A)		Persons in informal employment outside informal sector (B)		Persons in formal employment in the informal sector (C)	
	(x 1000)	(%)	(x 1000)	(%)	(x 1000)	(%)	(x 1000)	(%)
South Africa (2010)	4089	32.7	2225	17.8	1864	14.9	0.0	0.0
of which women	*2018*	*36.8*	*922*	*16.8*	*1096*	*20.0*	*0.0*	*0.0*
Zambia (2008)	920	69.5	854	64.6	155	11.7	89	6.7
of which women	*407*	*80.1*	*357*	*70.3*	*63*	*12.4*	*13*	*2.6*
Zimbabwe (2011)	1066	59.0	564	31.1	502	27.9	n.a.	n.a.
of which women	*491*	*63.4*	*284*	*36.7*	*207*	*26.7*	*n.a.*	*n.a.*
Ukraine (2009)	n.a.	n.a.	1525	9.4	n.a.	n.a.	n.a.	n.a.
of which women	*n.a.*	*n.a.*	*518*	*6.4*	*n.a.*	*n.a.*	*n.a.*	*n.a.*
Brazil (2009)	32493	42.2	18688	24.3	13862	18.0	57	0.1
of which women	*15909*	*45.9*	*6982*	*20.1*	*8944*	*25.8*	*18*	*0.1*
India (2009–10)	185876	83.6	150113	67.5	37409	16.8	1646	0.7
of which women	*34921*	*84.7*	*24475*	*59.4*	*10793*	*26.2*	*347*	*0.8*
Indonesia (2009) (only Banten and Yogyakarta)	3157	72.5	2822*	64.8*	532	12.2	197	4.5
of which women	*1180*	*72.9*	*1034*	*63.9*	*227*	*14.0*	*82*	*5.0*

Notes:
* Corrected calculation, except Zimbabwe: Zimstat (2012).
n.a. = not available.

Source: ILO (2013b).

(albeit for Indonesia only for one special district and one province out of a total 32, and for Ukraine only partially).

According to the figures assembled, the share of those in informal employment in the non-agricultural part of the economy (columns A + B – C) recently varied from 33 per cent in South Africa (37 per cent for women) up to 84 per cent in India (85 per cent for women). In all cases, the overall informality shares for women were higher than for men. Remarkably, in South Africa and in Brazil more women were in informal employment outside the informal sector, that is, in the formal sector (B), than in the informal sector as such (A). In these two countries they made up, respectively, 54 and 56 per cent of all women in informal employment; in Zimbabwe their share was also considerable. In all countries, the shares of those in formal employment in the informal sector (C) remained quite limited. (The South African statistics exclude this category by definition.) It can be added that similar overall shares (A + B – C) for the period 2005–10 have been made available for Mozambique (87.2 per cent) and Azerbaijan (45.8 per cent) (Charmes, 2012).

Due to the lack of survey data, as well as changes in definitions and methods of compilation, it is virtually impossible to trace long-term developments in the size of the informal economy for a substantial number of countries, let alone for the world's regions. Against this backdrop, the efforts of Charmes (2012: 114) in this direction, albeit limited to non-agricultural activities, generate highly questionable outcomes. As for the 14 countries we scrutinized, the statistics of only a few allow such tracing. Nevertheless, they generate illuminating insights.

An example is Brazil, where formal employment includes private salaried and domestic workers with a signed Labour Card (*Carteira Assinada*), government workers and military, as well as employers and self-employed contributing to the country's social security scheme. Between 1992 and 1999, when Brazilian domestic production and exports fell and jobs in exposed sectors were lost, the number of informal jobs grew at an annual rate of 3.0 per cent, whereas formal jobs increased at a rate of only 1.7 per cent annually. During 1999–2008 this pattern was reversed. By then, formal jobs grew by 5.3 per cent yearly, whereas the growth of informal jobs fell to an annual rate of 1.7 per cent. As a result, the national formality rate fell from 46.4 per cent in 1992 to 43.9 per cent in 1999, before rising to 49.6 per cent in 2008 (Berg, 2011) and 2009 (with 51.6 per cent formality among men and 47.2 per cent among women; authors' calculation based on IBGE, 2009). A number of factors fuelled such formalization, including Brazil's improved macroeconomic performance and rising domestic demand, though the effects of a more equitable and inclusive growth pattern, including the expansion of social security, should not be neglected. Other relevant factors were in demographics and education. Brazil's rapidly decreasing fertility rates and increasing secondary school enrolment rates resulted in reduced youth labour supply and falling amounts of young precariously employed. Finally, a 1996 tax law supporting the formalization of small firms, improved labour inspection and greater legal awareness amongst, notably, domestic workers have contributed to the rise of formalization in the 2000s (Berg, 2011).

Indonesia is another interesting case. At first sight its statistics show a trend similar to Brazil's, but they have to be interpreted very cautiously. According to the Indonesian statistics, formal employment – defined as employers with permanent workers and wage-earners, disaggregated according to occupational categories – recently increased rapidly. Though interrupted in the crisis years 2008–09, formal employment as a share of the labour force grew after 2005 by more than 9 percentage points to nearly 40 per cent in 2013. In particular, after 2010, the shares of self-employed and casual workers registered as 'informal' declined (ILO and IILS, 2011; Tjandra and Van Klaveren, 2015). However, women's share in formal employment remained about 6 percentage points below men's; job creation for women in the formal sector has been low, and constrained by discriminatory practices (Anwar and Supriyanto, 2012). Also, working in the Indonesian formal sector is far from a guarantee of job security and good conditions. Labour market flexibility, a key strategy of successive administrations in the last decade, has clearly triggered informalization and flexibilization processes within the formal sector (Tjandraningsih, 2013). For example, a few years ago the World Bank concluded that more than 80 per cent of wage-earners in the formal sector lacked any written contract. After 2005, the share of contract and outsourced workers in the ranks of the formally employed nearly doubled (Alatas, 2011; Anwar and Supriyanto, 2012).

As noted, the ILO–WIEGO statistical updates do not discuss the exclusion of agricultural employment. Drawing on his own, important role in shaping the measurement of informality, Charmes identifies two reasons why an indicator based on non-agricultural employment has been preferred. First, he argues that in countries where agriculture is predominant and occupies the bulk of the labour force, the share of employment in the informal economy, including agriculture, is above 90 per cent and changes over time may not be visible because of the volume of the labour force. Second, the importance of change may remain hidden by the dramatic flows of rural–urban migrations (Charmes, 2012: 112–13). We will return to these arguments in section 4.4. For the time being, by contrast, our position is that the exclusion of agriculture has to be questioned, and that such an exclusion may frustrate insights in particular as to the position

Table 4.2   *Agriculture (including forestry and fishing): total and female*
employment shares by country, first years (1999–2005) and
last years (2007–13)

	Empl. in agric. in % of total empl. (A)		Female empl. in agric. in % of total female empl. (B)		% females in empl. in agric. (C)	
	First year	Last year	First year	Last year	First year	Last year
Angola, 2000–2007	88	85	90	88	57	55
Botswana, 2010	n.a.	26	n.a.	21	n.a.	37
Malawi, 2005–13	83	64	89	70	48	52
Mozambique, 2002–12	80	73	89	83	62	63
South Africa, 2000–2013	11	5	10	4	40	33
Zambia, 2000–2008	72	71	80	77	50	52
Zimbabwe, 1999–2011	58	66	69	72	57	55
Azerbaijan, 2003–13	38	37	42	44	45	57
Belarus, 2009	n.a.	9	n.a.	7	n.a.	39
Kazakhstan, 2003–13	37	24	34	24	47	47
Ukraine, 2003–13	20	20	18	19	44	46
Brazil, 2003–13	21	14	14	10	32	30
India, 1999/00–2009/10	60	50	78	67	35	33
Indonesia, 2003–13	46	35	48	35	37	38

Sources: For Azerbaijan, Botswana, Brazil, Kazakhstan, Indonesia, Malawi,
Mozambique, South Africa, Ukraine, Zambia, Zimbabwe: ILOSTAT website and/or
national Labour Force Surveys/Household Surveys. Additional for Angola, Belarus, India,
South Africa, Zimbabwe: authors' estimates based on various sources (see Van Klaveren et
al., 2009b, 2009c, 2010a, 2010c, 2010d).

and perspectives of women in developing countries. We will underpin our
position with the help of Tables 4.2, 4.3 and 4.4.

Before going into these tables, we note that ILO's *Global Employment
Trends 2012* paid attention to developments in agriculture; notable, in
view of the earlier statistical exclusion of this sector. This ILO publication confirmed that a high incidence of vulnerable employment is often
associated with a large share of workers in (often subsistence) agriculture.
It pointed out that in the two regions with the highest shares of vulnerable
employment, sub-Saharan Africa and South Asia, the agricultural sector
has remained the largest in terms of employment, and concluded that 'a
major reduction in the incidence of vulnerable employment in developing regions will require a further shift of employment out of agriculture
and into higher value-added manufacturing and services sector activities'
(ILO, 2012b: 44). The next edition, *Global Employment Trends 2013*, noted
that in 2012, 1.46 billion workers in developing countries – 56 per cent of
all those employed in those countries – were in vulnerable employment, an

*Table 4.3   Shares of informal employment in total employment (incl.
            agriculture), by country and gender, latest year available*

	Total	Male	Female
Angola, 2007	81	72	89
Botswana, 2006	38	36	39
Malawi, 2013	89	84	94
Mozambique, 2006	87	84	90
South Africa, 2010	33	29	39
Zambia, 2008	89	85	94
Zimbabwe, 2011	88	83	93
Azerbaijan, 2008	55	47	62
Belarus, 2009	n.a.	n.a.	n.a.
Kazakhstan, 2008	32	31	34
Ukraine, 2010	23	20	28
Brazil, 2009	50	48	53
India, 2009–10	91	90	92
Indonesia, 2013	54	51	58

Note: n.a. = not available.

Sources: For Botswana, Malawi, Mozambique, South Africa, Zambia, Zimbabwe,
Azerbaijan, Kazakhstan, Ukraine, Brazil, Indonesia: national Labour Force Surveys;
for Angola, Mozambique, India: authors' estimates based on various sources (see Van
Klaveren et al., 2009a, 2009b, 2010a; Government of India, 2011; Papola and Sahu, 2012).

increase of more than 5 million from the previous year. In 2013, there was
a further increase of more than 13 million. The *Global Employment Trends
2014* report showed that vulnerable employment shares continued to be
extremely high in sub-Saharan Africa and South Asia, for women even
more so than men, with shares of females in vulnerable employment in
2012 of 85.6 and 81.1 per cent, respectively. ILO projections for 2013–18
predict for these two regions a slight fall in percentages but an increase
in numbers, adding during this period a further 22 million and 18 million
women, respectively, in vulnerable employment (ILO, 2013a: 39, 142–3;
ILO, 2014b: 98–9).

Table 4.2 allows a first indication of the quantitative implications
of leaving out agriculture, by showing shares of (female) workers in
agriculture for the 14 countries we scrutinized in the DFL project. We
used data as far as possible covering the last decade, though by neces-
sity the first and last years covered varied across countries. According
to the data from the most recent years (column A), apart from South
Africa (5 per cent) and Botswana (26 per cent), a majority of the total
labour force in the other five sub-Saharan countries was employed in

Table 4.4   *Shares of informal employment by sector, country and gender, latest year available*

	Total (A)			Agriculture (B)			Non-agr. economy (C)			Commerce (D)		
	Total	M	F	Total	M	F	Total	M	F	Total	M	F
Malawi, 2013	89	84	94	96	94	98	75	70	84	91	n.a.	n.a.
S. Africa, 2007	27	22	34	32	23	42	25	22	35	33	27	38
Zambia, 2008	89	85	94	98	98	99	70	59	80	90	85	97
Zimbabwe, 2011	88	83	93	99	98	99	64	57	75	86	80	93
Ukraine, 2010	23	20	28	24	21	32	23	20	27	14	n.a.	n.a.
Brazil, 2009	50	48	53	89	78	99	42	40	46	40	31	54
India, 2009–10	91	90	92	97	97	98	84	83	91	86	86	90
Indonesia, 2013	54	51	58	80	83	78	42	35	45	64	61	67

Note: n.a. = not available.

Sources: Columns A, B and D: authors' calculations/estimates based on ILOSTAT (n.d.) and national Labour Force Surveys (ILO, various dates; column C: ILO (2013b), except Ukraine, Labour Force Survey, 2010 (ILO, various dates); except columns A–D for Malawi: NSO (2014); for Zimbabwe: Zimstat (2012); for Indonesia: BPS (2013).

agriculture (including forestry and fishing). The shares of agricultural employment were also considerable in Azerbaijan, India and Indonesia, where they ranged from 30 to 50 per cent. The shares in agriculture were below 30 per cent in Belarus, Kazakhstan, Ukraine and Brazil. Comparison with the first period of observation shows that in ten of 12 countries for which we could compare, the proportion of the labour force in agriculture decreased, in half of them considerably, by 10–19 percentage points (Malawi, Kazakhstan, India, Indonesia) or by one-third (Brazil). Only in Zimbabwe did the share in agriculture increase, whereas in Ukraine it remained constant, indicating that particular political and social developments may induce diverging paths. The outcomes for 12 countries in the two observed years were strongly correlated ($R = 0.96$).

Column B shows, for the most recent year of observation, that in the five countries with the largest overall shares in agriculture, all in the sub-Saharan region, the shares of the female labour force involved in agriculture were 3–10 percentage points higher than the overall shares. In India, with half of its total labour force in agriculture, the proportion of women in this sector was 17 percentage points higher. Over the last decade, across countries the share of the female labour force developed largely similarly to the overall share. For the first year of observation, overall and female shares correlated strongly ($R = 0.98$), and for the last year even more strongly ($R = 0.99$). Three countries showed (slightly) increased shares of females in agriculture: Azerbaijan, Ukraine and Zimbabwe (though in the last case most likely caused by a change in statistical definitions). In the majority of countries, the shift of employment away from agriculture covered female and male workers alike, largely to the same extent.

Column C confirms that over the last decade the shares of women in the agricultural labour force remained fairly constant, again with the exception of Azerbaijan. Here, and in the five sub-Saharan countries (Angola, Malawi, Mozambique, Zambia and Zimbabwe), women recently made up majorities in the agricultural labour force. By contrast, recently in Kazakhstan and Ukraine their numbers were close to half of that labour force. By contrast, South Africa, Belarus and Brazil, the countries with the lowest overall shares of employment in agriculture (A), in recent years also showed rather low shares of female workers in agricultural employment (C). In this respect they joined Botswana, India and Indonesia, three countries with more substantial shares of agriculture in total employment. Taken together, these six countries all end up with less than 40 per cent female agricultural employment, although different explanations seem to apply. Particularly in South Africa and Brazil, large-scale commercial farming employing mainly male workers has come to dominate (cf. Van Klaveren et al., 2009c, 2009f).

In the case of India the relatively low numbers in column C may be related to the country's low female labour participation rate (LPR) of less than 26 per cent (Appendix, Table 4A.2). At the same time, especially in the case of India, it is strongly arguable that the amount of women's work has been under-reported. This could be a result of reliance on labour force, household or mixed surveys; the addition of time-use surveys (TUSs) might provide a more realistic picture because they capture short-term and simultaneous jobs as well as subsistence work. Previous use of TUS data has suggested that India's female LPR is higher than reported officially. Indeed, compared to data derived from the nationwide household survey, use of TUS data has shown that India's female LPR may in truth be nearly twice the figure derived from labour force, household or mixed surveys. It has also shown that the gap with the (also newly calculated) male LPR may be less than half of that which is officially reported (Hirway and Jose, 2011). Projecting these outcomes for 1998–2000 on India's 2009–10 household data would lift the proportion of females in agriculture from 33 per cent (Table 4.2, Column C) to approximately 45 per cent (authors' calculations, based on Hirway and Jose, 2011; Government of India, 2011).

In the next section of this chapter we consider the situation of women in the commerce sector, defined here as including wholesale and retail as well as hotels, restaurants and catering. By way of background, we present in Appendix Table 4A.2 the most recent available statistical information on this sector for the 14 countries in our study. In column A, this table shows that in nine countries women occupied 50–70 per cent of all jobs in commerce. In Azerbaijan (32 per cent) and particularly in India (14 per cent) their share was much lower, though for the latter country the under-reporting just discussed may have played a role. The shares of women in wholesale and retail are very similar. Indeed, women are employed far more often in these forms of work than they are in hotels, restaurants and catering. The differential ranges from four to five times as many (Botswana, South Africa, Brazil, India, Indonesia) to as much as 17–18 times as many (Malawi, Mozambique).

Column B also shows that the share of female employment in commerce as a proportion of total female employment varies widely across countries, ranging from 5 per cent in India to 10 per cent in Botswana, Mozambique and Zambia; and up to 28 per cent in Indonesia and 29 per cent in Brazil. We may assume that such gaps have widened during the last decade. National statistics indicate that in Indonesia and Brazil after 2000 female employment in commerce has increased both absolutely and relatively (as a percentage of total female employment), while in Mozambique and

Zambia, as well as in India, both the absolute increase of female employment and the increase of the employment share of commerce in female jobs remained quite limited (cf. Van Klaveren et al., 2009a, 2009d, 2009f, 2010a, 2010b). Obviously, specific national conditions have been decisive in this respect, partly related to national growth rates, and partly depending on the specific development of wholesale and retail, and of the hotels, restaurants and catering industry. The latter has turned in particular on the growth of tourism.

In summary, this section has shown that in the countries studied, informal work is predominantly found in the agricultural sector. Apart from Zimbabwe in the first decade of the 2000s, in all these countries the share of agricultural employment in total employment decreased. In this period of time the share of women remained stable, pointing to a decrease of women's informal employment. The finding that the shares of informality in non-agricultural employment were higher for women than for men only counteracted this trend to a limited extent.

4.4   MEASURES OF INFORMAL EMPLOYMENT IN AND OUTSIDE AGRICULTURE

We now turn our attention to informality. Table 4.3 provides the most recent figures available for the shares of informal employment in total employment, including agriculture. The table shows high rates of informality, more than 80 per cent, for Angola, Malawi, Mozambique, Zambia, Zimbabwe and India; although of these countries only India met the 90 per cent level of informality mentioned by Charmes. The other countries had substantially lower informality rates, with Azerbaijan and Indonesia forming a category in between. In all 13 countries for which data are available, the share of informality among women was higher than that for men, mostly by 3–9 percentage points; in Angola, South Africa and Azerbaijan however the differential was even greater. For the five countries for which these overall outcomes can be compared with those in Table 4.1 for the non-agricultural economy, only South Africa showed approximately the same total and female informality rates. The equivalent values for Zambia, Zimbabwe, Brazil and India were considerably higher: respectively 19, 29, 8 and 7 percentage points overall; and 14, 30, 7 and 7 percentage points for females. As Table 4.4 confirms, these differences imply high informality rates in agriculture for the latter four countries.

As noted in the ILO's *Global Employment Trends 2012*, the (further) shift of employment out of agriculture may be crucial for reducing vulnerable employment. Therefore, we tried to trace the development of agriculture and mining (the primary sector), manufacturing, construction and utilities (the secondary sector), and the tertiary sector for the respective countries over the time span indicated in Table 4.2. Unfortunately, the employment statistics used for Table 4.2 and Appendix Table 4A.2 facilitate this for only eight of the 14 countries. The four major countries in our sample (South Africa, Brazil, India and Indonesia) all showed a similar trend in the decade at stake, with 28–36 per cent of the outflow from agriculture absorbed by the secondary sector, and 64–72 per cent by the tertiary sector. For Kazakhstan the equivalent figures were 20–80 per cent. Zimbabwe, Azerbaijan and Ukraine displayed diverging development paths with decreasing shares of their tertiary sector as the common denominator. As most national statistics are not systematically disaggregated by gender, tracing changes in the sector division by gender was even more difficult. Yet the available evidence – notably for Brazil, India and Indonesia – suggests developments in the female labour force close to the overall trends, similar to what we have already noted for the respective magnitudes of the shift away from agriculture as such.

Statistical difficulties as noted above hold *a fortiori* for tracing informality across countries by sectors over time; we had to abstain from such an overview as few countries provided the necessary data. Therefore, Table 4.4 presents only for the latest year available, and only for eight countries, the shares of those informally employed in the labour force at large, agriculture, the non-agricultural economy and, as part of the latter, the commerce sector. It shows that in all eight countries informality was more widespread in agriculture than in non-agricultural activities, though for South Africa and particularly Ukraine the differences were small. In India, the share of informal employment remained high in both categories; whereas in Malawi and Zambia – and even more so in Zimbabwe, Brazil and Indonesia – there were massive gaps between the shares of informality in agriculture and non-agriculture. In five countries, gender differences were larger in the non-agricultural economy; whereas in South Africa, Ukraine and Brazil they were smaller. In Indonesia informality among females in non-agricultural activities was 10 percentage points higher than among men, whereas, surprisingly, in agriculture it was higher among men.

Finally, it is worthwhile comparing the shares of informal employment in commerce with those in non-agricultural employment at large. In four countries (South Africa, Zambia, Zimbabwe, Indonesia) these shares were higher in commerce for both males and females. In Brazil it was only higher for females, and in India only for males, although the differences in India were quite small. The figures for Malawi and Ukraine, although merely indicative, pointed to higher informality in Malawi's commerce sector, and lower in that of Ukraine. Compared with the shares of females in informal employment in agriculture, the outcomes in terms of informality for females in commerce in South Africa, Zambia, Zimbabwe, India and Indonesia suggested that the latter were to a limited extent – that is, 2–11 percentage points – better off. Only in Brazil were women in commerce much less employed informally (though still more than in non-agriculture at large).

Combining the falling shares of employment in agriculture, both total and female (Table 4.2), with the overall much lower share of informality in non-agricultural employment as recently noted (Table 4.4), suggests that in most countries scrutinized here the levels of informality are likely to decrease below those displayed in Table 4.3; for the countries included with older data this may actually be the case to a considerable extent. Yet, two reservations apply here. First, based on the trends detectable in the available statistics for most countries, the gender gap in informality may remain at the same level or may even widen for countries like Zambia and Zimbabwe. Second, if one regards levels of informality as main indicators for the incidence of vulnerable employment, the available employment statistics may already imply a warning against an overly optimistic outlook. In most countries the shift away from agriculture only partly translates into less vulnerable (and higher value added) activities elsewhere.

The figures in Table 4.4 (column D) already suggest that such a warning may in particular be relevant in view of the characteristics of employment in the commerce subsector. A qualitative indication of developments under way in commerce underlines this warning. The spread of supermarkets and department stores controlled by multinational retail chains, often linked with wholesale firms, will often be decisive for the development of employment in retail and wholesale. As has been documented for South Africa, Zambia, Malawi and Indonesia, the 'modern markets' as they are called in Indonesia may increase the opportunities for decent work; though in South Africa there has been a strong tendency towards casualization of formalized labour in the retail industry. Yet, evidence from the same countries also shows that the expansion of supermarkets is likely to destroy informal employment on a substantial scale; not only in retail, but also in agriculture. That expansion may outcompete small-scale trade and agriculture, currently still mostly the domains of women. There is quite some proof that local small-scale food producers have major problems meeting the quality, hygiene and packaging standards set by supermarkets and 'modern' wholesalers. For the time being, the net outcome of these processes may well be a decrease in female employment. In most countries of the 14 studied, the prospects of tourism operating as an impetus for (the formalization of) female labour may look brighter, but notably skills upgrading seems conditional for perspectives on sustainable and decent jobs in this industry. The development of nature-based tourism may be important in this respect as well (cf. Van Klaveren and Tijdens, 2012: 122–5). Moreover, even with strong growth rates of the hospitality industry, we expect its contribution to female employment to remain relatively limited for the years to come. The issue of the 'fall-back scenario', as noted in our introduction (section 4.1), and related individual considerations behind migration decisions, may hide a number of difficult and uneasy choices, in which on both sides vulnerability and job insecurity may play major roles.

4.5   OUR FINDINGS IN RELATION TO HARMONIZED LABOUR FORCE STATISTICS

Currently, the harmonized labour force statistics available at country level deliver only a limited contribution to the understanding of the opportunities and constraints that, in particular, women in agriculture face in their efforts to attain decent work and a decent living. For various reasons, leaving out employment data on agriculture may well diminish the possibilities of assessing these perspectives. First, it hampers the assessment of the specific conditions for the structural transformation of national economies that does justice to the role of employment. The most important processes here are related to the shift of employment from agriculture, with large shares of low-productive, own-account workers and contributing family members, to the manufacturing industry and in particular to the services sector. Our statistical exercise combined with industry information on the commerce sector suggests that in quite some developing countries the perspectives for notably (young) women on decent and sustainable employment linked with the shift away from agriculture may be much less rosy than value-added and productivity calculations may indicate. Better employment data at country and industry levels may clarify prospects and problems of particular worker categories, notably if combined with industry-based evidence.

Second, the lack of adequate national employment data hampers insight in the constraints of this transformation in terms of the lack of infrastructural provisions and basic services. For example, overviews of the situation of women in agriculture in sub-Saharan countries clarify that the persistent lack of such provisions and services turns out to be a major factor in the continuation of conditions of poverty and food insecurity where majorities of women are locked in; even more so if unbalanced transformation takes off and large-scale commercial agriculture starts to emerge. Time and time again, most of the burden of such developments is on girls and women (cf. Van Klaveren et al., 2009c, 2009e, 2009f, for South Africa, Malawi and Zambia; Van Klaveren and Tijdens, 2012: 117–19). Socio-economic policies aiming at decent work and decent living inclusive of the interests of girls and women, cannot do without adequate statistics. Such statistics should capture their large contributions to the informal economy, including in terms of time use. Here integration of labour force survey data with data from household survey and time-use surveys may be worthwhile. Our research also suggests that there is merit in the expansion of surveying employment status, wherever possible connected with surveying coverage of social security and infrastructural provisions. Such surveys may generate more shaded pictures of formality/informality, for example by using an informality index.

REFERENCES

Alatas, V. (2011) Leaving Poverty Behind: Policy Responses to help Indonesian Families Overcome Vulnerability to Poverty. *Indonesia 360 0* **1**(2): 69–81.

Anwar, R.P. and Supriyanto, A. (2012) *Non-Standard Work, Social Dialogue and Collective Bargaining in Indonesia.* Geneva: ILO – DIALOGUE/ILO Regional Office for Asia and the Pacific.

Bacchetta, M., Ernst, E., and Bustamante, J.P. (2009) *Globalization and Informal Jobs in Developing Countries.* Geneva: WTO and ILO.

Badan Pusan Statistik (BPS) (Statistics Indonesia) (2013) *Sakernas (Labour Force Survey) 2013-III.* Jakarta.

Berg, J. (2011) Laws or Luck? Understanding Rising Formality in Brazil in the 2000s. In S. Lee and D. McCann (eds) *Regulating for Decent Work. New Directions in Labour Market Regulation.* Basingstoke, UK and Geneva, Switzerland: Palgrave Macmillan and ILO, pp. 123–50.

Charmes, J. (2012) The Informal Economy Worldwide: Trends and Characteristics. *Margin – The Journal of Applied Economic Research* **6**(2): 103–32.

Government of India (2011) *Key Indicators of Employment and Unemployment in India 2009-2010. NSS 66th Round.* New Delhi: National Statistical Organisation.

Hirway, I. and Jose, S. (2011) Understanding Women's Work Using Time-Use Statistics: The Case of India. *Feminist Economics* **17**(4): 67–92.

Instituto Brasileiro de Geografia e Estatística (IBGE) (2009) *Pesquisa Nacional por Amostra de Domicílios (PNAD) Volume 30. 2009.* Rio de Janeiro.

International Conference of Labour Statisticians (ICLS) (1993) Resolution Concerning Statistics of Employment in the Informal Sector.

ICLS (2003) Guidelines Concerning a Statistical Definition of Informal Employment.

ILO LABORSTA (n.d.) Women and Men in the Informal Economy – Statistical Picture. http://laborsta.ilo.org/informal_economy_E.html, accessed 28 April 2015.

ILOSTAT (n.d.) Statistical Data. http://www.ilo.org/ilostat/faces/home/statistic

aldata?_afrLoop=627062185371031#%40%3F_afrLoop%3D627062185371031
%26_adf.ctrl-state%3D11b2kjmcaw_4, accessed 3 May 2015.
ILO (various dates) Labour Force Surveys (LFS). http://www.ilo.org/dyn/lfsur
vey/lfsurvey.list?p_lang=en, accessed 28 April 2015.
ILO (2002) Resolution Concerning Decent Work and the Informal Economy.
ILO (2010) *Global Employment Trends 2010*. Geneva: ILO.
ILO (2012a) *Measuring Informality: A Statistical Manual on the Informal Sector
and Informal Employment*. Geneva: ILO.
ILO (2012b) *Global Employment Trends 2012. Preventing a Deeper Jobs Crisis*.
Geneva: ILO.
ILO (2013a) *Global Employment Trends 2013. Recovering from a Second Jobs Dip*.
Geneva: ILO.
ILO (2013b) *Women and Men in the Informal Economy: A Statistical Picture
(Second Edition)*. Geneva: ILO/WIEGO.
ILO (2013c) *Transitioning from the Informal to the Formal Economy*. Geneva: ILO.
ILO (2014a) *World of Work Report 2014. Developing With Jobs*. Geneva: ILO.
ILO (2014b) *Global Employment Trends 2014. Risk of a Jobless Recovery?* Geneva:
ILO.
ILO and International Institute for Labour Studies (IILS) (2011) *Indonesia:
Reinforcing Domestic Demand in Times of Crisis*. Studies on Growth with
Equity. Geneva: ILO/IILS.
Luebker, M. (2008) Employment, Unemployment and Informality in Zimbabwe:
Concepts and Data for Coherent Policy-Making. Harare: ILO Sub-Regional
Office for Southern Africa, Issues Paper No. 32, Geneva: ILO Policy Integration
and Statistics Department, Integration Working Paper No. 90.
National Statistical Office (NSO) (Malawi) (2014) *Malawi Labour Force Survey
2013*. Zomba: NSO.
Papola, T.S. and Sahu, P. (2012) *Growth and Structure of Employment in India,
Long Term and Post Reform Performance and the Emerging Challenge*. New
Delhi: Institute for Human Development (IHD).
Statistics South Africa (SSA) (2013) *Quarterly Labour Force Survey, Quarter 4,
2013*. Pretoria: SSA.
Tjandra, S. and Van Klaveren, M. (2015) Indonesia. In M. van Klaveren,
D. Gregory and T. Schulten (eds), *Minimum Wages, Collective Bargaining and
Economic Development in Asia and Europe*. Basingstoke: Palgrave Macmillan,
pp. 139–55.
Tjandraningsih, I. (2013) State-Sponsored Precarious Work in Indonesia.
American Behavioral Scientist **57**(4): 403–19.
Tijdens, K., Besamusca, J., and Van Klaveren, M. (2015) Workers and Labour
Market Outcomes of Informal Jobs in Formal Establishments: A Job-Based
Informality Index for Nine Sub-Saharan African Countries. *European Journal
of Development Research* 15 January, doi:10.1057/ejdr2014.73.
Van Klaveren, M. and Tijdens, K. (2012) *Empowering Women in Work in
Developing Countries*. Basingstoke: Palgrave Macmillan.
Van Klaveren, M., Tijdens, K., Hughie-Williams, M., and Ramos Martin, N.
(2009a) An Overview of Women's Work and Employment in Mozambique.
Amsterdam: AIAS, Working Paper 09-77.
Van Klaveren, M., Tijdens, K., Hughie-Williams, M., and Ramos Martin, N.
(2009b) An Overview of Women's Work and Employment in Angola.
Amsterdam: AIAS, Working Paper 09-78.

Van Klaveren, M., Tijdens, K., Hughie-Williams, M., and Ramos Martin, N. (2009c) An Overview of Women's Work and Employment in South Africa. Amsterdam: AIAS, Working Paper 09-79.

Van Klaveren, M., Tijdens, K., Hughie-Williams, M., and Ramos Martin, N. (2009d) An Overview of Women's Work and Employment in Zambia. Amsterdam: AIAS, Working Paper 09-80.

Van Klaveren, M., Tijdens, K., Hughie-Williams, M., and Ramos Martin, N. (2009e) An Overview of Women's Work and Employment in Malawi. Amsterdam: AIAS, Working Paper 09-82.

Van Klaveren, M., Tijdens, K., Hughie-Williams, M., and Ramos Martin, N. (2009f) An Overview of Women's Work and Employment in Brazil. Amsterdam: AIAS, Working Paper 09-83.

Van Klaveren, M., Tijdens, K., Hughie-Williams, M., and Ramos Martin, N. (2010a) An Overview of Women's Work and Employment in India. Amsterdam: AIAS, Working Paper 10-90.

Van Klaveren, M., Tijdens, K., Hughie-Williams, M., and Ramos Martin, N. (2010b) An Overview of Women's Work and Employment in Indonesia. Amsterdam: AIAS, Working Paper 10-91.

Van Klaveren, M., Tijdens, K., Hughie-Williams, M., and Ramos Martin, N. (2010c) An Overview of Women's Work and Employment in Belarus. Amsterdam: AIAS, Working Paper 10-96.

Van Klaveren, M., Tijdens, K., Hughie-Williams, M., and Ramos Martin, N. (2010d) An Overview of Women's Work and Employment in Zimbabwe. Amsterdam: AIAS, Working Paper 10-97.

World Bank (2011) Policies to Reduce Informal Employment. An International Survey. Technical Note for the Government of Ukraine. Washington D.C.

Zimstat (2012) *2011 Labour Force Survey.* Harare: Zimstat.

APPENDIX

Table 4A.1   Labour force participation rate (LPR), 15+, by country and gender, latest year available

	Total	Male	Female
Angola (2010, EAPEP)	69.7	77.0	62.7
Botswana (2010, HS)	59.1	66.3	52.9
Malawi (2013, LFS)	74.6	75.1	74.2
Mozambique (2012, HS)	79.8	75.8	83.2
South Africa (2013, LFS)	55.8	63.6	51.0
Zambia (2012, LFS)	74.6	80.0	69.5
Zimbabwe (2011, LFS)	82.4	88.1	77.5
Azerbaijan (2013, LFS)	64.7	68.0	61.4
Belarus (2013, OE)	80.8	76.0	86.0
Kazakhstan (2013, LFS)	71.3	77.3	66.7
Ukraine (2013, LFS)	65.0	71.6	58.9
Brazil (2013, LFS)	65.5	77.3	54.6
India (2013–14, HS)	52.5	74.4	25.8
Indonesia (2013, LFS)	66.8	83.4	50.3

Note: EAPEP = ILO EAPEP projections; HS = Household Survey; LFS = Labour Force Survey; OE = Labour resource estimates.

Source: ILOSTAT (n.d.).

Table 4A.2   Wholesale/retail and hotels/restaurants/catering: female employment shares, latest year available

	Year	Status	% of females in employment of sector (A)			% female empl. in total female employment (B)		
			Commerce	Wholes. & retail	Hotels, rest., cat.	Commerce	Wholes. & retail	Hotels, rest., cat.
Angola	2007	formal	40			27		
Botswana	2010	total	66	65	73	10	8	2
Malawi	2013	total	56	56	64	18	17	1
Mozambique	2012	total	51			10		
South Africa	2012	total	49	45	63	23	18	5
Zambia	2008	total	52	54	50	10	9	1
Zimbabwe	2011	total	57	56	59	12	11	1
Azerbaijan	2013	total	32	33	24	19	18	1
Belarus	2009	total	68	68	61	14	13	1
Kazakhstan	2013	total	60	59	70	20	18	2
Ukraine	2013	total	59	57	71	23	20	3
Brazil	2013	total	45	42	57	29	24	5
India	2009–10	total	14	13	20	5	4	1
Indonesia	2013	total	50	50	55	28	23	5

Sources: Authors' calculations/estimates based on ILOSTAT (n.d.), except: Angola (Van Klaveren et al., 2009b), Malawi (NSO, 2014), South Africa (SSA, 2013), Zimbabwe (Zimstat, 2012), India (Government of India, 2011).

5. Regulating informal work at the interface between labour law and migration law*

Mark Freedland

5.1 INTRODUCTION

This chapter develops some ideas about the regulation of 'informal work'. They are ideas arrived at by reflecting on some legal and regulatory phenomena occurring at the interface between labour law and migration law, that is to say at the many points where migration law impacts upon labour law's regulation of labour markets and of employment relations. Three interconnected arguments are put forward.

First, it will be argued that reflection upon the impacts of migration law upon labour law's conception and regulation (or non-regulation) of informal work produces significant insights into the analytical complexity and imprecision of that conception and that regulation (or non-regulation) of informal work. It will be suggested that there are various different models of informal work, and that one of them, namely that of work by 'undocumented workers' is attributable to the influence of migration law. This set of propositions will form the 'imprecision argument'.

Second, it will be argued that reflection on the labour-law-generated and migration-law-generated models of informal work discloses a particular set of normative ambiguities about the culpability of the worker for being engaged in informal work which has very important implications for the ways in which informal work is regulated (or not regulated). It will

* The presentation of the original version of this chapter formed part of a large programme of work on the intersection between labour law and migration law which culminated in the publication of Cathryn Costello and Mark Freedland (eds), *Migrants at Work: Immigration and Vulnerability in Labour Law* (Oxford University Press, 2014). I am immensely indebted to Cathryn Costello both for opening up my own access to this area of intersection in the course of that programme of work and for drawing my attention to some recent developments in that field which are discussed in this version of the chapter.

be suggested that the migration-law-generated model of work by undocumented workers has especially strong connotations of culpability on the
part of the workers themselves. This set of propositions will constitute the
'normative ambiguity argument'.

Third and finally, some suggestions will be advanced as to how to
construct an appropriate regulatory response to those insights. This will
involve canvassing some ideas for improving the worker-protective regulation of informal work in ways which are inclusive of migrant workers
rather than unduly exclusive of undocumented workers. This set of suggestions will form the 'argument for inclusiveness'. The concluding section
of this chapter then reflects upon how these three arguments, taken as a
whole, apply to some significant recent developments in the articulation of
public policy at this crucial intersection between the regulation of informal
work and of labour migration.

5.2   THE IMPRECISION ARGUMENT

In this section of the chapter, it is asserted that the whole notion of the
regulation or non-regulation of informal work is characterised by deep
analytical complexities and imprecision, which are illustrated and thrown
into sharp relief when we come to consider the extent to which the idea of
informal work is itself partly generated by migration law. The notion of
informal work is one which we tend to assume has a simple, uncontroversial and accepted meaning; but that assumption quickly turns out to be
somewhat illusory when subjected to precise scrutiny, for example from
the perspective of migration law. Thus it is quite easy to say, and to regard
it as sufficient to say, that 'informal work' refers to work relations which
take place beyond the scope of formal (legal) regulation; but that is in
truth a very slippery notion.

One sense in which that notion, of work beyond the sphere of formal
regulation, is a slippery one is the ambiguity about the kind of formal
regulation which is being evaded. To focus on migration law as the type
of formal regulation for which informal work is the epiphenomenon (that
is, informal work as work in relation to which migration law is *not* being
observed) is to be reminded that migration law is only one of various kinds
of formal regulation by the absence of which informal work is characterised as such.

If one pursues that line of analysis of informal work, it soon becomes
apparent that there are in fact three main kinds of formal regulation to
which informal work is the epiphenomenon, as follows: (1) the regulation
of labour law and collective bargaining (the non-observance of which we

can think of as the 'sweatshop' typology); (2) the regulation of tax law and social security law (the non-observance of which we can think of as the 'black economy' typology; and (3) the regulation of migration law (the non-observance of which we can think of as the undocumented worker or 'illegal immigrant' typology). In each of these three regulatory contexts the notion of informal work is a complex and imprecise one, but the migration law context is one which it is especially fruitful to investigate in order to understand better the sources of complexity and imprecision.

A principal source or location of such complexity and imprecision is to be found in the notion of formal regulation or formal law-observance upon which it implicitly draws. The whole construct of 'informal work', as work carried out 'beyond the sphere of formal regulation', is apt to depend upon the assumption that there is a relatively clear and precise applicable body of formal legal regulation which is *de facto* not observed or evaded in the particular work relationship or work environment in question. However, even a superficial scrutiny of the ways in which migration control regimes operate upon work relationships reveals the oversimplicity of any such assumption. Thus we find that restrictions which migration control regimes place upon the freedom and entitlement of non-nationals to work in any given nation-state are typically immensely complex and may be deeply imprecise; the assessment of whether a given worker is working 'legally' at any given moment may be a very difficult one. The distinction between the *de jure* work status of a migrant worker and the *de facto* implementation of work status restrictions may be a great deal less obvious in day-to-day practice than it appears to be in abstract legal theory.

Having arrived at that observation with regard to the regulation imposed by migration law, it quickly becomes evident that similar observations might be made for the other two main sources of 'informality' which I have identified, namely those of labour law's regulation of work relations and the regulation of those relations by tax and social security law. If we bear in mind, moreover, that the ascription of 'informal work' is typically accorded on the basis of perceived non-observance of some combination of all three types of regulation, then we can easily see how very complex and imprecise the assessment of 'informality' may become. This leads on to an argument about the normative ambiguity of the notion of informal work which is pursued in the next section of this chapter.

5.3   THE NORMATIVE AMBIGUITY ARGUMENT

In the previous section, I observed the extent of the complexity and imprecision which attends the notion of informal work, taking the regulation of migration law as my starting point for doing so. This heightened the awareness of the variety of types of regulation, the non-observation of which may contribute to the informality of the work situation or work relationship in question. This section builds upon those analytical foundations to try to construct an argument about the normative ambiguity of the idea of informal work, again taking the regulation of migration law as its main starting point.

The argument here advanced is that if we take migration law as a starting point in the analysis of the 'informality' of work, that serves to focus attention not only, as we have seen, upon the variety and complexity and imprecision of the different types of regulation the non-observance of which characterises work as informal, but also upon the different normative constructs of informal work which tend to be associated with those different kinds of regulation. It will be argued that the failure fully to separate out these different normative constructs gives rise to a normative ambiguity which can become a besetting problem for the working out of the most appropriate regulatory approaches to the whole large and growing set of issues about informal work.

Accordingly, I suggest that an initial focus upon migration law and its non-observance in informal work relations points up some significant contrasts in the rationales for trying to extend into the domain of informal work each of the three different main types of regulation which I have identified as the counterparts of informal work. Thus it is a safe assertion that migration law, as it impacts upon employment or other personal work relations, has the rationale of protecting the integrity and functioning of the national or international labour market in question by controlling access to that labour market on the basis of national citizenship, and by excluding non-citizens from that labour market or severely restricting their access to it. This rationale, therefore, is not one which is primarily concerned with the protection of the migrant worker, but rather with the protection of a perceived public interest which may appear to require or justify action against the migrant worker. It should be emphasised, moreover, that this rationale will itself reflect the political agenda of the legal system in question, an agenda which may sometimes itself be both neo-liberal and anti-immigrant in character. In other words, migration law, and the social construction of the relevant concepts, may be used to shape employment law and to bring about the deregulation of employment.

That analysis of the migration-law-based rationale for trying to regulate informal work throws into relief a somewhat contrasting rationale for trying to extend tax and social security law's regulation into that domain, and an even more contrasting rationale for trying to enforce labour law's regulation in that domain. Thus tax and social security law's regulation has a rationale which, like that of migration law, is primarily concerned with the protection of a general public interest – this time in the viability of the economy and social welfare system of the nation-state in question – but it is a rationale which is nevertheless partly that of directly protecting the workers in question by trying to ensure that they are fully entitled to the contribution-based benefits of citizenship.

Moreover the contrast in rationales becomes an even sharper one when we turn to labour law's regulation and to the concern for extending that regulation into the sphere of informal work. For even in an era in which theorists and policy-makers are increasingly disposed to view labour law as having the purpose of labour market regulation or deregulation in the interests of job creation and economic growth, it is still relatively uncontroversial to assert that labour law's concern with informal work is still primarily a worker-protective one, to do with the implementing and maintaining of labour standards.

By reason of these contrasts between different rationales for regulating informal work attached to different types of regulation, and by reason of the fact that each of these types of regulation may be in play with regard to any given situation of informal work, there is therefore a considerable degree of uncertainty about the overall rationale for trying to enhance the regulation of informal work; it is this phenomenon which this chapter has tried to capture with the description of the 'normative ambiguity' of regulating informal work. There is one particular respect in which this normative ambiguity manifests itself especially strongly, and this stage of the overall argument is completed by concentrating upon it.

That further point is as follows: I suggest that we can discern as creeping into the public policy discussion of the regulation of informal work a particular kind of normative ambiguity which is derived from the contrasts which I have drawn earlier in this chapter between the different types of regulation which we might wish to extend into the sphere of informal work, and between the rationales associated with each of those types. This particular kind of normative ambiguity concerns the extent to which workers can be seen as culpable for the 'informality' of the work relations in which they are engaged, and therefore less deserving of regulation to protect them and more justly susceptible to regulation which penalises them. The variation in approaches in this regard as between the different types of regulation is, yet again, thrown into sharp relief by concentrating on migration-law-based regulation of informal work. For it is in the context of migration-law-based regulation that the worker is especially liable to be seen as culpable for the informal character of the work relation, which in this context is very likely to be conflated with notions of illegality or criminality: the undocumented worker is readily seen as primarily culpable for, or at least as being the reprehensible source of, the informality of the work relation in question, by having engaged in the work relationship or remained in the work relationship when not entitled to do so by reason of lacking the requisite migration status.

In partial contrast, in the context of tax-law-based and social-security-law-based regulation, there is a greater disposition to regard the employer or employing organisation as at least equally responsible with the worker for the informality of the work relation, insofar as the informality consists in the failure to comply with the requirements of the applicable tax and social security regime. Moreover, in even sharper contrast, in the context of labour-law-based regulation, it is normally regarded as counter-intuitive (though it is not unknown) to treat the worker as primarily culpable for informality consisting of failures of observance of labour standards which are primarily directed at protecting workers themselves; and it would normally be seen to follow that the worker should not be penalised for this kind of informality but should rather be regarded as the victim of it. These are the general and the particular grounds upon which the normative ambiguity argument is advanced. The concluding section of this chapter will seek to show how the problem of normative ambiguity, like the problem of imprecision, manifests itself in the actual practice of regulation of informal work, and attempts to put forward some suggested responses to the difficulties which result.

5.4 THE ARGUMENT FOR INCLUSIVENESS IN THE REGULATION OF INFORMAL WORK

My concluding argument is a very tentative one, more in the nature of a call for further discussion as to where my two previous arguments might be seen to lead. The two previous arguments point to difficulties in the regulation of informal work, consisting both in the imprecision of the idea of 'informal work', and in a set of normative ambiguities about the purposes of such regulation and the means of pursuing those purposes. I suggest that those difficulties are on the one hand usefully focused, but on the other hand more than somewhat exacerbated, by the increasingly dominant presence in the regulatory apparatus of a special concern with migration law and the control of labour migration. However, those arguments were not advanced as in any sense arguments against efforts to advance labour law's regulation into the sphere of informal work. On the contrary, I would see them as arguments for the refashioning of the tools of labour law's regulation of informal work, and as pointers towards particular obstacles in the path of such regulation which need to be overcome.

There are certain specific impediments to labour law's regulation of informal work which my earlier arguments might help to address. British labour lawyers have been much concerned about a trend which reached its zenith (so far at least) in the decision of the Court of Appeal in the case of *Hounga v Allen*,[1] of prioritising the perceived importance of not condoning illegal immigration over the importance of allowing any workers within the territory to claim their fundamental labour rights even if they have by their own actions located themselves in the informal work sector as undocumented workers. The Supreme Court reversed the decision,[2] holding that the claimant's status as an illegal immigrant was 'no more than the context in which Mrs Allen then perpetrated the acts of physical, verbal and emotional abuse by which, among other things, she dismissed Miss Hounga from her employment'.[3] That view was reinforced by reference to international laws on human trafficking and the balancing of competing public policy concerns, the defence of illegality running 'strikingly counter to the prominent strain of current public policy against trafficking and in favour of the protection of its victims'.[4]

I would view my earlier arguments as suggesting that the former decision represented the wrong way and the latter decision represented the right way to resolve a normative ambiguity between labour law's regulation and migration law's regulation of the sphere of informal work;[5] and

---

[1]   In the Court of Appeal, [2012] EWCA Civ 609.
[2]   In the Supreme Court, [2014] UKSC 47.
[3]   [2014] UKSC 47 at para [40].
[4]   [2014] UKSC 47 at para [52].
[5]   See, for further discussion, Alan Bogg and Virginia Mantouvalou (2014), 'Illegality, Human Rights and Employment: A Watershed Moment for the United Kingdom Supreme Court?', http://ukconstitutionallaw.org/2014/03/13/alan-bogg-and-virginia-mantouvalou-illegality-human-rights-and-employment-a-watershed-moment-for-the-united-kingdom-supreme-court/; Alan Bogg and Sarah Green (2015), 'Rights Are Not Just for the Virtuous: What *Hounga* Means for the Illegality Defence in the Discrimination Torts', 44 *Industrial Law Journal* 101; and, more generally, Alan Bogg and Tonia Novitz (2014), 'Links between Individual Employment Law and Collective Labour Law – Their Implications for Migrant Workers', Chapter 19 of Cathryn Costello and Mark Freedland (eds), *Migrants at Work: Immigration and Vulnerability in Labour Law*, Oxford: Oxford University Press, especially at pp. 366–72. Comparison may also usefully be made between the handling of the *Hounga* case by the UK Supreme Court and the approach of the CJEU to an associated set of issues in the case of *Tümer v Raad van bestuur van het Uitvoeringsinstituut werknemersverzekeringen* Case C-311/13 (2014), http://curia.europa.eu/juris/document/document.jsf;jsessionid=9ea7d0f130d55b267cccb66a4729ada7fe79df7776cd.e34KaxiLc3eQc40LaxqMbN4ObNuRe0?text=&docid=159243&pageIndex=0&doclang=EN&mode=lst&dir=&occ=first&part=1&cid=197713.

I would seek to construct on that basis a general 'argument for inclusiveness' in the regulation of informal work. In the next, concluding, section of this chapter, it is considered how this analysis applies to, and it is hoped serves to illuminate, some significant recent developments in the articulation of public policy at this crucial intersection between the regulation of informal work and of labour migration.

5.5 INFORMAL WORK AND LABOUR MIGRATION: THE THREE ARGUMENTS APPLIED

By way of conclusion to this chapter, this section reflects upon the application of my three arguments to two very recent articulations of regulatory policy, each of which in its own way concerns itself with or touches upon the regulation of informal work in the context of labour migration. One of these is the International Labour Organization (ILO) Transition from the Informal to the Formal Economy Recommendation, 2015 (No. 204);[6] the other is the report, also of June 2015, from the EU Fundamental Rights Agency on 'Severe Labour Exploitation: Workers Moving Within or Into the European Union'.[7] Between them, the Transition Recommendation and the Severe Exploitation Report throw into stark relief all three of the arguments which have been advanced earlier in this chapter, in different ways revealing the degree of definitional imprecision, the normative ambiguity, and the problems of inclusion and exclusion which attend upon even the best-thought-through initiatives to regulate the sphere of informal work, most especially when labour migration is involved.

A comparison of two very different regulatory approaches to this intersection, taken, respectively, by the Recommendation and the Report enables the pinpointing of a particular deep-seated regulatory problem which has been emerging from the preceding sections of this chapter: it concerns the complex and difficult role of criminality in this sphere of regulation. My suggestion is that criminality may figure in two sharply contrasting, almost diametrically opposed, ways in the regulation of informal work, most especially in the context of labour migration. In one mode, criminality may operate as a limiting or exclusionary factor in the shaping of this kind of regulation. In the contrasting mode, criminality may figure as a justificatory or inclusionary factor

---

6   http://www.ilo.org/dyn/normlex/en/f?p=NORMLEXPUB:12100:0::NO::P1
2100_ILO_CODE:R204.
7   http://fra.europa.eu/sites/default/files/fra-2015-severe-labour-exploitation
_en.pdf.

in the shaping of such regulation. The tension between these two tendencies is considerable and unresolved: one could almost say that there is a 'criminality fault-line' which threatens to destabilise this whole area of regulation.

This notion of a criminality fault-line in the regulation of informal work will become somewhat clearer, and understanding of the significance of the Recommendation and the Report will be increased, if we consider for a moment the close, though elusive, relationship between the ideas of informal work and 'decent work'. They are in some measure, though by no means completely, counterparts of each other; informal work is very apt not to be decent work, and work that is not decent is very apt to be informal. Moreover, illegal or undocumented migrants loom large in the personification of both informal work and decent work; they are especially likely to be in situations of informal work, and they are especially likely not to be in situations of decent work. For both of these two closely associated, though still distinct, regulatory notions there is a real problem of how far criminality, on the part of the employer or the worker, or associated intermediaries, is a defining or limiting feature. There are very real, and indeed surprisingly difficult, issues of whether and how far the presence of criminality is on the one hand a defining feature of informal work, or on the other hand a limiting feature of decent work; and these issues become especially fraught where 'illegal immigration' is involved. These complex associations between the ideas of informal work, decent work and criminality are soon encountered when we examine the provisions, and the supporting discourse, of ILO Recommendation No. 204. In the framing of the Recommendation, there is a real concern to present informal work as a problematical but not a criminal phenomenon; however, in one particular respect this regulatory enterprise does nevertheless seem, potentially at least, to encounter the criminality fault-line in both a definitional and a normative sense. The whole tenor of the Recommendation is to promote 'the transition from the informal economy to the formal economy' as a way of realising the positive goals of labour law and employment policy, without however unduly castigating either employers or workers who happen for the time being to be located in the informal sector; a forbearance which is no doubt tailored to the sensitivity of many developing countries about the large extent of informal work and enterprise within their systems.[8] Hence the care which the Recommendation takes to define the

---

[8]   Illuminating in this respect is a presentation about the Recommendation made by Malensu Kapaipi of ILO Lusaka in June 2015: http://www.saspen.org/home/wp-content/uploads/2015/07/ILO-PRESENTATION_Lusaka-Social-Protection-Colloquium_SASPEN-PSP-FES_15072015.pdf.

'informal economy' in minimally condemnatory terms: 'For the purposes of this Recommendation, the term "informal economy" . . . refers to all economic activities by workers and economic units that are – in law or in practice – not covered or insufficiently covered by formal arrangements.'[9]

However, the framers of the Recommendation felt that it was also necessary to distinguish sharply the informal economy, as thus defined, from a contrasting sphere of 'illicit activity':

> For the purposes of this Recommendation, the term 'informal economy' . . . does not cover illicit activities, in particular the provision of services or the production, sale, possession or use of goods forbidden by law, including the illicit production and trafficking of drugs, the illicit manufacturing of and trafficking in firearms, trafficking in persons, and money laundering, as defined in the relevant international treaties.[10]

It is of course politically understandable that the Recommendation should distance itself from the sphere of 'illicit activities', but this exclusion of criminality or near-criminality takes place at some risk of reintroducing the definitional and normative ambiguities which the Recommendation's initial formulation of the 'informal economy' seems designed to avoid. That risk seems especially to attach to the notoriously slippery notion of 'trafficking in persons', or human trafficking; it is an idea whose deployment might all too easily produce unintended exclusionary effects in the labour migration sphere of the informal economy.

When we turn our attention to the Severe Exploitation Report, we encounter a contrasting, indeed almost diametrically opposed, set of issues arising from the importation of notions of criminality into this regulatory discourse. Like the Recommendation, the Report is centrally concerned with the promotion of decent work, and it is even more obviously focused on the situation of migrants – in particular, irregular migrants – working in the informal economy, since its point of departure consists of a generic observation or hypothesis that it is in this very sphere that 'severe labour exploitation' will be disproportionately experienced by workers migrating into the European Union or between its member states.

Most significantly for the purposes of the present argument, the Report's central normative notion of 'severe labour exploitation' invokes the idea of exploitation of workers, by employing enterprises or their agents or intermediaries, which is so extreme as to constitute criminal conduct or conduct which is virtually criminal. In other words, for this

---

[9] Recommendation No. 204, para 2(a).
[10] Recommendation No. 204, para 2(b).

exercise in regulatory observation and analysis, criminality, far from being a ground of limitation of the scope of the inquiry, figures as its guiding rationale. Thus, the Report declares that:

> The term 'exploitation' denotes work situations that deviate significantly from standard working conditions as defined by legislation or other binding legal regulations, concerning in particular remuneration, working hours, leave entitlements, health and safety standards and decent treatment. The term 'severe' refers to forms of exploitation of workers which are criminal under the legislation of the EU Member State where the exploitation occurs. Hence, severe labour exploitation includes coercive forms of exploitation, such as slavery, servitude, forced or compulsory labour and trafficking (Article 5 of the Fundamental Rights Charter), as well as severe exploitation within the framework of an employment relationship, in particular employment situations covered by Article 9 (1) of the Employer Sanctions Directive.[11]

However, the trenchant simplicity of this reliance upon a notion of criminality to define the idea of severe labour exploitation is quickly eroded. The Report acknowledges the difficulty with its nationally specific notion of criminality: 'Hence, what constitutes severe labour exploitation in one EU Member State may not in another.'[12]

Moreover, the definitional and normative problems go even further than this, for the Report has to admit from the outset that a strict conception of outright criminality will not suffice to capture the whole of its idea of 'severe labour exploitation':

> The various forms of labour exploitation form a continuum of severity of abuses spanning from slavery to relatively less serious forms of exploitation which fall short of constituting severe labour exploitation and a criminal offence. The term 'severe labour exploitation' also covers situations referred to by Article 9 (1) of the Employer Sanctions Directive – the employment of a worker in an irregular situation under 'particularly exploitative working conditions'. This means – according to Article 2 of the directive – working conditions 'where there is a striking disproportion compared with the terms of employment of legally employed workers which, for example, affects workers' health and safety, and which offends against human dignity'.[13]

Indeed, so severe does this conceptual difficulty become for the framers of the Report that they devote a section of the Report to what they identify as the 'no-name problem', which is articulated in the following way:

---

[11] Report, p. 10, Glossary, entry for 'severe labour exploitation'.
[12] Report, p. 12, Executive Summary. The problem is amplified in section 1.2 of the Report under the heading of 'Criminalisation of labour exploitation and trafficking at Member State level'.
[13] Ibid.

> Throughout the project, researchers encountered a remarkable discrepancy: the phenomenon of workers moving within or into the EU [European Union] accepting, because of personal situations of poverty and marginalisation, work under conditions that are – judged by the standards of the country of their workplace – clearly irregular and exploitative has no label commonly attached to it and receives little attention. While the traditional categories of 'slavery' or 'forced labour'– which imply a lack of consent on the part of the worker – are common, the severe exploitation of workers from other countries in employment relationships lacks a categorisation and hence is often not perceived.[14]

The 'no-name problem' amounts to an admission of the normative insufficiency of the categories of criminality upon which the Report has ostensibly based itself.

Let me say in conclusion that it would be presumptuous and inappropriate to regard the exposure of these difficulties as demonstrating a lack of logic or rigour in the formulation of either ILO Recommendation No. 204 or the Severe Exploitation Report. These are difficulties which inherently confront any agency seeking to promote labour standards, and to control the disregard or abuse of those standards in the sphere of the informal economy, even more especially where labour migration is involved. This chapter is intended to confront those difficulties, but in no way to denigrate those who seek to resolve them. There is much further work to be done in fleshing out this set of arguments; but my starting point for so doing would be a conviction that there are great dangers in allowing labour law's regulation to falter and fall short in the difficult or 'informal' territory where it is in fact most needed. This chapter has tried to focus attention upon the problematical and increasingly sensitive interface between labour law and migration law as a way of pointing up the need for an argument or discourse of inclusiveness with regard to the regulation of a social and economic phenomenon of informal work. Moreover, I have tried by that path of reasoning to show that the very notion of informal work is analytically and normatively fragile. It should not, I suggest, be allowed to confer legitimacy upon the recognition of an outer zone of work relations in which the writ of labour law's regulation does not run, whether by reason of the perceived exigencies of migration control or on any similar ground.

---

[14]   Report, section 1.3, pp. 38–9.

6. Partial protection? The regulation of home care workers' working conditions*

Sara Charlesworth

6.1 INTRODUCTION

This chapter is concerned with a specific group of workers: those who provide care – both domestic and personal care, to the frail aged and other vulnerable groups – inside people's homes. Home care workers are thus a subset of domestic workers, and fall into the definition set out in Article 1 of the International Labour Organization (ILO) Domestic Workers Convention, 2011 (No. 189) of workers who perform work in or for a household within an employment relationship. In most developed countries the majority of workers are covered by formal employment and labour regulation. Home care workers are a partial exception. They are often expressly excluded from certain minimum labour standards, such as in North American jurisdictions (Applebaum and Leana, 2011; Zeytinoglu et al., 2015), or have poorer minimum conditions than other workers, including those in the feminised care sector, such as in New Zealand (NZHRC, 2012) and the United Kingdom (Hussein and Manthorpe, 2014).

In the world of paid employment, home care work is distinctive in that it trespasses not only the boundaries between the informal and formal economies but also those boundaries between market work and family work, and between public and private spaces (Fudge, 2012: 3). To understand how employment conditions for home care work are produced and reproduced it is important to move beyond what are often presented as

---

*   This chapter draws on research conducted as part of an Australian Research Council Future Fellowship (FT120100346): Prospects for Decent Work and Gender Equality in Frontline Care Work. Many thanks to Somayeh Parvazian for her analysis of the 2012 National Aged Care Workforce Census and Survey dataset used in the chapter.

static categories of formal/informal work or as a regulated/unregulated division of the reach of employment law. The concept of a continuum is a helpful one, with formalisation/informalisation seen as a dynamic process (Fudge, 2012; Freedland and Kountouris, 2012). In the case of home care, then, formalisation can be seen as the process that facilitates the regulatory recognition of home care work as 'work' (Le Bihan, 2012). As with other forms of work in developed economies there has not been a linear move towards formalisation. There is now a growing informalisation of employment in this sector, following shifts to the subcontracting out of services (Williams and Lansky, 2013).

A substantial literature problematises the (de)valuation of paid care work as a consequence of its connection to the unpaid caring work women have traditionally performed in the home and community (England, 2005; Folbre, 2008; Palmer and Eveline, 2012). The gendered norms that underpin the devaluation of care work are premised on an ideology of domesticity (Williams, 2000) that positions the care women do, both in the home and as paid work, as natural and therefore unskilled. This ideology is justified by an essentialised view of women as female homemakers and of men as male breadwinners, unencumbered by caring responsibilities. Because women are born to do caring work they are not primary breadwinners and need not be paid as much (Charlesworth and Marshall, 2011: 674). Thus the focus on the 'care' in paid care work obscures its characteristics as employment and affects its valuing in relation to other paid work (Martin, 2007).

The spatial location of paid care work is also crucially important. Even where it is formal care work, rather than semi-formal care work such as that undertaken by family members in the context of welfare or cash payments (Pfau-Effinger et al., 2009: 6), the proximity of care work undertaken in a care recipient's home to the work women do for free imbues it with the aura of 'non-work'. Indeed in many countries employment regulation distinguishes between formal care work undertaken in the home and that undertaken in an institution, or for a government or a community services agency (Charlesworth, 2012: 123). These demarcations underpin poorer employment standards for home care workers who undertake similar work to other care workers such as in residential aged care.

This chapter aims to contribute to better understandings of the wider regulatory context in which the remuneration and working conditions for home care work are negotiated and determined. Focusing on the Australian case, it highlights the contradictory shifts in employment standards by outlining, firstly, the incomplete process of formalisation in respect to home care work until the late 1990s; and secondly, the more patchy process of informalisation since that time, driven as much by outsourcing and government funding models as by changes in labour regulation.

The next section outlines the broader Australian and international contexts that inform the analysis of home care work and its employment regulation in this chapter. Section 6.3 examines the historical and regulatory mechanisms that have produced current working conditions for different groups of home care workers in Australia, underpinned by contradictory shifts in the in/formalisation of employment standards and by employer type. The Conclusion (section 6.4) briefly canvasses the potential within Australian labour regulation more broadly to address the marginalisation of home care workers and prospects for change.

6.2   HOME CARE WORK IN CONTEXT

What Do Home Care Workers Do?

The type of work undertaken by home care workers very much reflects the distinctive long-term care funding models employed in developed countries, in turn reflecting particular welfare regimes (Mundlak, 2012: 190). In most systems these regimes support essentially two classes of home care services: personal care, such as assistance with dressing, bathing, personal hygiene, eating and drinking; and domestic assistance or 'home help', such as cleaning, tidying and preparing meals (Genet et al., 2011). The types of tasks taken on also reflect the extent of the marketisation of care in any one context with different types of employer – government, not-for-profit and private – providing different ranges of services. In the Australian context for example, the Home and Community Care Program (HACC) funding programme, which until recently was the main funding model used to deliver home care services,[1] provided a different unit price for the two main types of funded direct care services delivered to clients (Australian Government, 2012: 60).

The unit price paid by the Commonwealth government for services differs along similar lines, reflecting the 'value' attached to each type of home care service, but is specific to different Australian states. In Victoria, for example, providers in 2013–14 received A\$31.51 per hour to provide domestic assistance and A\$36.00 per hour for personal care (Victorian Government, 2013a). These unit prices cover the salary and on-costs

---

[1]   From 1 July 2015, this programme was consolidated into the Commonwealth Home Support Programme.

for the home care worker: staff salary and on-costs, supervision, in-service training and induction, operational support and management costs (Victorian Government, 2013b: 49). While travel costs are also supposed to be covered by the unit price, there is no recognition of the time home care workers require to travel between clients to deliver an hour (or a part-hour) of service. The different costs of providing services in different regions are not accounted for in the unit price and the capacity of service providers to cover the costs incurred in the delivery of home care services depend very much on the extent to which they are able and/or willing to cross-subsidise home care services from other services they provide. One study suggests that Victorian local councils have significantly subsidised the HACC funding received in order to provide home care services to residents (Vella, 2008).

Unlike the Netherlands, for example, where different services provide personal care or domestic assistance services (Genet et al., 2011), most home care services in Australia employ workers to provide both types of service. Nevertheless, the bifurcation of personal and domestic work is reflected in Australian wage classifications in the federal industry award, the Social, Community, Home Care and Disability Services (SCHCDS) Industry Award that provides minimum wages and working time conditions for the majority of home care workers,[2] who work for not-for-profit or for-profit employers.

The SCHCDS Award provides far more detailed labour minima than in many other countries. However, the skill classifications on which pay is based do not cover the 'articulation' work required to actually do home care work. Articulation work has been described as the 'linking activities, such as follow-through and follow-up, and continuity of awareness in the management, establishment, maintenance and termination of relationships' (Hampson and Junor, 2010: 531). This linking work is integral to the labour process in home care work, yet it remains substantially unrecognised both in funding models and in industrial descriptions of the skills and work required. Home care workers work away from direct supervision

---

[2] In Australia, there are 122 different federal 'modern' awards that operate with the force of law, regulating the terms on which specified types of workers in a specific industry or occupational grouping can be employed. Awards establish wage rates for workers in different skill classifications as well as detailed working time minima (Stewart, 2013: at 7.1). These provisions are in addition to the ten National Employment Standards that provide statutory minima for most employees. Award conditions are determined by the Fair Work Commission, with increases in the annual minimum wage flowing on to minimum wages set in industry awards.

in a client's home, and to do their work they need the skills to establish and build relationships with a wide range of clients, and to monitor and report on the health and well-being of these clients to their employer.

Counting Home Care Workers

Despite the increased reliance on home care services to deliver long-term care in Organisation for Economic Co-operation and Development (OECD) countries, just how many home care workers there are in the formal care sector is difficult to estimate, let alone the characteristics of these workers and their employment conditions. Difficulties in accurately counting home care workers in the formal economy have more to do with the distinctions made between groups of workers funded by different funding programmes and how national government statistics classify the employer industry and worker occupation,[3] than with any differences in the collection of domestic and personal care job tasks undertaken (Armstrong et al., 2008; Howes, 2014). In 2010 in the United States, there were an estimated 2.3 million home care and personal assistance workers in the formal sector, largely employed by organisations delivering in-home services as well as directly by consumers able to hire their own personal care worker under publicly financed programmes (PHI, 2011: 4). In England it is estimated that there were some 485000 workers working in adult domiciliary care in 2014, although these figures do not include the self-employed or those employed through other funding streams or by self-funding care recipients (Skills for Care, 2015: 30, 19). In Australia it is estimated that in 2012 there were some 76000 home care workers, although these figures, drawn from the National Aged Care Workforce Census and Survey (NACWCS) do not include workers employed privately by households, through labour hire or aged care brokering agencies, or the so-called 'self-employed' (King et al., 2013).

Home care represents a major government expense. For example in the United States in 2012, Medicaid provided in excess of US$12 billion annually for the provision of in-home personal care to older people and adults with disabilities (Eiken et al., 2014: Table B), while United Kingdom (UK) gross annual expenditure for older people's home care in 2011/12 was

---

[3]   In Australia, for example, while residential aged care is recognized in the industry classifications used in the national Census, community-based aged care is aggregated with many other very different social care sectors under an industry category of 'social assistance'. At the occupational level the national Census distinguishes only an aggregate group of 'aged and disabled workers' who provide in-home care.

an estimated £1.83 billion (US$2.39 billion), down from an £1.95 billion (US$2.55 billion) in the previous year (HSCIC, 2013: 21). In Australia, Commonwealth expenditure on home care totalled A$2.8 billion (US$2.14 billion) in 2012/13 (Aged Care Financing Authority, 2014: xii).

National-level data across many developed countries, however imprecise, indicates a shift in funding and in workforce numbers towards in-home aged care and away from residential aged care facilities (e.g., Eurofound, 2013). Nevertheless, while in many countries the in-home care workforce is expanding, in some countries such as the Netherlands and England it is actually decreasing because of austerity-driven government funding cuts, despite growing demand (Eurofound, 2013; Ismail et al., 2014). These funding cuts mean that fewer elderly people in need will be able to access formal in-home care services, and will be reliant instead on informal family care where it is available (Maarse and Jeurissen, 2016; CLES, 2014).

Home Care Workers and Labour Minima

This chapter focuses on home care employment in the formal sector, which in most developed economies is typically regulated by minimum labour standards. What is striking is that in such jurisdictions home care workers are nevertheless expressly excluded from certain minimum standards, or are entitled to poorer minima than other workers. For example, in the United States until 2015 there was a 'companionship' exemption for home care workers under the Fair Labor Standards Act (FLSA) that exempted employers from paying minimum wages and overtime benefits to care workers who provide what is considered as personal and unskilled assistance, classifying them as 'companions' (Boris and Klein, 2012). This exclusion – estimated to exclude almost two-thirds of all home care workers – was originally put in place back in the 1970s when domestic servants came under the protection of the FLSA. Home health care aides were distinguished from domestic servants on the basis that they provide 'companionship' rather than undertake 'work' per se (Klein and Boris, 2013). In September 2013, this exemption was partially repealed with effect from January 2015. While it has been removed for third parties such as agencies, it is still in place for families and individuals directly employing home care workers.

In Canada, employment standards outside of federal employment are essentially a provincial responsibility. Under the Ontario Employment Standards Act (ESA), for example, home care workers employed by agencies or designated as 'elect to work' workers have no rights to notice of termination (or termination pay in lieu of notice), nor to severance pay.

However, this situation represents an improvement on previous exclusions. Before 2009, home care workers were also excluded from the public holiday provisions of the ESA that entitle workers scheduled to work on public holidays to have the day off with pay (Charlesworth, 2010: 386).

In Australia the partial protection afforded home care workers under the ten federal National Employment Standards (NES) and the minima set out in industry awards is more indirect, and mainly a consequence of employment status. For example, under the Fair Work Act 2009 (FWA), these labour standards do not cover workers who are self-employed, while employees who are on casual contracts are excluded from a number of entitlements in the NES. Under the SCHCDS Award that provides industry-specific minimum standards for the majority of Australian home care workers, workers are entitled to poorer minima than home care workers employed directly by government, as discussed below.

6.3   HOME CARE: THE AUSTRALIAN CASE

The main focus of this section is on the historical and regulatory mechanisms that have produced current working conditions for different groups of home care workers in Australia. This analysis underpins the argument about the dynamic process of formalisation and informalisation of home care work; less a narrative of incremental formalisation than one of shifts forward and backward on the in/formalisation continuum. To set the context and render the workers on whom this chapter focuses a little more visible, the main socio-demographic characteristics of the Australian home care workforce and their employment conditions is first set out.

Socio-Demographic and Employment Characteristics of Home Care Workers

I draw here on the 2012 Australian NACWCS survey of aged care providers and aged care workers, and an analysis of the specific employment regulation that sets different employment minima for workers employed by the government and non-government sectors.

The profile of home care workers in Table 6.1 does not include those who are employed in labour hire arrangements or who are in self-employment.[4] The data are disaggregated according to three types of employment

---

[4]   The data exclude those not employed directly by aged care organisations surveyed. Data collected from these organisations indicate that 21 per cent employ

*Table 6.1   Key characteristics of directly employed home care workers by
employment contract*

Characteristics	Casual	Part-time	Full-time	Total
Sex = female	92%	90%	92%	91%
Median age	51 years	50 years	49 years	50 years
Overseas born	43.9%	24%	23.3%	28.7%
(NESB)	(33.9%)	(14%)	(10.1%)	(17.5%)
Employer type				
Not-for-profit	24.8%	66.2%	9.0%	100% (76.1%)
For-profit	36.4%	53.8%	9.8%	100% (6.7%)
Government	7.1%	88.0%	4.9%	100% (17.1%)
Employer size				
1–20 employees	32.4%	59.3%	8.4%	100% (16.9%)
21–40 employees	29.1%	63.3%	7.7%	100% (13.8%)
40+ employees	21.7%	69.9%	8.4%	100% (69.3%)
Average weekly hours	19	26	45	26
Want more hours	28.9%	31.8%	43.1%	32%
Multiple job holder	20.9%	12.2%	8.8%	14.0%
Total	30.4%	62.9%	6.7%	100%

Note: The table follows Australian employment regulatory demarcations rather than the
Australian Bureau of Statistics (ABS) demarcation of full-time/part-time hours (35 hours
a week or more/less than 35 hours a week). Workers included as full-time/part-time are
as those working 38 hours or more/less than 38 hours per week on an ongoing or fixed-
term basis. Casual workers may work full-time or part-time hours, their contract status
dependent on being designated as such under the Award.

Source: 2012 National Aged Care Workforce Census and Survey database.

contracts set down under the SCHCDS Award, as with other Australian
industry awards: full-time, part-time and casual. As highlighted in Table
6.1, more than 30 per cent of home care workers are employed on a casual
basis, well above the 24 per cent casualisation rate for all Australian
employees (ABS, 2013). In the Australian regulatory context, casual
employment attracts a 25 per cent premium above ordinary time pay rates.
However, casual status removes any rights to notice of termination or
severance pay and excludes workers from coverage by the statutory NES
in respect of paid leave such as sick, annual, carers' leave and rights in
respect of public holidays. Further, casuals' NES rights to unpaid parental
leave and to request flexible work arrangements are dependent on being

other home care workers via external agencies (8.3 per cent), through brokers (12.1
per cent) or self-employment (3 per cent) (King et al., 2013: 184).

in 'regular and systematic' employment with a reasonable prospect of continuing employment (Charlesworth and Heron, 2012: 172).

Part-time is the most common type of employment contract for home care workers, with only 7 per cent working on a full-time basis. However, while the SCHCDS Award provides that part-time employees are entitled to pro rata conditions of full-time work, the Award working time provisions arguably render part-time employment inferior to full-time employment. This facilitates a casual-like flexibility for employers, paid for at ordinary time rates (Charlesworth and Heron, 2012: 175).

Table 6.1 underscores the fact that the Australian home care workforce in aged care, like in other developed countries, is a highly feminised and ageing one. The proportion of those born in outside Australia and in non-English-speaking background (NESB) countries is similar to that for all Australian employees. However, while migrant status is a key feature of analyses of the home care workforce in many countries, in Australia the presence of migrants has received little attention. This may be because, as Howe suggests, historically many non-Australian-born migrants working in aged care have been long-term permanent migrants. Recent skill-based migration policies largely preclude the entry of workers classified as low-skilled, and until recently the cash for care schemes that have fostered the employment of migrant care workers in other countries have not been part of the policy landscape in Australia (Howe, 2009: 388). Both temporary and permanent migrants are entitled under Australian law to the same wages and conditions of other workers. Nevertheless, the data in Table 6.1 show that casual workers are more than twice as likely as part-time workers to be born in NESB countries.

Employer type can shape employment conditions; an issue taken up further below. Unlike the UK, where the private sector is now the major employer of home care workers (Skills for Care, 2015), most home care work in Australia is carried out for not-for-profit employers in the charitable sector. However, the for-profit sector, which is growing, is more likely to employ casual workers than either not-for-profit or government employers.

Home care workers, and in particular casual workers, work relatively short hours.[5] Underemployment is an issue, reflected in the fact that 32 per cent of home care workers want to work more hours than they currently do. Interestingly it is full-time workers who are more likely than casual workers to want more hours of work. This may be related to the

---

[5] On average, Australian non-managerial employees work 31.2 hours per week (ABS, 2014).

higher relative rate of multiple job holding among casuals (21 per cent) than full-time workers (8.8 per cent). The comparable multiple job holding rate for all Australian employees is 5.2 per cent (King et al., 2013: 130).

Towards Formalisation: The Industrial Recognition of Home Care Work

In most developed economies, the sort of work undertaken by home care workers today was historically relegated to the family. With the emergence of the welfare state this type of work was taken on by the state where the family was unable to provide this care (Mundlak, 2012: 190). In Australia the post-war period saw the increasing use of services provided by charities to support the elderly and others in their homes. While there were different developments in different Australian states, both state and local governments started to assume some responsibility for the delivery of what is now known as 'home care' services.

The nature of the care provided also expanded rapidly from the provision of domestic and support services to personal care delivered to an increasingly targeted group of more dependent older people. At the same time there was a decline in the direct government provision of home care services with an increasing contracting out by state and local governments and strong growth in publically subsidised not-for-profit and for-profit provision (Briggs et al., 2007: 501). By the early 1970s, home care workers employed directly by state and or local governments started to be included in the relevant industry awards that provided the minimum wages and employment conditions for those sectors, although home care workers were the lowest-paid of all workers and the classification structure did not provide for any progression in those awards (Charlesworth, 1993). In some government awards a change in work value was recognised in the late 1980s–1990s, despite there having been no initial assessment of work value. In Victorian local government, for example, in 1986 the Australian Industrial Relations Commission held that there had been a change in the skill levels required by home care workers and introduced an additional skill classification to recognise personal care work (Charlesworth, 1993: 18).

In 1985, under the Home and Community Care Act 1985, the federal government and the eight state and territory governments agreed to jointly fund the Home and Community Care (HACC) programme. The HACC programme 'replaced a range of disparate community care services that were being delivered to older people and those with a disability in their homes', with its objectives being to 'provide care in the community without the need for institutionalisation' and 'to reduce the demand and financial pressures being placed on residential facilities' (Productivity Commission,

2011: 14–15). Importantly, the HACC programme formalised joint state and federal funding of home care, providing a fixed unit cost per service. Thus, while a key rationale for the shift to home care was to respond to the preferences of older people and their families, cost containment remains a key driver for the shift from institutional to home-based aged care services, where the care provided is broken down into discrete tasks rather than holistic services.

Until 1991, home care workers employed by the growing non-profit sector were excluded from Australian 'industrial citizenship', including coverage by an industry award, minimum wage rates and other employment conditions (Briggs et al., 2007). In 1991 the first Social and Community Sector (SACS) Award was won in the New South Wales (NSW) jurisdiction, covering non-government SACS workers. The state government and the charitable sector fought long and vigorously against the establishment of this award, which only came into being after a High Court challenge. In the mid-1990s, the NSW SACS award was followed by the winning of similar awards in other states and territories (Briggs et al., 2007).

In the early 1990s, as part of an award restructuring process in local and state governments, the typically one- or two-level skill and pay classifications for home care work began to be unpacked, in recognition of the more intensive work and different skill levels required (Kenna, 1993). The taking on of personal care was a defining feature of this reclassification, with increases in the complexity and difficulty of that work being recognised over three skill levels, with a fourth level recognising team leadership or supervisory responsibilities. The unpacking of home care skills classifications was incorporated, at least in part, into the various state-based and federal SACS awards. Today under the SCHCDS Award, as shown in Table 6.2, there are two skill classifications for direct home care work, with a third level applying to those employed in team or supervisory roles.[6]

The work value of work performed in the social and community services sector changed considerably during the 1990s and 2000s, including in home care work, with more complex and demanding personal care work required by an increased targeting of HACC services to the very frail and dependent. However there was never any initial assessment of 'work value' undertaken in the NSW award, nor in the other state SACS awards that

---

[6] This chapter focuses on formal employment minima rather than actual compliance with these minima. However, in practice some home care workers have been placed on and remained on the lowest classification of the SCHCDS Award, whatever the work they do, as a way of smaller agencies, often in regional locations, managing within HACC funding allocations.

followed. Nor were any subsequent changes in work value recognised in these awards (Charlesworth, 2012: 115).

Towards Informalisation?

Three main shifts have contributed to the incomplete process of the regulatory recognition of home care work as work and, for many home care workers, a move backwards on the in/formalisation continuum. These include the increasing contracting out of home care services including requirements in some states for the compulsory tendering of local government services, the structural underfunding of social care and the award modernisation process under the Fair Work Act 2006 (FWA).

In the 1990s, several state governments forced local governments into compulsory competitive tendering for their services, such as home care, as part of a broader shift of the state to neoliberal governance. This put an end to union attempts to properly revalue home care work and the relativities between this work and other local government work. Through the 1990s and into the 2000s, the low rates set in the many awards in the social and community services industry were underpinned by state and federal governments' lack of preparedness to fund additional payments above the basic level set down in the relevant award (Productivity Commission, 2011: 359). Indeed the gendered undervaluing of care work in labour regulation is reinforced and structured by a care market in which the price for labour is set through funding allocation decisions made by governments underpinned by social norms about care (Charlesworth, 2012: 128). That is, the industrial recognition of home care work was an incomplete one, shaped not only by a reluctance to fully recognize caring work undertaken in the home as 'work', but also by inadequate government funding based on assumptions that the work undertaken was unskilled 'women's work'.

Another step towards informalisation came as part of the award modernisation process introduced in 2009/2010 under the FWA, where more than 23 state and federal SACS awards were aggregated into one federal award: the SCHCDS Award. Some of the improvements won in several individual predecessor awards, such as a casual conversation clause, the right to a written agreement to hours worked and changes to hours, and payment for travel time between clients, were lost in this process as were some of the premia paid to workers who worked unsocial hours. The view of many unions involved in the award modernisation process is that what is now the Fair Work Commission (FWC) used a 'lowest common denominator' approach to balance differences in conditions in diverse predecessor awards. This approach compounded the disadvantage for community services workers, including home care workers, where any improvements in conditions were very hard fought and won in a patchy fashion in different jurisdictions.

However it is not only governments and industrial tribunals that have undervalued home care work. While unions are parties to industrial awards, those unions covering the non-government sector have not improved conditions for home care workers who remain at the bottom of the SCHCDS Award classification structure. This is due to the lack of presence of home care workers within workplaces and in union membership, as well as more recently to union efforts being focused on maintaining existing minima in the face of pressure from employers for care work to be made more flexible. The relatively limited attention to home care work played out in the equal-pay claim pursued by unions under the then new SCHCDS Award in 2011. By the mid-2000s there was an average of around 30 per cent difference in pay rates between social and community services (SACS) workers employed by the non-government sector, and those employed directly by state and local governments. It was this differential that underpinned a successful SACS industry pay equity case run in the Queensland jurisdiction in 2009, and then the first successful case run under the SCHCDS Award in 2011/12 (Charlesworth, 2012: 121–3). The Fair Work Australia determination provided wage increases of between 19 per cent and 41 per cent for different groups of workers covered by the award, which were to be phased in over eight years (Cortis and Meagher, 2012: 381).

Home care workers were, however, excluded from the federal case despite the fact most are employed under the SCHCDS Award. There appear to be two main reasons for this exclusion.[7] First, the federal case was a 'derived case' that built directly on a successful Queensland case for those covered by the relevant Queensland SACS state award, which had expressly excluded home care workers. Second, the union agreement with the federal Labor government to support the case was contingent on the case not covering home care workers who were funded out of the health budget, as it was feared the case might open up 'flow on' equal-pay claims in the much larger aged care residential and hospital sectors.[8] As a result of this exclusion, the small 2 per cent pay relativity between disability support workers and home care workers before the 2012 equal pay case will increase to some 24 per cent over the eight years of the phased-in wage increase.

---

[7]   Based on discussions with union officials at the Australian Services Union, the main union in the equal pay claim.
[8]   The Labor government committed more than $2 billion to fund the wage increases (Cortis and Meagher, 2012: 383).

In Australia we can see the results of the truncated process of formalisation in pay and conditions of home care workers in the SCHCDS Award. It can be seen, firstly, in comparison to the rapidly dwindling numbers of home care workers still employed directly by government; and secondly, in comparison to workers who perform similar tasks but perform this work in the institutional setting of residential aged care.

The Impact of Employer Type on Working Conditions

Table 6.2 highlights the importance of the type of employer to the conditions of home care workers and the impact different funding models have on working conditions. In NSW, more than 4000 home care workers were employed directly by the state government until 19 February 2016, when the service was contracted out to a not-for-profit employer, Australian Unity. The relevant industrial award that covered these workers was the NSW Care Worker Employees–Department of Family and Community Services Aging, Disability and Home Care (State) Award 2014.[9] As set out in Table 6.2, the NSW Award represents the (limited) heights of the formalisation process of home care work in direct government employment that was truncated for those in the non-government sector, today reflected in the federal SCHCDS Award.

While the SCHCDS Award provides in effect for just two skill levels for 'hands-on' home care work, the NSW Award has three skill levels. The NSW Award provided detailed guidelines covering the grading of care work that account for not only the types of tasks performed and level of interpersonal skills required, but also the impact of factors such as client behaviour illustrated with vignette examples. Grade 1 is for basic domestic assistance work only; while Grade 2 is for domestic work that requires some capacity to adjust around clients' needs and/or personal care work that requires some assistance such as helping a client wash and dry their own hair. Grade 3 home care workers take on domestic work with clients who are very difficult or aggressive, and/or complex personal care tasks such as those concerned with 'bodily intrusion' such as assisting

---

[9]   This award was replaced by an updated award with similar conditions, the NSW Care Worker Employees – Department of Family and Community Services Ageing, Disability and Home Care (State) Award 2015. The conditions and pay rates of this new award mirror the 2014 award and cover those workers whose employment was transferred to Australian Unity for at least two years. After this time the former state government employees will be entitled only to the 'safety net' of poorer conditions in the SCHCDS Award, unless an enterprise agreement with improved conditions is struck with United Voice.

Table 6.2   *Employer type and employment minima*

Minimum condition/ award	SCHCDS Modern Award 2010	NSW Ageing, Disability and Home Care (State) Award 2014
Hourly pay rates[a]	HCW 1 – $18.15 HCW 2 – $19.24–$19.37 HCW 3 – $19.63–$20.24	CW 1 – $20.64 CW 2 – $21.67 CW 3 – $23.43
Written agreement: • on hours on commence-ment	✓ FT/PT only	✓On commencement, casuals advised in writing of Award conditions and entitlements
• to changes of hours (FT/PT only)	✓[b]	✓
Rostering (FT & PT only)	Roster posted at least 2 weeks in advance, 7 days notice of change in roster except where another employee absent on sick leave or in emergency	Roster to be received for following fortnight's work based on agreed availabilities of worker
Client cancellation	If notified by 5 pm the day prior no payment; if FT/PT employee not so notified will be paid min specified hours for that day	If notified by 5 pm the day prior, no payment; if FT/ PT employee not so notified replacement work to be found or payment for cancelled task of one hour max
Weekend premia (FT/PT)	50% loading for Saturday work, and 100% loading for Sunday work	50% loading for Saturday work, and 100% loading for Sunday work
Overtime (FT/PT)[c]	Where work more than 38 hours a week or 10 hours a day, loading of 50% for the 1st 2 hrs and 100% for further hrs	Where work more than 8 hours a day or 76 hours per fortnight, loading of 50% for the 1st 2 hrs and 100% for further hrs
Casuals	25% loading only, including on weekends and for overtime	20% loading plus weekend and overtime premia as for FT/PT
Casual to permanent conversion	No	After 6 months 'regular' casual can elect to be permanent. Can only be refused on 'reasonable grounds'
Casual minimum engagement	1 hour	2 hours unless 'genuine inability' when it is 1 hour
Paid travel time between clients	No	✓

Table 6.2   (continued)

Notes:
[a]   As of July 2014 for the SCHCDS Award and September 2014 for the NSW Award.
[b]   These provisions for written agreement were not present in the original SCHCDS Award. They were introduced by the FWC, with effect from August 2013, after a union claim in the 2012 Interim Modern Award Review.
[c]   The requirement for those on part-time contracts to work more than full-time hours to be entitled to overtime is typical of many awards in feminised industries, although not all. Like awards that cover male-dominated industries such as manufacturing, the Restaurant Industry Award provides that part-time workers who work more than their contacted hours are entitled to be paid overtime.

with bowel management, cathertisation, changing colostomy and drainage bags, and changing wound dressings. In contrast, the classification descriptors for the two hands-on levels in the SCHCDS Award are more rudimentary, with the lack of detail enabling these skill levels to be 'read down' in practice. This means, for example, that while the Level 1 classification is only for those with less than 12 months of experience and who undertake routine domestic tasks, industry practice suggests that many home care workers who undertake domestic work only are employed at this level even where they have 12 months or more experience.

What is immediately striking in Table 6.2 is that at Level/Grade 2 where workers undertake a range of personal care tasks, those covered by the SCHCDS Award can be paid up to $2.40 less per hour than workers undertaking similar work under the NSW Award. This differential may increase in some cases to $4.06 per hour, given that in practice complex personal care work under the NSW Award is paid at Grade 3.[10] These wage differentials highlight the effect of state and local government contracting out of home care services, and the limited involvement of unions in collective bargaining on behalf of home care workers in non-government employment.

Apart from hourly pay rates, the comparison in Table 6.2 is based on several key working time minima identified in the Draft Model Working Time Law for Domestic Workers (Model Law), which was developed as an ILO resource for the design of regulatory measures on working time in domestic work (McCann and Murray, 2010). The Model Law combines elements of conventional working time laws in 'framing standards', together with 'flexibility standards' that support both employer and employee-orientated flexibility, and provides a useful benchmark in assess-

[10]   Data provided to the author by United Voice indicate that in 2014 some 11 per cent of home care workers in the NSW Service were paid at Grade 3 rates.

ing Australian minima for home care workers. Framing standards include written agreement to hours and changes to hours, premia on night work, work on rest days and public holidays, payment for travel time, what is essentially a two-hour minimum engagement, and prohibition on employing domestic workers on a casual or 'as and when required' basis (McCann and Murray, 2010: 44–54). In the Australian context, where casual employment is formally recognised in regulation, this latter standard could be interpreted as a right to conversion from a casual to an ongoing contract, present in the NSW Award but not the SCHCDS Award.

The Model Law minima suggest that a written contract specifying the quantum and schedule of hours is central to decent work (McCann and Murray, 2010: 43). While this standard is provided for in the NSW Award for all workers, it was only recently introduced in the SCHCDS Award and excludes casuals. The SCHCDS Award provides a very low minimum engagement for casuals of just one hour, half that provided for in the NSW Award in most circumstances and recommended in the Model Law. This means that a casual worker (and, as highlighted above, almost one-third of home care workers are employed on a casual basis) can be allocated and paid for just one hour of work. In the same Award casual disability support workers, who also provide care in the home, are entitled to a two-hour minimum engagement whereas all other casual community services workers covered under the Award have three hours minimum engagement (Charlesworth and Heron, 2012).

The hours required in home care work can vary, given their dependence on clients. The Model Law suggests that flexibility standards can be designed to recognise and facilitate unpredictable demands while ensuring protection for workers (McCann and Murray, 2010: 28). In both Australian awards, requirements for a written agreement to changes to hours is limited to those in part-time or full-time employment. Further, under both awards where a client cancels a scheduled visit and the required notice is provided, employees are not paid for this time. This does not meet flexibility standard suggested in the Model Law, where a worker required to be available for work but not called out to work must be paid at least 25 per cent of the hourly wage (McCann and Murray, 2010: 51).

While casual home care workers under the NSW Award have had better minima than those under the SCHCDS Award, it is noteworthy that the former are much less likely to be casual,[11] and thus more likely

---

[11] Data provided by United Voice indicate that 17 per cent of the NSW Home Care Service employees were casual, compared to more than 30 per cent of home care workers under the SCHCDS Award (Table 6.1).

to be entitled to the better minima for part-time workers in the NSW Award. The lower incidence of casualisation may be due in part to the NSW Award provision that only those who work less than 20 hours per fortnight can be employed as casual. Casual workers under the SCHCDS Award are not compensated for working unsocial hours, receiving only their 25 per cent loading, whereas under the NSW Award premia for working on the weekends are paid on top of the casual loading of 20 per cent. Transferring from casual to ongoing status is only provided for in the NSW Award. While this condition had been part of several of the predecessor SACS awards, as noted above, in the award modernisation process this condition was lost.[12] Finally, while both awards make provision for the some reimbursement of fuel costs incurred in driving between clients, payment for the time taken for this travel – essential to the work of home care – is only provided for in the NSW Award. The issue of including such travel time as working time remains a contentious one for home care workers in most countries, although more recently some steps have been taken in the United Kingdom and New Zealand towards recognising it.

The Impact of Location on Working Conditions

The gendered architecture of both funding and labour regulation constructs home care work undertaken in the private sphere as a lesser form of care work than that undertaken in institutional settings in the public sphere (Lily, 2008; Le Bihan, 2012; Charlesworth, 2012). To illustrate how this is reflected in the Australian case, it is useful to compare the employment minima for personal care workers (PCWs) who work in residential aged care, covered under the Aged Care Award, with non-government home care workers covered under the SCHCDS Award.[13] PCWs undertake broadly similar personal care tasks to home care workers, although their domestic tasks are more limited. PCWs are directly supervised and

---

[12]   In the four-yearly Modern Award Review conducted by the FWC, the Australian Council of Trade Unions (ACTU) lodged a general claim for a casual conversion clause in industry awards without such a clause, such as the SCHCDS Award, a claim that was accepted by the Full Bench of the FWC in July 2017. However, the ACTU claim that a deeming clause be inserted where there was an existing casual conversion clause in an award to convert casual to ongoing employment was rejected (*4 Yearly Review Of Modern Awards – Casual Employment and Part-Time Employment* [2017] FWCFB 3541).

[13]   When the FWC first produced the Aged Care Award there was a provision for home care workers employed by aged care residential providers. After an application by employers in 2011 the FWC varied the Award to exclude care work undertaken in the home, with that work to be covered by the SCHCDS Award.

tend to undertake more routine tasks in the fixed schedules that typify residential aged care. The nature of the labour process in residential aged care with more predicable schedules also means that PCWs work more average weekly hours than home care workers (Parvazian et al., 2014).

In the Aged Care Award there are three main PCW skill classification levels, with an additional two provided for those undertaking supervisory and work organisation tasks. Overall, PCW minimum wages are only very marginally higher than those of home care workers under the SCHCDS Award, ranging from A$18.67 at Level 1, where workers are 'responsible for work performed with a limited level of accountability or discretion', to A$19.64 at Level 3, where workers are 'responsible for work performed with a medium level of accountability or discretion'. It is only Level 3 PCWs who are required to have Certificate 3 aged care qualifications, typically expected of Level 2 home care workers.[14]

Those PCWs who are casual – and PCWs are less likely to be so than home care workers[15] – have better working time conditions than casual home care workers. They have a two-hour minimum engagement, and overtime premia where applicable are paid in addition to the 25 per cent casual loading. And while a poorer standard than in many other industry awards, weekend premia are paid in substitution of the casual loading, which provides some compensation for working unsocial hours. The Aged Care Award provides that if employees are travelling on duty, all their costs are to be covered, which in practice would include their time. In contrast, the SCHCDS Award assumes for home care workers that each episode of care is a separate one, no matter how the roster is worked out, with no recognition of the time spent travelling between clients.

The institutional setting in which work is performed shapes both the nature and the scope of labour regulation (Fudge, 2012: 17). The location of aged care work in clients' homes renders it distant both from the normative worker, and from the workplaces around which labour regulation and its enforcement have been built. While PCWs' regulatory entitlements are still poor in the Australian context, both the nature of the work and the

---

[14]   Home care workers and PSWs have broadly similar qualification levels, including in respect of Certificate 3 aged care qualifications (King et al., 2013: 33, 118). United Voice officials report that in the current Modern Award Review they are seeking to ensure that where PCWs hold a Certificate 3, they are paid at Level 3 rates, unlike the current Award provisions which allow employers discretion over whether or not to pay PCWs with those qualifications at Level 3 rates.

[15]   NACWCS data indicate that 19.5 per cent of all directly employed PCWs are casual (King et al., 2013: 39), compared to 30.4 per cent of home care workers (Table 6.1).

relatively predicable organisation of working time in recognisable work-places provide the basis for more formalised employment regulation than is in place for home care workers, whose work remains largely invisible.

6.4 CONCLUSION

This chapter has focused on analysing the broader regulatory context in which the remuneration and employment standards for home care work have been produced in the Australian context. As in other countries, while shifts in government policy have driven the marketised provision of care in client's homes rather than in institutions, employment regulation continues to underscore the exceptionalism of this form of care work (McCann and Murray, 2014: 323). Over time there has been an increased regulatory recognition of home care work as 'work'. However, this recognition continues to be a partial one, shaped by shifts forward and backward on the in/formalisation continuum.

Unlike in many other countries, in Australia there are no formal regulatory exclusions of home care workers from specific labour minima, apart from those who are self-employed contractors. Further, their wages, while low, have arguably been protected by historically robust Australian minimum-wage-setting processes. Nevertheless, the casual status of a large number of home care workers has the effect of reducing access to both certain NES employment standards and comparable working time minima under the SCHCDS Award. Casual status allows employers to schedule workers whenever they wish, with the only obligation being a one-hour minimum engagement, and excludes them from the premia to which full-time and part-time workers are entitled in relation to overtime and unsocial hours. Part-time status offers only some limited protection, as workers' hours can be flexed up to almost full-time hours without entitlement to overtime premia. Home care workers in the not-for-profit and for-profit sectors are entitled to poorer minimum labour standards than workers in other feminized low-paid industries, particularly in respect to travel time and the cancellation of scheduled hours for full-time and part-time workers. They are also entitled to poorer minima than the diminishing number of home care workers who remain employed by governments, and those personal care workers undertaking similar tasks in the institutional setting of residential aged care.

The development of employment minima in home care has been very much shaped by the expansion of formal home care on the one hand, and on the other hand by inadequate government price-setting and indexation of aged care subsidies to providers. Following the Productivity

Commission Inquiry into Aged Care, industry groups had proposed a 'cost of care' study to ensure that the pricing of aged care services by government was reflective of wages and other labour costs, and to provide the basis for adequate review and adjustment over time to maintain competitive wage levels (NACA, 2013). To date, neither the former Labor government nor the current Coalition government have taken up this proposal.

Government funding models in aged care draw on powerful gendered norms about the value of home care, and place both downward pressure on the development of more expansive and inclusive minima, and pressure on employers to employ workers on non-standard contracts. The apparent similarity of the work home care workers undertake to the work women do for free within the private sphere has proved a powerful force in the valuing and recognition of this form of work in labour regulation, and indeed to the wilful blindness in calculating its true cost. The marketisation of care has been central to reinforcing and contributing directly to this undervaluation in home-based aged care. The significant contracting out of home care services formerly provided by local and state governments to the not-for-profit and for-profit sectors covered by the poorer minima in the SCHCDS Award has worked to undercut the recognition of home care work as work representing a shift backwards towards informalisation. Contracting out has a practical effect on wages and access to decent working time standards under the SCHCDS Award, with those working for not-for-profit and for-profit employers more likely to be casual and underemployed than those employed directly by government.

In Australia, the push towards informalisation and the fragmentation of the labour regulation of home care work are set to continue – amplified through direct payments and self-employment – modelling similar shifts in the UK marketisation of care (Glendinning, 2012: 297). A funding model of individual allocations to home care recipients rather than to agencies is now part of Australian aged care policy. There was another shift from the consumer-directed funding introduced in mid-2015, and initially confined to employer provision of a coordinated package of services designed to meet the specific care needs of individual home care recipients. From 2017, untied aged care funding is paid to providers to manage on behalf of individual recipients, who will be able to choose their providers and the services they wish to 'purchase' with the funds allocated to them (Belardi, 2015).

There is some concern in the industry, and in particular by unions, about the impact of individualised funding on the scheduling of home care services with flow-on consequences for a further erosion of employment conditions. A further policy shift to the full cashing out of home care, with direct payments to individuals, is planned by the current government

(Austin, 2015), similar to UK and Canadian cash-for-care home care systems. Analyses of the impact of those funding models suggest that there will be further downward pressure on employment conditions, with consequences also for the quality of care (Glendinning, 2012; Zeytinoglu et al., 2015). A review of a pilot of a similar Australian model under the National Disability Insurance Scheme (NDIS) and its impact on employment conditions suggests that the underfunding of unit prices paid for care is leading to employers exploiting gaps in the SCHCDS Award, and to the encouragement of 'self-employment' as a mechanism to provide the 'flexibility' of individualised care delivery (Macdonald and Charlesworth, 2016).

Nevertheless, the formalisation/informalisation process in the employment regulation of home care work remains a dynamic one. This process is illustrated by union action around the NSW government's 2016 contracting out of the NSW Home Care Service, where workers have been covered by better conditions, as discussed above. While United Voice was not able to prevent this contracting out, it negotiated with the state government to ensure that a single not-for-profit provider be the successful tenderer to take over the service. While ultimately the conditions under the NSW state award will be lost, unions have successfully pushed back against earlier shifts to informalisation, resulting from the 2010 award modernisation process. In the 2012 Interim Modern Award Review, unions won changes in the SCHCDS Award that now provide for a written contract of hours, and written agreement to changes to hours for permanent full-time and part-time workers.

The four-yearly Modern Award Review being undertaken by the FWC – focused on the operation of individual industry awards as well as common issues across them – potentially provided the necessary sectoral focus advocated by McCann and Murray (2014) and Albin (2012) that could address the specific disadvantage faced by home care workers. One hurdle has been that the SCHCDS Award covers a wide gamut of professional and quasi-professional community services workers, and as the 2012 Equal Pay case demonstrated, home care workers can easily be excluded from rights claims under the Award. Driven by burgeoning labour costs in the roll-out of the NDIS, there were some industry proposals for a separate in-home care industry award, which would cover home care workers in both aged care and disability support. To date, however, discussions and negotiation in the Modern Award Review has focused on making the meagre existing working time minima even more 'flexible' including through reducing overtime and unsocial hours premia and minimum shift requirements (Morton, 2014).

A rethinking of employment regulation so that it can accommodate both the specific nature of home care work and its value as 'work', worthy of full regulation, would require a fundamental commitment by the FWC, unions and employers. That commitment is not yet in place and it seems likely that the current Modern Award Review of the SCHCDS Award will provide only piecemeal changes forwards and backwards along the in/formalisation continuum. Canvassed in detail before the FWC in 2017, there were a number of claims by employers and unions. Several employer associations indicated that they wanted to further increase the flexibility of part-time hours in home care, while unions sought to increase the periods of notice for cancellations for part- and full-time workers and pursued the issue of payment for travel time between clients. Drawing on Australian policy goals of providing quality care to the aged and to people with disabilities, and the increased visibility that the ILO Domestic Workers Convention, 2011 (No. 189) provides to in-home care workers, may provide a more realistic platform for union and community coalitions to rethink the basis of decent working standards for home care workers in the next Modern Award Review scheduled for 2018.

REFERENCES

Aged Care Financing Authority. 2014. 'Report on the funding and financing of the aged care industry', available at http://www.dss.gov.au.

Albin, E. 2012. 'From "domestic servant" to "domestic worker"', in J. Fudge, S. McCrystal and K. Sankaran (eds), *Challenging the Legal Boundaries of Work Regulation* (Oxford, Hart Publishing), pp. 231–50.

Appelbaum, E. and Leana, C. 2011. 'Improving job quality: Direct care workers in the US', Center for Economic and Policy, September.

Armstrong, P., Armstrong, H. and Scott-Dixon, K. 2008. *Critical to Care: The Invisible Women in Health Services* (Toronto, University of Toronto Press).

Austin, S. 2015. Radio interview with Minister Mitch Fifield, Assistant Minister for Social Services, ABC Radio 612 Brisbane, 20 May.

Australian Bureau of Statistics (ABS). 2013. 'Forms of employment, Australia, November 2013', Cat No 6359.0.

Australian Bureau of Statistics (ABS). 2014. 'Employee earnings and hours, Australia, May 2014', Data Cube 63060DO004_201405.

Australian Government. 2012. 'Commonwealth HACC Program Guidelines 2012–2015', available at: https://www.dss.gov.au.

Belardi, L. 2015. 'Budget: ACAR to end in move to market system in home care'. Australian Aging Agenda, 13 May, available at http://www.australianageingagenda.com.au.

Briggs, C., Meagher, G. and Healy, K. 2007. 'Becoming an industry: The struggle of social and community workers for award coverage, 1976–2001', *Journal of Industrial Relations*, **49**(4), 497–521.

Boris, E. and Klein, J. 2012. 'Home-care workers aren't just "companions"', *New York Times*, 1 July.

Centre for Local Economic Strategies (CLES) (2014) 'Austerity uncovered', Executive Summary. Presented to Trades Union Congress. Available at https://www.tuc.org.uk/.

Charlesworth, S. 1993. 'Making the grade: Community services and pay equity', Report for the Pay Equity Unit, Department of Industrial Relations (Canberra: Commonwealth of Australia).

Charlesworth, S. 2010. 'The regulation of paid care workers' wages and conditions in the non-profit sector: A Toronto case study', *Relations Industrielles/Industrial Relations*, **65**(3), 380–99.

Charlesworth, S. 2012. 'Decent working conditions for care workers? The intersections of employment regulation, the funding market and gender norms', *Australian Journal of Labour Law*, **25**(2), 107–27.

Charlesworth, S. and Heron, A. 2012. 'New Australian working time minimum standards: reproducing the same old gendered architecture?', *Journal of Industrial Relations*, **54**(2), 164–81.

Charlesworth, S. and Marshall, H. 2011. 'Sacrificing workers? The curious case of salary sacrificing in non-profit community services in Australia', *International Journal of Public Sector Management*, **24**(7), 673–83.

Cortis, N. and Meagher, G. 2012. 'Recognition at last: Care work and the equal remuneration case', *Journal of Industrial Relations*, **54**(3), 377–85.

Eiken, S., Sredl, K., Gold, L., Kasten, J., Burwell, B. and Saucier, P. 2014. 'Medicaid expenditures for long-term services and supports in FFY 2012', Truven Health Analytics, available at http://www.medicaid.gov.

England, P. 2005. 'Emerging theories of care work', *Annual Review of Sociology*, 381–99.

Eurofound. 2013. *More and Better Jobs in Home-Care Services* (Luxembourg: Publications Office of the European Union).

Folbre, N. 2008. 'Reforming care', *Politics and Society*, **36**(3), 373–87.

Freedland, M. and Kountouris, N. 2012. *The Legal Construction of Personal Work Relations* (Oxford: Oxford University Press).

Fudge, J. 2012. 'Blurring legal boundaries: Regulating for decent work', in J. Fudge, S. McCrystal and K. Sankaran (eds), *Challenging the Legal Boundaries of Work Regulation* (Oxford: Hart Publishing), pp. 1–26.

Genet, N., Boerma, W.G., Kringos, D.S., Bouman, A., Francke, A.L., Fagerström, C., Melchiorre, M., Grecos, C. and Devillé, W. 2011. 'Home care in Europe: A systematic literature review', *BMC Health Services Research*, **11**(1), 207–21.

Glendinning, V. 2012. 'Home care in England: Markets in the context of underfunding', *Health and Social Care in the Community*, **20**(3), 292–9.

Hampson, I. and Junor, A. 2010. 'Putting the process back in: Rethinking service sector skill', *Work, Employment and Society*, **24**(3), 526–45.

Health and Social Care Information Centre (HSCIC). 2013. *Personal Social Services: Expenditure and Unit Costs, England 2012–13*, Final release (London: Health and Social Care Information Centre).

Howe, A. 2009. 'Migrant care workers or migrants working in long-term care? A review of Australian Experience', *Journal of Aging and Social Policy*, **21**(4), 374–92.

Howes, C. 2014. 'Raising wages for home care workers: Paths and impediments', in Institute for Research on Labor and Employment (ed.), *A Paper Series Commemorating the 75th Anniversary of the Fair Labor Standards Act* (Berkeley, CA: University of California), pp. 241–79.

Hussein, S. and Manthorpe, J. 2014. 'Structural marginalisation among the long-term care workforce in England: Evidence from mixed-effect models of national pay data', *Ageing and Society*, **34**(1), 21–41.

Ismail, S., Thorlby, R. and Holder, H. 2014. *Focus On: Social Care for Older People: Reductions in Adult Social Services for Older People in England* (London: Health Foundation and Nuffield Trust).

Kenna, S. 1993. *Skilled Work: A Skills Analysis of Community Services Workers*, Women's Research and Employment Initiatives Program (Canberra: Australian Government Publication Service).

King, D., Mavromaras, K., Wei, Z., He, B., Healy, J., Macaitis, K., Moskos, M. and Smith, L. 2013. *2012 National Aged Care Workforce Census and Survey – The Aged Care Workforce, 2012 – Final Report* (Canberra: Australian Department of Health and Ageing).

Klein, J. and Boris, E. 2013. 'We have to take it to the top: Workers, state policy, and the making of home care', *Buffalo Law Review*, **61**, 293–321.

Le Bihan, B. 2012. 'The redefinition of the familialist home care model in France: The complex formalization of care through cash payment', *Health and Social Care in the Community*, **20**(3), 238–46.

Lily, M. 2008. 'Medical versus social work-places: Constructing and compensating the personal support worker across health care settings in Ontario, Canada', *Gender Place and Culture*, **15**(3), 285–99.

Maarse, J. and Jeurissen, P. 2016. 'The policy and politics of the 2015 long-term care reform in the Netherlands', *Health Policy*, **120**(3), 241–5.

Macdonald, F. and Charlesworth, S. 2016. 'Cash for care under the NDIS: Shaping care workers' working conditions?', *Journal of Industrial Relations*, **58**(5), 627–46.

Martin, B. 2007. 'Good jobs, bad jobs? Understanding the quality of aged care jobs, and why it matters', *Australian Journal of Social Issues*, **42**(2), 183–97.

McCann, D. and Murray, J. 2010. *The Legal Regulation of Working Time in Domestic Work*, International Labour Office Conditions of Work and Employment Series (Geneva: International Labour Office).

McCann, D. and Murray, J. 2014. 'Prompting formalisation through labour market regulation: A "framed flexibility" model for domestic work', *Industrial Law Journal*, **43**(3), 319–48.

Morton, R. 2014. 'Secret Fair Work talk on NDIS "workplace" reform', *Australian*, 1 December.

Mundlak, G. 2012. 'The wages of care-workers: From structure to agency', in J. Fudge, S. McCrystal and K. Sankaran (eds), *Challenging the Legal Boundaries of Work Regulation* (Oxford: Hart Publishing), pp. 189–212.

National Aged Care Alliance (NACA). 2013. *Aged Care Reform Series – Workforce*. Available at http://www.naca.asn.au.

New Zealand Human Rights Commission (NZHRC). 2012. Caring Counts: Report of the Inquiry into the Aged Care Workforce (Wellington: New Zealand Human Rights Commission).

Palmer, E. and Eveline, J. 2012. 'Sustaining low pay in aged care work', *Gender, Work and Organization*, **19**(3), 254–75.

Parvazian, S., Charlesworth, S., King, D. and Skinner, N. 2014. *Developing Job Quality Benchmarks in Australian Aged Care Services* (Adelaide: Centre for Work+Life University of South Australia).

Pfau-Effinger, B., Flaquer, L. and Jensen, P. (eds). 2009. *Formal and Informal Work in Europe: The Hidden Work Regime* (New York: Routledge).

PHI National – Quality Care through Quality Jobs (PHI). 2011. *Caring in America: A Comprehensive Analysis of the Nation's Fastest-Growing Jobs: Home Health and Personal Care Aides*. Available at www.phinational.org.

Productivity Commission. 2011. *Caring for Older Australians: Final Inquiry Report*, Vol. 2 (Canberra: Productivity Commission).

Skills for Care. 2015. 'The state of the adult social care sector and workforce in England, 2014', available at www.skillsforcare.org.uk.

Stewart, A. 2013. *Stewart's Guide to Employment Law*, 4th edn (Sydney: Federation Press).

Vella, K. 2008. 'Home and community care in Australia: Why the Victorian service delivery model is best for people who need care and their carers' (Carlton: Australian Services Union).

Victorian Government. 2013a. 'Home and community care unit prices 2013–14', available at http://www.health.vic.gov.au.

Victorian Government. 2013b. *Victorian Home and Community Care Program Manual 2013*, available at http://www.health.vic.gov.au.

Williams, C.C. and Lansky, M.A. 2013. 'Informal employment in developed and developing economies: Perspectives and policy responses', *International Labour Review*, **152**(3/4), 355–80.

Williams, J. (2000) *Why Work and Family Conflict and What To Do About It* (New York: Oxford University Press).

Zeytinoglu, I. U., Denton, M., Plenderleith, J. and Chowhan, J. 2015. 'Associations between workers' health, and non-standard hours and insecurity: The case of home care workers in Ontario, Canada', *International Journal of Human Resource Management*, DOI: 10.1080/09585192.2014.1003082.

PART III

Labour Market Regulation and Informality

7. Informal work in the Republic of Korea: Non-regulation or non-compliance?*

Byung-Hee Lee

7.1 INTRODUCTION

Since the financial crisis in late 1997, the labour market has changed drastically in the Republic of Korea. Market-driven flexibility has been implemented in ways that shift the accompanying costs to vulnerable groups of workers. This has been especially true in the area of hiring and firing. The changes have encouraged non-regular work and intensified labour market segmentation (Lee and Yoo, 2008). Of course, labour market dualization is not an issue that is unique to the Republic of Korea. Advanced countries have sought to restructure their social security systems in response to the dualization of their labour markets. The Republic of Korea also attempted to reduce the cost of market-driven changes. A series of policies including minimum wage and other labour standards were introduced to protect vulnerable groups, while the scope of social insurance coverage has continued to expand. Nonetheless, a considerable number of employees are still not effectively protected either by labour laws or by social insurance (Hwang and Lee, 2012). Furthermore, although the country is equipped with institutions and policies such as collective bargaining, minimum wage, unemployment benefits, and in-work benefits for the purpose of improving conditions in the low-wage labour market, the proportion of low-wage workers in the Republic of Korea is the highest among Organisation for Economic Co-operation and Development (OECD) economies. In addition, the proportion has continued to increase over the past decade, indicating that existing institutions and policies have not been helpful in improving conditions in the low-wage labour market. The mere

* The original version of this chapter was published as 'Informal work in Korea: Measurement, causes and characteristics'. *Journal of Korean Economic Development*, **19**(2), 81–109 (in Korean).

existence of a policy menu cannot guarantee on its own that policies will be effective (Hwang and Lee, 2012).

In this context, this chapter addresses the puzzling question of why informal work is widespread in the Republic of Korea even though labour law and the social insurance system have been developed towards universal application. Special attention will be paid to regulation and enforcement. The prevalence of informal work will be related closely to the lack of relevant regulation or lack of compliance. The evidence examined suggests that about 80 per cent of informal work in the Republic of Korea occurs within the regulatory framework, and that this is explained by the low level of policy enforcement. Therefore, these findings emphasize the need to reinforce the enforcement of protective policies.

7.2 DEFINING AND MEASURING INFORMALITY IN EMPLOYMENT

There is no universally accepted definition of informal work. The International Conference of Labour Statisticians has determined that workers have informal jobs if their employment relationship is, in law or in practice, not subject to national labour legislation, income taxation, social protection or entitlement to certain employment benefits (advance notice of dismissal, severance pay, paid annual or sick leave, and so on) (ILO, 2003). However, this definition is based on a social protection perspective and poses various difficulties when it comes to measuring informality in employment. Among other things, accurate measurement and empirical research depend on the availability of data and the purpose of the research. Hussmanns (2004) and ILO (2012) proposed that a labour force survey would be useful were it to include several questions on issues such as the existence of written labour contracts, subscription to social insurance, availability of paid leave, requirements for advance notice of dismissal, and the application of labour standards as provided for by labour laws. Previous empirical studies have adopted similar definitions referring to the existence of written labour contracts, subscription to social insurance programmes, income tax payment requirements, and so on.

In the Korean context, it is problematic to rely on empirical definitions of informality in employment that were developed in other countries. Among other things, written contracts are not very common in the Republic of Korea, even for employees in formal employment.[1] The

---

[1] In its comparison of informal employment in seven middle-income economies including the Republic of Korea, the OECD (2008) uses non-subscription

country also has quite a few tax-exempt employees who are not required to pay income tax, but lacks reliable survey data on whether individuals do in fact pay taxes on their income. In this study, jobs which are not subject to minimum wage legislation, mandatory retirement allowance,[2] and public pension at the principal employment are used as a proxy for informal work. These three policy areas were chosen because they are all characterized by their universal application across all workplaces. A brief description of the development of each of these policies follows.

The minimum wage system was first introduced in 1988 for permanent employees in manufacturing workplaces with ten or more employees. From October 2000 it was gradually expanded to cover all employees in all workplaces across all industries. The mandatory retirement allowance system stipulates that the employer must pay a retired employee the equivalent of 30 days' average pay for each year of tenure. Retirement allowance was introduced as a voluntary programme in the Labour Standards Act in 1953, but was made mandatory for workplaces with 30 or more employees from 1961. In 1989, it was gradually expanded to smaller workplaces with five or more employees. Finally, it was expanded to workplaces of all sizes, including those with fewer than five employees, from December 2010. To be eligible for a retirement allowance, an employee must have worked consecutively at the workplace for at least one year, for 15 or more contractual working hours each week. All Korean nationals from the ages of 18 to 59 who engage in income-earning activities are required to subscribe to a public pension scheme – either the National Pension Scheme (either workplace-based or individually insured) – or a Special Occupational Pension Scheme for public servants or teachers. The National Pension Scheme was first introduced in 1988 in workplaces with ten or more employees, and was expanded to include workplaces with five or more employees in 1992, farmers and fishermen in July 1995, and all urban residents in April 1999, so as to provide coverage for all citizens. From 2006, all employees in workplaces with more than one employee have been required to subscribe to the National Pension Scheme as workplace-based insured persons.

---

to social insurance programmes and the absence of written labour contracts as proxy variables for informal employment, but is unable to provide statistics on the proportion of workers without written labour contracts in the Republic of Korea.

[2] The important provisions in the Labour Standard Act – for example, overtime pay, paid leave, advance notice of dismissal – do not apply to workplaces with fewer than five workers. This chapter looks only at the universal requirement for the payment of retirement allowance when determining compliance with labour standards.

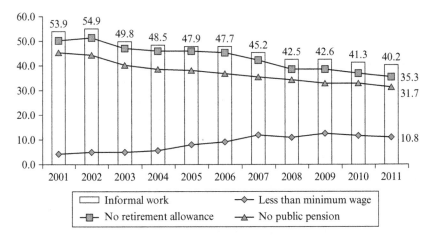

Source: Korea Statistical Office, Supplementary Survey of the Economically Active
Population Survey, August, yearly.

Figure 7.1   Trends in the incidence of informal work (%)

This chapter uses data from two surveys. The Supplementary Survey of
the Economically Active Population Survey (conducted by the Korea
Statistical Office) is used to analyse trends and characteristics of informal
employment. The Korean Labour and Income Panel Study (conducted by
the Korea Labor Institute) is used in the dynamic analysis of informality
in employment.

7.3   KEY TRENDS OF INFORMAL EMPLOYMENT

Figure 7.1 shows the share of informality among all employees. In 2011,
40.2 per cent of all wage workers were excluded from social protection
provided under the minimum wage system, labour standards or the social
insurance system. Of all waged workers, 10.8 per cent received less than
the minimum wage; 35.3 per cent were not eligible for mandatory retirement allowance; and 31.7 per cent did not subscribe to workplace-based
public pension schemes.

The incidence of informality has steadily declined over the past decade
from 53.9 per cent in 2001 to 40.2 per cent in 2011. This decline is explained
by the increase in the number of workers eligible to receive a retirement
allowance or subscribe to a public pension. The proportion of employees
not receiving the minimum wage increased significantly, however, to 10.8

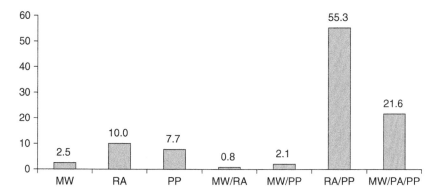

Note: MW = minimum wage; RA = mandatory retirement allowance; PP = public pension.

Source: Korea Statistical Office, Supplementary Survey of the Economically Active Population Survey, August 2011.

Figure 7.2 *Distribution of informal employees excluded from minimum wage, retirement allowance and public pensions (%)*

per cent in 2011 from 4.3 per cent in 2001. Although the relative level of the minimum wage has been increasing to curb low-wage work in the 2000s, the high degree of non-compliance with the system suggests a significant level of policy failure.

7.4 OCCURRENCE TYPE OF INFORMAL EMPLOYMENT

Figure 7.2 illustrates the distribution of informality among employees in terms of their exclusion from the three policies – minimum wage, retirement allowance and public pensions – that define informal employment in this study. Only 20.2 per cent are excluded from only one of these policies, while 79.8 per cent are excluded from two or more.

Table 7.1 presents a more detailed look at the extent of overlap in exclusion from the three policies. More than 80 per cent of those who do not receive the minimum wage are excluded from both retirement allowance and public pension coverage. Among employees who cannot receive a retirement allowance, one quarter receive less than the minimum wage, while 87.7 per cent are excluded from subscribing to a workplace-based public pension scheme. Of employees who are excluded from the public pension, 27.3 per cent do not receive minimum wage while 88.7 per cent

Table 7.1   Overlap in exclusion from minimum wage, retirement allowance and public pensions (%)

	Minimum wage		Retirement allowance		Public pension	
	Equal or above	Less than	Yes	No	Yes	No
Employees receiving less than minimum wage			16.9	83.1	12.1	87.9
Employees with no retirement allowance	74.5	25.5			12.3	87.7
Employees with no public pensions	72.7	27.3	11.3	88.7		

Source: Korea Statistical Office, Supplementary Survey of the Economically Active Population Survey, August 2011.

are excluded from retirement allowance benefits. These results suggest that exclusion from one policy usually entails exclusion from the others.

As noted, lack of coverage or effective application of regulation can be considered a defining characteristic of informal employment (ILO, 2003). One type of informality caused by non-regulation is 'independent contracting'. Workers who are considered independent contractors are excluded from coverage by law because they are not viewed as employees, even though they may be economically dependent upon the employer. Many of them provide labour in a manner that is identical or similar to an employee, but because they sign service contracts with employers they are not recognized as employees who are protected by law. A second type of informality due to non-regulation involves domestic workers, those tending to the sick, caring for babies at home and working as housemaids. These workers are specifically exempted from labour laws and social insurance. A third group is employees with less than one year of tenure, as they are excluded from retirement allowance benefits. A fourth group comprises part-time employees who work for less than 15 contractual hours per week; they are excluded from both retirement allowance benefits and subscription to workplace-based public pensions.[3] Any other cases of informality are categorized as resulting from non-compliance.

---

[3]   Daily workers are excluded from workplace-based subscription to health insurance and the National Pension Plan, but are included in employment insurance and industrial accident compensation insurance. Because this study

Table 7.2   Occurrence type of informal employment (%)

	Less than minimum wage	No retirement allowance	No subscription to public pension	Total
Non-regulation	7.4	73.2	19.0	20.6
Independent contractor	3.9	9.8	9.7	
Domestic service industry	3.5	2.4	2.4	
Less than 1 year of tenure		64.3		
Part-time work		7.3	7.4	
Non-compliance	92.6	26.8	81.0	79.4

Source: Korea Statistical Office, Supplementary Survey of the Economically Active Population Survey, August 2011.

Table 7.2 shows that a considerable level of informal work occurs not because workers are excluded from the scope of application of labour laws, but due to a lack of compliance with existing labour laws.[4] Of the employees who receive less than the minimum wage, only 7.4 per cent were informal employees because of non-regulation, while most were receiving less than the minimum wage due to employer non-compliance with minimum wage laws. Among employees excluded from retirement allowance benefits, a high proportion engaged in informal work as a result of non-regulation: 64.3 per cent of these employees had less than one year of consecutive service. Regarding employees excluded from subscription to workplace-based public pension schemes, 81 per cent were excluded in practice even though the law requires that they have such coverage. When informal employment due to non-compliance is defined as employment in which the employer does not comply with one or more of the statutory requirements for fully eligible employees, 79.4 per cent of all informal employees are in informal work situations due to non-compliance on the part of the employer, while 20.6 per cent are engaged in informal employment due to non-regulation.

Kanbur (2009) has argued that the issue of informal employment must

determines informal employment on the basis of compliance to social insurance requirements, it does not classify the informal employment of daily workers as being caused by non-regulation.

[4]   Due to limitations in data on domestic workers, information in this table represents the situation for waged workers in the domestic services industry. Part-time workers with less than 15 contractual working hours per week have been replaced by workers with usual weekly working hours of less than 15 hours.

Table 7.3   Status of workplace labour inspections (workplaces, persons, %)

	Workplaces potentially subject to labour inspection	Labour inspectors	Inspected workplaces	Workplaces to cover per inspector	Workplaces inspected per inspector	Proportion of inspected workplaces
	(A)	(B)	(C)	(A/B)	(C/B)	(C/A, %)
2007	1 401 784	1276	26 976	1099	21.1	1.9
2008	1 432 812	1227	21 546	1168	17.6	1.5
2009	1 422 261	1209	19 873	1176	16.4	1.4

Source: Ministry of Employment and Labour, White Paper in Employment and Labour, each year (cited from Kim, 2012).

be examined through the lens of state intervention. If it is highly unlikely that non-compliance will be detected, or if the penalty for non-compliance is lower than the cost of compliance, it is quite natural for employers to choose not to comply with the law. For the large part, the occurrence of informal employment is linked to the level of policy enforcement. Therefore, it is primarily the responsibility of the government to detect and discipline employers' non-compliance. In this respect, the labour administration and inspection system is a critical actor in state efforts to block informal employment due to non-compliance: these institutions safeguard standards for working conditions by inspecting for compliance with statutes on labour relations, and, where necessary, taking action to require corrective measures.

Table 7.3 reveals the current state of labour inspections in Korean workplaces. In 2009 each labour inspector was responsible for 1176 workplaces. Of these, only 16 were actually inspected: that is, only 1.4 per cent of all workplaces potentially subject to labour inspections were actually inspected. This indicates that it is quite likely that labour inspection does not reach workplaces with high concentrations of informality.

Table 7.4 demonstrates that violations are rampant. In the three years from 2007 to 2009, 70.3 per cent of inspected workplaces were found to be in violation of the Labour Relations Act in some respect. However, the data reveal that only 1.1 per cent of these workplaces were disciplined through judicial action, fines or administrative measures. This low level of policy enforcement and the negligible disciplinary measures may be contributing to higher non-compliance.

In Table 7.5, the working conditions of informal employees are compared with those of formal employees. While there is little difference in

Table 7.4 Workplace labour inspection implementation and sanctions (workplaces)

		2007	2008	2009	Total
Inspected workplaces		26976	29173	31467	87616
Inspected workplaces in violation		16281	21828	23465	61574
(%)		(60.4)	(74.8)	(74.6)	(70.3)
Measures:	Judicial action	58	79	46	183
	Fine	46	18	24	88
	Administrative measures	175	100	149	424

Source: Ministry of Employment and Labour, White Paper in Employment and Labour, each year (cited from Kim, 2012).

Table 7.5 Comparison of working conditions for formal and informal employees

	Formal employment	Informal employment
Usual weekly working hours (hours)	43.2	42.1
Hourly wage (1000 KRW)	14.0	7.1
Monthly average wage (1000 KRW)	257.0	123.3
Tenure (years)	7.1	2.1
Employees with written labour contracts (%)	66.3	27.3
Implementation of the 40-hour workweek (%)	70.9	27.8
Job training in the past year (%)	47.6	17.4
Union membership (%)	17.6	1.0
Job choice motive (%) Voluntary	85.2	38.3
Involuntary	14.8	61.7

Source: Korea Statistical Office, Supplementary Survey of the Economically Active Population Survey, August 2011.

working hours, the wage level for informal employees was only about half of that for formal employees. Informal employees served an average of only 2.1 years of tenure, compared to 7.1 years for formal employees, indicating the highly insecure nature of informal employment. The compliance rates for written labour contracts and the 40-hour work week – required for all workplaces with five or more employees – also remained below 30 per cent for informal employees. Opportunities to move to better jobs through career development were also quite limited for informal employees, given that only 17.4 per cent of informal employees participated in job training programmes in the past year. Informal employees are already excluded from protection by labour laws and social insurance programmes, yet only 1 per cent of these employees are union members, indicating that they are also excluded from any protection offered by the unions.

Data on job choice motives give an even clearer indication of the relationship between informal employment and non-compliance. While 61.7 per cent of informal employees reported that their job choice was involuntarily motivated, only 14.8 per cent of formal employees reported the same. This raises the question of whether informal employment should be viewed as an involuntary exclusion from state-provided protection, as opposed to a voluntary exit from formal employment because the benefits of formality do not outweigh the costs involved (Perry et al., 2007). The fact that many employees are involuntarily engaging in informal work suggests that their exclusion from social protection is directly connected to their involuntarily chosen informal work rather than being a choice made because the cost of exclusion is limited.[5]

7.5   INCIDENCE AND COMPOSITION OF INFORMAL EMPLOYMENT

Table 7.6 outlines the incidence and the composition of informal employment by job characteristics. With respect to enterprise size, the proportion of informal employment is higher among smaller businesses. Informal employment is particularly concentrated in workplaces with fewer than five employees, where 78.5 per cent of all workers are informal. In turn, they comprise 37.4 per cent of all informal workers. It must be recalled that the three policies in this study – minimum wage, retirement allowance and subscription to public pension plans – apply to all workplaces with fewer than five workers. In these workplaces, 66.3 per cent of the workers are engaged in informal employment as a result of non-compliance with legal requirements; they account for 39.8 per cent of all informal work due to employer non-compliance. Even though this phenomenon can in part be attributed to the low level of profitability in small firms, it is also closely related to the fact that other major labour law provisions do not apply to these small workplaces. The core provisions of the Labour Standards Act (such as

---

[5]   In a comparative analysis of the size and causes of informal employment in 30 European countries, Hazans (2011) also noted that exclusivity and discrimination are the major causes of informal employment in the context of waged work.

*Table 7.6   Incidence and composition of informal employment by job
characteristics (%)*

		Incidence			Composition		
		Total	Non-regulation	Non-compliance	Total	Non-regulation	Non-compliance
All workers		40.2	8.3	31.9	100.0	100.0	100.0
Firm size	1–4	78.5	12.1	66.3	37.4	28.1	39.8
	5–9	55.3	6.7	48.6	23.4	13.7	25.9
	10–29	39.1	9.7	29.4	22.0	26.6	20.9
	30–99	23.4	9.6	13.8	11.5	23.0	8.5
	100–299	12.8	3.4	9.4	3.2	4.2	3.0
	300–	8.8	3.3	5.5	2.5	4.5	1.9
Employment type	Regular	25.4	2.1	23.4	41.6	16.6	48.1
	Non-regular	68.6	20.2	48.4	58.4	83.4	51.9

Source: Korea Statistical Office, Supplementary Survey of the Economically Active
Population Survey, August 2011.

those restricting lay-offs or those regulating overtime, night, holiday work
and paid annual leave) and the Act on the Protection of Fixed-Term and
Part-Time Employees do not apply to workplaces with fewer than five
workers. Neither do other important provisions, including those mandat-
ing a 40-hour work week. These discrepancies in the application of laws
and regulations have led to greater non-compliance with requirements for
the minimum wage, retirement allowance and public pensions.

In terms of employment type, 68.6 per cent of all non-regular workers
engage in informal employment. Informal employment as a result of non-
compliance with any one of the three criteria accounts for 48.4 per cent
of all non-regular workers. It is also important to note that the issues of
non-regular and informal employment are quite closely correlated, and yet
are still distinct. The proportion of informal employment among regular
workers is 25.4 per cent. This is because there is a class of workers who are
categorized as regular, but excluded from social protection.

In order to identify the closely related job characteristics of informal
employment, logit regression analysis is applied (Table 7.7). 'Informal
employment' and 'informal employment due to employer non-compliance'
are set as the two dependent variables. Job characteristics such as workplace size, employment type, industry, occupation and union dummy are
included in the estimation. The personal characteristics of workers are
not taken into consideration in this analysis, because compliance with
minimum wage, labour standards and social insurance requirements are
compulsory, irrespective of personal characteristics. 'Less than one year of

Table 7.7   Logit analysis for the probability of being in informal employment

		Sample characteristics		Informal employment		Informal employment due to non-compliance	
		Mean (SD)		Marginal effect (SE)		Marginal effect (SE)	
Firm size	1–4	0.192	(0.320)	0.519	(0.018) ***	0.488	(0.023) ***
	5–9	0.170	(0.305)	0.339	(0.022) ***	0.367	(0.025) ***
	10–29	0.227	(0.340)	0.206	(0.023) ***	0.209	(0.023) ***
	30–99	0.198	(0.324)	0.093	(0.023) ***	0.071	(0.022) ***
	100–299	0.101	(0.245)	−0.012	(0.025)	0.026	(0.024)
Employment type	Non-regular	0.342	(0.386)	0.338	(0.010) ***	0.091	(0.009) ***
Industry	Agriculture, forestry & fishing	0.011	(0.083)	0.372	(0.037) ***	0.369	(0.038) ***
	Construction	0.080	(0.220)	0.167	(0.021) ***	0.156	(0.017) ***
	Producer services	0.213	(0.333)	0.006	(0.017)	−0.018	(0.012)
	Distributive services	0.161	(0.299)	0.072	(0.018) ***	0.070	(0.014) ***
	Social services	0.204	(0.328)	0.117	(0.018) ***	−0.002	(0.013)
	Personal services	0.126	(0.270)	0.331	(0.019) ***	0.087	(0.017) ***
Occupation	Managers	0.022	(0.118)	−0.108	(0.035) ***	−0.055	(0.027) **
	Professionals	0.220	(0.337)	−0.128	(0.017) ***	−0.073	(0.013) ***
	Clerks	0.215	(0.334)	−0.188	(0.015)***	−0.141	(0.011) ***
	Service workers	0.090	(0.232)	0.051	(0.023) **	0.188	(0.022) ***
	Sales workers	0.083	(0.224)	0.228	(0.024) ***	−0.007	(0.017)
	Skilled Agriculture, forestry & fishery workers	0.004	(0.048)	0.109	(0.069)	0.128	(0.064) **
	Craft and related trades workers	0.092	(0.235)	0.061	(0.021) ***	0.110	(0.018) ***
	Elementary occupations	0.168	(0.304)	0.288	(0.019) ***	0.228	(0.018) ***
Unions	Non	0.760	(0.347)	0.123	(0.012) ***	0.092	(0.009) ***
Tenure	Less than 1 year	0.359	(0.390)	0.255	(0.010) ***	0.132	(0.008) ***
Pseudo R^2				0.412		0.314	
N				26 522			

Table 7.7   (continued)

Notes:
1. Reference group was regular, assembly employees with one or more year of tenure in unionized workplaces with 300 or more employees in the manufacturing and electricity, gas and water supply industries.
2. *** denotes significant at the 1 per cent level, ** significant at the 5 per cent level.

Source: Korea Statistical Office, Supplementary Survey of the Economically Active Population Survey, August 2011.

tenure' is added to this analytic model as a control variable to reflect the reality that employers are not required to provide a retirement allowance to employees who have worked for less than one year.

It is evident that informal employment is more likely in smaller businesses. In particular, the likelihood of a worker who should be legally protected being engaged in informal employment due to employer non-compliance is 48.8 per cent higher in firms with fewer than five workers than in firms with 300 or more workers. Compared to firms with 300 or more workers, the probability of informal employment due to non-compliance is 36.7 per cent higher in firms with 5–9 workers, 20.9 per cent higher in those with 10–29 workers, and 7.1 per cent higher in workplaces with 30–99 workers.

Regarding employment type, the probability of non-regular workers engaging in informal employment is 33.8 per cent higher than for regular workers, and with all other variables controlled, the probability of workers being engaged in informal work due to employer non-compliance is 9.1 per cent higher for non-regular workers than for regular workers. By industry, it is more likely for workers in construction, personal services and distributive services to be engaged in informal employment due to employer non-compliance. It is interesting to note that although the probability of informal employment in social services is significantly higher than in the manufacturing industry, there is no statistically significant difference between the two in terms of informal employment due to employer non-compliance. This difference is most likely because of the high number of care service workers in the social services industry who are excluded from protection under labour laws. By occupation, the data tell us that informal employment due to employer non-compliance is significantly higher for blue-collar workers and service workers. Meanwhile, the likelihood of informal employment due to employer non-compliance is 9.2 per cent higher in non-unionized workplaces than in unionized workplaces, pointing to the role that unions play in limiting informal employment. Lastly, there is a significantly higher probability that workers who have worked for less than one year will engage in informal employment.

Table 7.8   Yearly transition probability, 2002–08 (%)

t \ t + 1	Formal employment	Informal employment	Non-waged work	Non-employment
Formal employment	81.4	10.7	1.5	6.4
Informal employment	15.3	65.3	4.5	15.0
Non-waged work	1.0	3.3	88.9	6.8
Non-employment	3.6	7.4	2.0	87.0

Source: KLI, Korean Labour and Income Panel Study, 2002–2008 pooled data.

7.6   PERSISTENCE OF INFORMALITY

If employees experience informal work only temporarily in their working lives, it may be of little concern. However, if the prospect of a transition to formal employment is limited, they are likely to experience the difficulties associated with repeated spells of informal work. An analysis of mobility between different types of employment over a one-year period was conducted using the Korean Labour and Income Panel Study.

Table 7.8 shows that the likelihood of transition to formal employment the year after being engaged in informal employment is only 15.3 per cent, while 65.3 per cent remained in informal jobs. Those in informal jobs face a much higher risk of job loss than their formal counterparts. For example, 15 per cent became unemployed, which is more than double the rate for formal employees. For persons who are not employed, the probability that they will be working informally in the following year is 7.4 per cent, which is more than two times higher than the probability that they will gain formal employment. Those who are in informal work also have a 4.5 per cent chance of transitioning into self-employment, which is again higher than that of formal employees. When non-waged workers transition to waged work, it is more likely that they will move into informal work than formal work. All these data reveal that it is highly likely that workers will become entrenched in informal employment, or move back and forth between informal employment and a state of non-employment.

Further analysis shows how informal work persists over long periods. Figure 7.3 reports the number of years spent in informal jobs over the seven-year period from 2002 to 2008, according to each person's type of employment activity in 2002. This measure is better than simple transition rates because it takes into account work intermittence and repeat spells of informal employment. Informal workers in 2002 experienced 4.0 years of informal jobs and 1.3 years of non-employment over seven years,

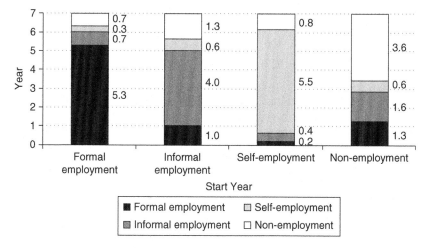

Source: KLI, Korean Labour and Income Panel Study, 2002–2008.

Figure 7.3   *Cumulative years of informality over seven years for persons engaged in informal jobs at the beginning of the period*

with only one (1.0) year spent in formal jobs. This indicates that workers engaged in informal situations are likely to become entrenched in informal employment in the long term.

The persistence of informal work comes about through two different mechanisms. First, individual heterogeneity may make the incidence of informal work increase the likelihood of informal work in the future. Heterogeneity refers to observable personal characteristics or unobservable properties such as making an effort to work. Second, state dependence exists if informal work in a particular period has an effect on the probability of informal work over the subsequent period. State dependence may take place when there is a low level of labour policy enforcement within a segmented labour market structure. In this case, employers are likely to have more incentive to offer informal employment; thus, it becomes more difficult for workers who have already been excluded from social protection to break away from informal employment (Akay and Khamis, 2011; Perry et al., 2007).

Heterogeneity that affects informal work should be controlled in order to identify state dependence.[6] Because informal work status is a discrete

---

[6]   For the estimation method, we refer to Stewart (2007), Clark and Kanellopoulos (2009) and Akay and Khamis (2011).

dependent variable, the dynamic random effects probit model of equation (7.1) is used:

$$I_{it}^* = \gamma I_{it-1} + \mathbf{X}_{it}'\beta + \varepsilon_i + u_{it}(i = 1, ..., N; t = 2, ...T) \qquad (7.1)$$

I_{it}^* is a latent variable of an individual i being in an informal job at the time t. I_{t-1} is the informal job status of an individual i in the previous period. X_{it} is a vector of explanatory variables (see Table 7.9). Error terms are comprised of two terms. Individual specific error term ε_i captures time-invariant, unobserved heterogeneity. The u_{it} is a usual error term for which

Table 7.9   Sample characteristics

		All		Formal employment		Informal employment	
		Mean	(SD)	Mean	(SD)	Mean	(SD)
Informal employment		0.453	(0.453)				
Informal employment at t − 1		0.470	(0.470)	0.151	(0.359)	0.853	(0.354)
First-time informal employment		0.498	(0.498)	0.228	(0.420)	0.823	(0.382)
Gender	Female	0.358	(0.358)	0.289	(0.454)	0.441	(0.497)
Age	15–29	0.141	(0.141)	0.159	(0.366)	0.119	(0.324)
	30–59	0.164	(0.164)	0.138	(0.345)	0.197	(0.397)
	60 or more	0.063	(0.063)	0.010	(0.102)	0.126	(0.332)
Education	Middle or lower	0.263	(0.263)	0.138	(0.345)	0.413	(0.492)
	Technical college	0.124	(0.124)	0.172	(0.377)	0.067	(0.250)
	University or higher	0.213	(0.213)	0.301	(0.459)	0.107	(0.310)
Marital status	Unmarried	0.201	(0.201)	0.217	(0.412)	0.181	(0.385)
	Divorced/widowed	0.080	(0.080)	0.037	(0.189)	0.131	(0.338)
Firm size	1–4 persons	0.164	(0.164)	0.056	(0.229)	0.296	(0.456)
	5–9 persons	0.153	(0.153)	0.104	(0.305)	0.213	(0.409)
	10–29 persons	0.224	(0.224)	0.244	(0.429)	0.200	(0.400)
Employment type	Non-regular work	0.259	(0.259)	0.143	(0.350)	0.399	(0.490)
Industry	Agriculture, forestry & fishing	0.008	(0.008)	0.003	(0.051)	0.015	(0.123)
	Construction	0.082	(0.082)	0.038	(0.192)	0.135	(0.342)
	Producer services	0.157	(0.157)	0.164	(0.370)	0.149	(0.356)
	Distributive services	0.204	(0.204)	0.210	(0.407)	0.198	(0.399)
	Social services	0.112	(0.112)	0.126	(0.332)	0.096	(0.294)
	Personal services	0.085	(0.085)	0.029	(0.166)	0.154	(0.361)
Unions	Unionized workplaces	0.219	(0.219)	0.361	(0.480)	0.048	(0.214)
Number of workers		2980		1886		1838	
Number of jobs		11 223		6134		5089	

Source: KLI, Korean Labour and Income Panel Study, 2002–2008.

the properties are zero mean, uncorrelated with itself, uncorrelated with X_{it} and ε_i, and homoscedastic.

The assumption that ε_i is uncorrelated with X_{it} is frequently thought of as unrealistic. According to the Mundlak (1978) method, a correlation between ε_i and X_{it} is allowed by assuming a relationship in the form $\varepsilon_i = \overline{X}_i'\delta + \alpha_i$, where $\alpha_i \sim$ iid N(o, σ_α^2). Substituting in equation (7.1), we get the following equation:

$$I_{it}^* = \gamma I_{it-1} + X_{it}'\beta + \overline{X}_i'\delta + \alpha_i + u_{it} \tag{7.2}$$

Even when heterogeneity is well controlled using panel data, an initial conditions problem may arise, which is why the initial observation of a dependent variable I_{i1} may have a correlation with unobserved hetero-geneity ε_i. If a correlation exists, the estimation result of equation (7.2) overestimates state dependence. As proposed by Wooldridge (2005), we specify $\alpha_i = \alpha_0 + \alpha_1 I_{i1} + \alpha_2 \overline{X}_i + \zeta_i$, independent of $I_{i1}, X_{it.}$

If put into equation (7.2), we end up with estimation equation (7.3) as follows:

$$I_{it}^* = \gamma I_{it-1} + X_{it}'\beta + \alpha_1 I_{i1} + \alpha_2 \overline{X}_i + \zeta_i + u_{it} \tag{7.3}$$

γ is the magnitude of genuine state dependence.

Table 7.9 presents the characteristics of the samples used in the analysis. Here the sample is restricted to waged workers over two consecutive years. In the estimation model, job characteristics such as firm size, employment type, industry and unionization are controlled, while personal characteristics – such as gender, age, level of educational attainment and marital status – are also included to control individual heterogeneity.

Table 7.10 reveals the marginal effects of explanatory variables on the probability of the persistence of being engaged in an informal job. Column (1) presents results by using a pooled probit model. γ has a significant positive value. Column (2) presents estimation results in a dynamic random effects model using the same sample. Explanatory variables, though not shown separately, include the average of time-varying variables and year dummies. The null hypothesis that ρ is 0 is rejected, demonstrating that it is more desirable to engage in estimation with individual heterogeneity controlled. Even after heterogeneity and initial conditions are controlled, γ still has a statistically significant, positive value. The experience of informal work in the previous year increases the probability of current informal work by 28.3 per cent compared to the probability of a formal work experience.

Table 7.10   Estimation of persistence of informal employment

	(1) Pooled probit model[a]		(2) Dynamic random effects probit[b, c]	
	Marginal effect	(SE)	Marginal effect	(SE)
Informal employment at t − 1	0.552	(0.010) ***	0.283	(0.021) ***
Female	0.021	(0.014)	0.006	(0.024)
15–29	−0.055	(0.022) **	0.048	(0.051)
30–59	0.015	(0.019)	−0.072	(0.052)
60 or more	0.291	(0.031) ***	0.212	(0.102) **
Middle school or lower	0.098	(0.018) ***	0.153	(0.222)
Technical college graduate	−0.135	(0.019) ***	−0.145	(0.108)
University or higher	−0.113	(0.017) ***	−0.121	(0.135)
Unmarried	0.021	(0.019)	0.023	(0.067)
Divorced/widowed	0.095	(0.026) ***	−0.034	(0.089)
1–4 persons	0.346	(0.018) ***	0.325	(0.035) ***
5–9 persons	0.177	(0.019) ***	0.153	(0.033) ***
10–29 persons	0.042	(0.016) **	−0.011	(0.028)
Non-regular work	0.199	(0.015) ***	0.104	(0.024) ***
Agriculture, forestry & fishing	0.159	(0.077) **	0.201	(0.192)
Construction	0.243	(0.026) ***	0.200	(0.086) *
Producer services	0.052	(0.020) **	0.169	(0.069) **
Distributive services	0.063	(0.018) ***	0.023	(0.059)
Social services	0.077	(0.023) ***	0.223	(0.086) **
Personal services	0.243	(0.026) ***	0.336	(0.071) ***
Unionized workplaces	−0.224	(0.017) ***	−0.192	(0.033) ***
Informal work at the first year			0.373	(0.026) ***
Log likelihood	−3907.7		−3679.5	
N		8720		

Notes:
[a]   The year dummy in the pooled probit model were additionally controlled.
[b]   The year dummy and the mean of time-varying variables in the dynamic random effects probit model were additionally controlled.
[c]   Likelihood ratio test result for $\rho = 0$: chibar2(01) = 187.02 Prob >= chibar2 = 0.000. Reference group was married, male, high school graduate, regular workers, aged 30 to 49 in non-unionized workplaces with 30 or more workers in the manufacturing and the electricity, gas and water supply industries.
*   Significant at 10 per cent level; ** significant at 5 per cent level; *** significant at 1 per cent level.

Source: KLI, Korean Labour and Income Panel Study, 2002–2008.

7.7 SUMMARY AND POLICY IMPLICATIONS

After the 1997 financial crisis, the Republic of Korea sought to introduce greater flexibility in the labour market while also implementing reforms to expand social protection. While the dark side of such reforms was the sharp increase in non-regular work and increased inequality in the labour market, the bright side was the advance towards a universal institution that sought to integrate all workers into a single system.

This chapter addresses the reasons behind the widespread occurrence of informal work, despite the presence of a wide variety of protective policies. Informal work accompanies lack of regulation or lack of compliance. The relationship between informal work and non-regulation or non-compliance has been analysed. The following policy implications can be derived from the results of this analysis.

First, the finding that 80 per cent of socially unprotected informal employment can be attributed not to non-regulation but to non-compliance indicates that, beyond just making legislative efforts to expand the scope of coverage for social protection, the level of policy enforcement should be strengthened. It is necessary to deter the occurrence of informal employment through means such as labour administration and inspection, while also providing policy incentives for employers to comply with rules and policies and to formalize employment.

Second, the fact that an overlap is present in the blind spots of minimum wage, labour standards and social insurance coverage implies that measures to heighten the effectiveness of any protective policies may contribute to improving the level of compliance with other policies. To promote formal employment, states should explore a policy mix combining labour laws, labour policies, social insurance programmes and taxation policies.

Finally, policies should target vulnerable groups with characteristics that increase the probability of being persistently in informal employment. The results of analysis pointing to the existence of statistically significant state dependence in informal work also indicates the need for encompassing policies to curb informal work and to promote formal work.

REFERENCES

Akay, A. and Khamis, M. (2011). 'The persistence of informality: Evidence from panel data'. IZA Discussion Paper No. 6163.

Clark, K. and Kanellopoulos, N.C. (2009). 'Low pay persistence in European countries'. IZA Discussion Paper No. 4183.

Hazans, M. (2011). 'Informal workers across Europe: Evidence from 30 countries'. IZA Discussion Paper No. 5871.

Hussmanns, R. (2004). 'Measuring the informal economy: From the employment in the informal economy to informal employment'. ILO Policy Integration Department Working Paper No. 53.

Hwang, D. and Lee, B. (2012). 'Low wages and policy options in the Republic of Korea: Are policies working?'. *International Labour Review*, **151**(3), 243–59.

International Labour Office (ILO) (2003). 'Guidelines concerning a statistical definition of informal employment'. Endorsed by the Seventeenth International Conference of Labour Statisticians (Geneva, 24 November–3 December), Report of the Conference, Doc. ICLS/17/2003/R, Geneva: ILO.

International Labour Office (ILO) (2012). *Measuring Informality: A Statistical Manual on the Informal Sector and Informal Employment*. Geneva: ILO.

Kanbur, R. (2009). 'Conceptualising informality: Regulation and enforcement'. IZA Discussion Paper No. 4186.

Kim, H.-Y. (2012). 'Informal employment and labour inspections in micro-businesses'. In B. Lee et al., *Informal Employment in Korea*. Seoul: Korea Labor Institute (in Korean).

Lee, B. and Yoo, B. (2008). 'The Republic of Korea: From flexibility to segmentation'. In S. Lee and F. Eyraud (eds), *Globalization, Flexibilization and Working Conditions in Asia and the Pacific*. Geneva and Oxford: International Labour Office and Chandos Publishing, pp. 187–234.

Mundlak, Y. (1978). 'On the pooling of time series and cross section data'. *Econometrica*, **46**(1), 69–85.

OECD (2008), 'Declaring work or staying underground: Informal employment in seven OECD countries'. *OECD Employment Outlook 2008*. Paris: OECD.

Perry, G.E., Maloney, W.F., Arias, O.S., Fajnzylber, P., Mason, A.D. and Saavedra-Chanduvi, J. (2007). *Informality: Exit and Exclusion*. Washington, DC: World Bank.

Stewart, M.B. (2007). 'The inter-related dynamics of unemployment and low-wage employment'. *Journal of Applied Econometrics*, **22**(3), 511–31.

Wooldridge, J.M. (2005). 'Simple solutions to the initial conditions problem in dynamic, nonlinear panel data models with unobserved heterogeneity'. *Journal of Applied Econometrics*, **20**(1), 39–54.

8. Employment formalization in Argentina: Recurring and new challenges for public policies

Fabio Bertranou and Luis Casanova

8.1 INTRODUCTION

Informality has serious consequences for workers, their families and enterprises, as well as society as a whole. On the one hand, informal employment constitutes an obstacle to the recognition of worker rights and it is often associated with poverty and social exclusion. Informal workers are rarely protected against a number of social risks such as workplace accidents, unemployment and old-age poverty and disability. On the other hand, informality can lead to low levels of productivity and a limited capacity for business expansion; this can also create unfair competition for formal firms and, therefore, a 'race to the bottom'. On a more aggregate level, informal employment has an impact on equity, efficiency, the state's ability to collect taxes, the reach of social security, productivity and growth (ILO, 2002, 2013; Jüting and de Laiglesia, 2009; Packard et al., 2013).

The meaning of the term 'informality' has changed since it was first introduced in the early 1970s. While it initially referred to subsistence self-employment, it now refers to a wide range of jobs in both the formal and informal economy. This expanded definition of informality represents an attempt to encompass different components of a complex and multidimensional phenomenon.[1] Several factors limit the scope of public policies and reduce their effectiveness, among them the persistence of informality even during periods of economic growth and rising employment; the connection between the formal and informal sectors; the presence of informal employment in the formal economy; and the great variety of jobs affected by informality. Due to these and other aspects, there is now consensus on

---

[1] For a review of the different perspectives on informality and its implications for public policies, see Bertranou and Casanova (2013).

173

the need for a comprehensive policy package that takes into account all of the characteristics of the informal economy in order to reduce its scope (ILO, 2013).

This chapter analyses the process of registered employment formalization in Argentina during the 2000s, particularly the drop in non-registered salaried employment.[2] Non-registered work is one of the main types of informal employment and the target of most relevant public policy measures in Argentina. The chapter also identifies the labour segments where informality is deeply rooted, as well as the challenges to advancing in the process of formalization. In this description, we present the notable drop in informality (mainly between 2003 and 2008) and the subsequent levelling off of informal employment indicators (particularly since 2011).

The chapter is organized as follows. After this introduction, section 8.2 describes the evolution of non-registered salaried employment, along with an estimate of the percentage of informal employment among all employed workers. Section 8.3 identifies the critical segments with high levels of informality and/or a high concentration of informal employment. Section 8.4 describes the implemented policies and presents the general guidelines of the Ley de Promoción del Empleo Registrado y Prevención del Fraude Laboral (2014) – the Law for the Promotion of Registered Employment and Labour Fraud Prevention. Finally, section 8.5 presents closing remarks.

8.2   TRENDS IN EMPLOYMENT FORMALIZATION

The macroeconomic scheme implemented after the economic crisis in 2001–02 encouraged the creation of formal jobs, reversing the previous trend towards informalization in the 1990s. Between 2003 and 2014, non-registered salaried employment dropped nearly 15 percentage points, from 49.0 to 33.4 per cent (Figure 8.1). Due to this drop, in addition to the increase in salaried employment (which rose from 73.3 to 76.5 per cent among all employed workers in the same period), the percentage of informality in total employment decreased.

As a result, there was an interruption of the rising trend in non-registered salaried employment, which had increased gradually since the mid-1970s (the first years for which systematic data are available) with

---

[2]   This statistical indicator refers to wage employment where employers do not make mandatory contributions to social security.

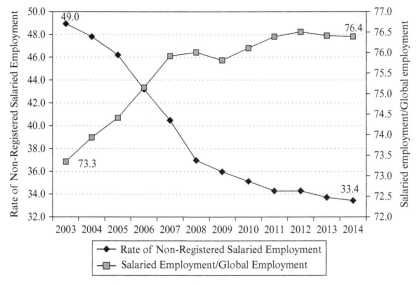

Note: Annual average of quarterly rates.

Source: Bertranou and Casanova (2013), based on the Encuesta Permanente de Hogares (Annual Household Survey).

Figure 8.1 *Evolution of non-registered salaried employment and of the percentage of salaried employment in overall employment, 2003–14*

more pronounced rises during the 1990s. During that decade, not only did non-registered employment increase, but also a portion of the formal employment created can be considered precarious due to the labour flexibility schemes put into effect during that period (Altimir and Beccaria, 1999; Schleser, 2007; Jiménez, 2013). Despite the significant drop, particularly between 2003 and 2008, the levels of non-registered employment are still higher than those recorded in Argentina at the beginning of the 1990s.

Due to the available information, it is not possible to track changes over time in terms of independent workers (that is, own-account workers and employers) not registered with the social security system; it is possible to track those changes only in the case of salaried employment. However, several studies conducted over the past decade have found that the rate of non-registration in the social security system is higher for the self-employed than it is for salaried workers. Unlike salaried workers, the rate of registration with the social security system has remained stagnant among independent workers at around 60 per cent (Bertranou and Casanova, 2013).

Considering all employed workers (that is, salaried workers, independent workers and unpaid family workers), informal employment represented 44 per cent of all employment in 2010. On the basis of the distribution of workers between different types of jobs and their respective informality rates, it can be concluded that two out of three informal workers are salaried workers and one out of three is an independent worker (Bertranou and Casanova, 2013). In terms of production units, 25 per cent of informal salaried workers work at home; 31 per cent in a production unit with some formal employment; and 44 per cent in a production unit with no formal employment[3] (MTEySS, 2013a, 2013b).

As in other countries in Latin America, in Argentina informal employment is one of the most visible signs of the heterogeneous productive structure (ECLAC, 2010). In fact, in Argentina the growth of informal employment between the mid-1970s and the early 2000s – and the subsequent slowdown of this trend, mainly between 2003 and 2008 – is associated to a certain degree with changes in the productive structure. The first period mentioned (mid-1970s to the early 2000s) coincides with the fragmentation and disintegration of the industrial linkages and the dismantling of industrialization policies and institutions. Both were the result of the Washington Consensus approach that included deregulation and the sudden opening of the domestic market to foreign trade, which tended to increase international productivity gaps (in relation to developed countries) as well as domestic gaps. The second period (2003 to 2008), though, witnessed a turnaround in term of the dynamics of the heterogeneous structures (de Miguel and Woyecheszen, 2015; Coatz and Sarabia, 2015). Nevertheless, the most dynamic economic sectors in the 2000s were responsible for only a small portion of the country's economic growth, due to their low impact on the gross domestic product (GDP). Despite recent advances, the productive matrix continues to show signs of fragmented industrialization, the result of decades of production fragmentation. All of this restricts the creation of quality employment (de Miguel and Woyecheszen, 2015; Coatz and Sarabia, 2015).

Although a few countries in the world have been able to reduce informality as fast as Argentina, the amount of informal employment is still high; it affects more than 40 per cent of employed workers, two-thirds

---

[3]   This information was taken from the National Social Security and Protection Survey (ENAPROSS).

of whom are salaried workers and one-third of whom are independent workers. Due to the persistence of this phenomenon, certain public policies must be analysed and reconsidered.

8.3 MULTIDIMENSIONAL DESCRIPTION OF INFORMAL EMPLOYMENT IN ARGENTINA: CRITICAL SEGMENTS[4]

The economic sectors to experience the largest reductions in non-registered employment in the 2000s were social and health services,[5] commerce, construction and the manufacturing industry. Due to the structure of salaried employment, these sectors combined with domestic work account for 75 per cent of the total reduction in non-registered salaried employment.

Aggregate reductions in the levels of non-registered employment can hide substantial differences by sector, company size, and worker qualification. In general, the segments with high levels of informal employment in 2003 continued to have high levels in 2014, although the concentration by sector increased: domestic work, self-employment, agriculture (the rural sector), and salaried employment in construction and commerce. In these last two sectors, micro-enterprises had high rates of informality and accounted for a high proportion of the global amount of non-registered employment (Figure 8.2). Even in economic sectors where the rate of informal employment was relatively low, it occurred more frequently in certain segments. This is the case of the clothing industry within the manufacturing sector. Thus, domestic work along with small and medium-sized enterprises in five sectors (construction, commerce, transport, storage and communications, hotels and restaurants, and industry) accounted for nearly 70 per cent of non-registered employment in 2014 (Figure 8.2).

Precise information and detailed understanding of the many dimensions of informality are necessary both to go beyond the aggregate data, and to develop a comprehensive policy approach. For this reason, we will now analyse the main characteristics of the critical segments of the job market in terms of their impact on informality (that is, their rates of informal employment), and the concentration of informal employment. The critical segments identified include: domestic work, the clothing industry,

---

[4]   This section is based on Bertranou and Casanova (2013, 2015).
[5]   Social services play a role in reducing non-registered employment due to the formalization of a large number of beneficiaries of the employment programmes created as a response to the 2001–02 economic crisis.

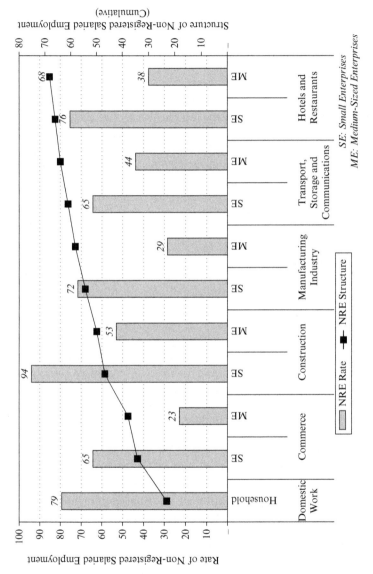

Note: Second quarter 2014 (latest microdata available).

Source: Based on the Encuesta Permanente de Hogares.

Figure 8.2 Rate and structure of non-registered employment (NRE) according to sector and type of enterprise, 2014

micro-enterprises in commerce and construction, self-employment and rural employment.

Domestic Work

The level of informal employment among domestic workers was more than twice the average for the Argentine economy as a whole (the level was 79 per cent in 2014). In addition to the high level of informality in this segment, job precariousness in domestic work is a multifaceted phenomenon. It is important to note these workers – more than 90 per cent of whom are women – represent 23 per cent of all the non-registered salaried workers in the country.

The bulk of the demand for domestic workers in Argentina lies in upper-middle-class households where both the husband and the wife work outside the home (in most cases they both hold formal jobs); domestic workers allow them to balance their own work and family life. Although a number of tax incentives encourage employers to register their domestic workers, the levels of informality and precariousness in the sector continue to be among the highest in the economy. Other problems that contribute to informality include: (1) the difficulties of conducting labour inspections and getting those who hire domestic workers to recognize their status as employers;[6] and (2) cultural and social perceptions that domestic work does not require a formal labour relationship.

Domestic workers are not only subject to exclusion due to non-compliance with employment regulations, but are also less protected by the law than other employees. At the beginning of 2013, the Régimen Especial de Contrato de Trabajo para el Personal de Casas (Special Employment Contract Scheme for Domestic Employees) was passed by Congress to replace the regulations that had been in effect since 1956. The new legislation protects the rights of domestic workers, granting them rights similar to those of other workers. There is still much to be done by the state, including conducting inspections and informing workers of their rights, to ensure that all domestic workers enjoy their rights and due protection.

Another aspect to consider is the number of migrant workers in the sector. Despite the progress made thanks to new legislation and the legal status of immigrants, many have not been able to formalize their jobs (Messina, 2015).

---

[6] Another characteristic of domestic work is the high mobility of workers who shift between not being employed and non-registered employment.

The Clothing Industry

This sector is characterized by informal employment and other forms of precarious work, and even forced labour at illegal sweatshops. In 2014, just 32.6 per cent of all workers in the clothing industry were formally employed and registered with the social security system. The rest consist of informal salaried employees (37.2 per cent of the total) and the self-employed (30.1 per cent).

The 2000s witnessed sharper growth in this sector than in industry as a whole. In terms of new jobs by sector (particularly registered jobs), though, it ranked significantly lower. This is partly due to changes in the industrial organization of the sector, some of which date back to the 1970s and others to the 1990s. Due to these changes, long-standing manufacturers have outsourced some stages of production to concentrate on the more profitable facets of the activity. As a result, the business risk has shifted to the sweatshops where the garments are manufactured and, in turn, to the employees themselves.

Within this area, it is essential to differentiate between the textile and clothing sectors. The textile sector is characterized by higher levels of formal employment, and the clothing sector by widespread informal employment. While 64 per cent of textile manufacturing workers are formal salaried employees, the rate in the clothing sector is 30 per cent lower. The high level of self-employment in the clothing industry (in comparison to the textile industry and to the rest of industry) is due to the concentration in this area of the weakest actors in this production chain, for example garment outsourcers, the self-employed and those who work in their homes. While these textile workers appear to have a degree of autonomy, they are actually subject to a form of precarious employment.

The high levels of non-registered employment in the clothing industry can be explained by an array of technical and production factors that create low entry and exit barriers due to the small requirements for physical capital, the relative ease of learning the trade, and the fact that it is not necessary for the entire production process to be carried out at a single location. Due to the sector's lack of competitiveness, manufacturers may resort to subsistence strategies that, in turn, partly explain the high levels of non-registered employment. This sector is also characterized by its informal production units, which explains the high levels of informal employment.

Though the sector experienced an economic upswing after 2001, the number of illegal sweatshops also rose, with serious infractions of local labour laws. An important factor was the large number of immigrants working in these sweatshops, many of whom were brought to Argentina through human trafficking networks.

Micro-Enterprises: Commerce and Construction

Enterprises with less than 40 employees account for the 83.2 per cent of all informal employment. In mid-2014, the rate of non-registered employment among firms with five workers or less was 71.6 per cent, while that figure stood at 8.8 per cent for large firms. With regards to small firms, the problem is twofold, since informal workers are often performing their tasks in establishments that do not meet legal requirements. At micro-enterprises in construction, 70 per cent of workers work at informal construction sites. For this reason, public policy challenges are not limited to increasing formal employment, but also encompass formalizing the economic activity in general.

Inspection poses a particular problem for micro-enterprises and, as a result, the cost of informality (that is, fines) is lower for micro-enterprises given how difficult it is for government departments to detect non-compliance with labour and tax legislation at such firms. Furthermore, micro-enterprises face greater difficulties in complying with regulations due to factors such as low levels of productivity.

In the construction sector, workers in economic units employing five or fewer people generally do not work at construction sites: instead, they perform tasks that mostly go unregistered, such as home repairs and remodelling, and constructing extensions to existing properties. Furthermore, many workers are hired by homeowners, rather than firms, to carry out such repairs. Of the total number of salaried construction workers at small firms, nearly 80 per cent perform their tasks at the client's home or store. Such employment is not stable (many jobs are temporary), which makes it more difficult to get workers registered with social security. The nature of the jobs themselves, which are generally performed solely in interiors, presents difficulties to government inspection offices. The cultural patterns associated with work of this sort (that is, employment relationships based on pre-existing personal ties) are also key to understanding the high level of informality (Bertranou and Casanova, 2013).

In the commerce sector, three out of four workers carry out their tasks at a storefront or office, while the rest perform their tasks at roadside stands or street markets. The highest levels of precarious work (informal salaried work and independent workers) are found in the food, beverage and tobacco sector (for example, neighbourhood stores) and in the sale and repair of motor vehicles and motorcycles (for example, small auto shops). Though commerce has its own particular traits, obstacles to formalization are similar for all micro-enterprises: how to formalize employment while maintaining a productive and profitable business. Within commerce, workers at street markets and roadside stands (street vendors)

Table 8.1   Distribution of informal salaried workers at production units according to type of unit, by activity and size of enterprise, 2011

	Production units			
	With formal employment (%)	Without formal employment (%)	Not specified (%)	Total (%) (A + B + C)
	(A)	(B)	(C)	
Total	31.5	46.4	22.1	100.0
Economic Sector				
Primary Sector	22.6	42.3	35.2	100.0
Manufacturing	33.7	40.6	25.7	100.0
Construction	12.8	70.0	17.3	100.0
Commerce	31.6	51.9	16.5	100.0
Hotels and Restaurants	21.3	52.1	26.5	100.0
Transport, Storage and Communications	22.5	55.2	22.3	100.0
Financial Services, Real Estate, Rentals and Companies	48.1	27.6	24.3	100.0
Public Service and Defence	100.0	0.0	0.0	100.0
Teaching	48.8	24.5	26.7	100.0
Social and Healthcare Services	51.3	19.2	29.5	100.0
Other Community, Social and Personal Services	30.8	48.4	20.8	100.0
Not specified	30.2	23.2	46.6	100.0
Size of the Enterprise				
Five employees or less	20.8	60.7	18.4	100.0
Between 6 and 40 employees	44.8	35.4	19.8	100.0
41 employees or more	64.8	12.1	23.1	100.0

Source: Contartese et al. (2015) based on ENAPROSS 2011.

face additional problems such as the lack of a physical space for carrying out their business, and the difficulties of advancing from street vendor to market entrepreneur.[7]

As Tables 8.1 and 8.2 show, the core issue at many micro-enterprises

[7]   Like domestic workers, many workers in the commerce sector move frequently between unemployment and non-registered employment (Bertranou and Casanova, 2013).

Table 8.2 Distribution of informal salaried workers at production units according to type of unit, by activity and size of enterprise, 2011

	Production units		
	With formal employment (%)	Without formal employment (%)	Total (%)
Total	100.0	100.0	100.0
Economic Sector			
Primary Sector	1.9	2.4	2.6
Manufacturing	15.2	12.5	14.3
Construction	6.6	24.6	16.3
Commerce	21.7	24.3	21.7
Hotels and Restaurants	3.9	6.5	5.8
Transport, Storage and Communications	7.1	11.9	10.0
Financial Services, Real Estate, Rentals and Companies	11.5	4.5	7.6
Public Service and Defence	6.2	0.0	1.9
Teaching	8.2	2.8	5.3
Social and Healthcare Services	8.6	2.2	5.3
Other Community, Social and Personal Services	6.6	7.0	6.7
Not specified	2.3	1.2	2.4
Size of the Enterprise			
Five employees of less	36.2	71.8	54.8
Between 6 and 40 employees	43.6	23.5	30.7
41 employees or more	17.8	2.3	8.7
Not specified	2.4	2.4	5.8

Source: Contartese et al. (2015) based on ENAPROSS 2011.

is informal production units (nearly 60 per cent of employees at micro-enterprises are non-registered). Construction and commerce are jointly responsible for 50 per cent of non-registered employees at production units.

Self-Employment

Approximately 60 per cent (or perhaps even more) of independent workers, including employers and own-account workers, are not registered with the social security system, and do not pay income tax on a regular basis. This is particularly the case among self-employed workers.

Among independent workers, the rate of informal employment is higher for those who perform unskilled work or operational tasks; those with a low education level and/or not working full-time; those who work at enterprises with low levels of capital investments and at single-person economic units; those who remain independent because they cannot find salaried employment; and those with low incomes.[8]

According to recent estimates, one out of three informal workers is self-employed. Informal employment among independent workers is concentrated in three sectors: commerce, construction and industry. Two-thirds of self-employment is concentrated in these three sectors, where skills are relatively low and the incidence of subsistence workers is above 75 per cent. A high percentage of self-employee workers are located in the quintiles with the lowest income. The situation is similar for non-registered salaried workers (Contartese et al., 2015; Bertranou and Casanova, 2013).

In the past 15 years in Argentina, the main instrument for ensuring tax registration and social security coverage for independent workers has been the simplified tax scheme known as Monotributo. The number of workers registered in this scheme has grown steadily. However, this instrument needs to be re-evaluated not only in terms of its role in formalizing economic activity, but also as a means for transitioning to the general tax regime (Cetrángolo et al., 2013).

Rural Employment

Informal employment is a major problem in the rural sector, including agriculture (which represents 60 per cent of rural employment). In agriculture, non-registered employment is most common among salaried workers, while unskilled labourers represent the majority of independent workers in the sector.

It is difficult to detect informal employment and to formalize it in the rural sectors due to a range of factors. Changes in the job insertion of agricultural workers partly accounts for the problem. Technological changes and the restructuring of production in the sector over the past few decades have also contributed to transforming the job market.

The level of direct employment has decreased and there have been modifications in workforce requirements. This has led to a decrease in the number of permanent workers and an increase in temporary positions, a change in the skills required, the relocating of the workforce to urban areas, an increase of jobs associated with services for primary produc-

---

[8]   For more on this topic, see Bertranou and Maurizio (2011).

tion, and the appearance of employment intermediaries (temporary work agencies) for the hire of temporary workers. At the same time, modifications in the production process and in workforce requirements have not only increased the participation of temporary workers, but also altered the profile of these workers, with a higher percentage of youth, urban dwellers, workers with job experience outside agriculture and a greater number of migrant workers.

8.4 MEASURES FOR PROMOTING EMPLOYMENT FORMALIZATION IN ARGENTINA

Since 2003, policy-makers in Argentina have begun gradually approaching informal employment in a new way. This new focus consists of integrating and coordinating programmes and a range of social, socio-occupational and economic strategies associated with the different factors that give rise to informal work (Table 8.3, 'Outstanding programmes and policies' column) (Bertranou and Casanova, 2013; Novick, 2007).

One aspect that merits special attention is the connection between economic growth and the creation of salaried employment. Growth remained steady until 2009, when certain domestic factors and the international financial crisis affected the domestic economy. From 2003 to 2008, average annual growth was 8.5 per cent, while from 2009 to 2014, that rate fell to 3.6 per cent, with three years of sluggish economic activity (2009, 2012 and 2014). This suggests that growth is a necessary condition for systematic reduction in informal employment, though it does not suffice alone. In other words, specific public interventions (such as inspections, vocational training and other micro-level policies) geared towards diminishing informality are less likely to have a significant impact in the absence of sustained growth (Beccaria, 2015).

Regardless of the relative success of the efforts that followed the 2001–02 economic crisis, the combination of persistent high levels of informal employment – seemingly entrenched in certain segments of the labour market – and the drop in economic growth since 2009 requires the consolidation and redesign of the formalization strategy. Beccaria (2015) argues that it is necessary to strengthen policies in three major areas: (1) simplified registration processes and lower tax and social security requirements for smaller companies; (2) support for production at small and medium-sized enterprises (since low efficiency is a factor that encourages either total or partial evasion of tax obligations, social security contributions, and so forth); and (3) inspections at work sites. Efforts should be coordinated among the different public institutions (and different levels

Table 8.3 Policy strategies and new measures within the framework of the Law for the Promotion of Registered Employment and Labor Fraud Prevention (2014)

Pillar	Outstanding programmes and policies, 2003–2015	Law for the Promotion of Registered Employment and Labor Fraud Prevention
Macroeconomic scheme	Characteristics of the macroeconomic policies that foster the demand for decent work. Improvements to the tax administration. Coordination with labour institutions (collective bargaining and minimum wage). Active role of the state.	
Regulation of informal activities	Simplification of rules and procedures, reductions of entry costs and mechanisms for accessing formality. Tax simplification programmes, e-government and one-stop source at the municipal and provincial levels.	Strengthening of work site inspections. Specific interventions in critical sectors (creation of the Special Auditing Unit for Job Irregularities).
Actions targeting informal workers at formal companies	Regime for the Promotion of Legal Employment and Registered Work. The reduction of social security contributions and flexible payment plans for old debts (Law 26,476). These measures were designed to have a counter-cyclical effect during the international crisis.	Economic incentives to formalize workers at micro-enterprises. Creation of a permanent regime of social security contributions for micro-employers (permanent reduction of employer contributions). Re-adaptation of the Regime for the Promotion of Registered Employment: temporary reductions of employer contributions will vary according to company size (and limited to firms with 80 workers or less).
	National Plan for Employment Regularization. In effect since 2003. Strengthening of the state's	Strengthening of work site inspections, particularly the role of the Ministry of Labor. Creation of a Special

Labor Fraud Investigative Unit (indicators by sector, monitoring of value chains, etc.).

Expansion of the CCG. Additional benefits (temporary reduction of employer contributions).

Creation of a public registry of employers who have been sanctioned for labour offenses (REPSAL). Once listed in the registry, companies are barred from accessing other government assistance programmes for business.

Strengthening of work site inspections. Specific interventions in critical sectors (creation of the Special Auditing Unit for Job Irregularities).

auditing and inspection capacities. Significant increase in the number of inspectors and regular reporting on the process.

Government estimates or presumptions on the social security contributions and payments a firm should be making. Sectors include construction, the textile industry and domestic work.

Perfecting the payment methods of employer obligations. Co-responsibility Agreements (*Convenios de Corresponsabilidad Gremial*, CCG) in rural production, by which employers can differ monthly social security payments until a more favourable moment of the production process.

Social security regime for domestic workers. Income tax deductions for domestic work employers. Presumption – unless evidence is provided to the contrary – that any individual earning a certain income or owning certain assets employs a domestic worker.

Modifications to the immigrations policy. The new Immigration Law (Law 25,871) and measures

Formalization of ambiguous employment relationships and employment relationships at informal companies

Table 8.3 (continued)

Pillar	Outstanding programmes and policies, 2003–2015	Law for the Promotion of Registered Employment and Labor Fraud Prevention
	aimed at providing identification documentation to immigrants. New labour regime for domestic workers. Domestic workers enjoy the same rights as other workers. New regime for work in agriculture. Joint Trade Union–Employer Agreements (CCG) for rural workers. Modification of the regime of temporary employment companies. Adaptation of the regulations to the concept of decent work, new guidelines established.	
Improvements to employability	Measures for vocational training. Programmes for professional training, second-chance education programmes, registry of labour qualification norms and worker certification.	
Social awareness of the issue	Systematic media awareness campaign on the advantages of complying with labour and tax obligations and the social protection associated with these. Through the Corporate Social Responsibility Plan, major companies inform clients and suppliers about the need and obligation to comply with labour regulations.	

| Formal employment protection before economic crisis/shocks | Protection of formal employment. The Preventive Crisis Programs and the Production Recovery Program (wage subsidies). |
| Social protection for informal workers and their families | Income transfer programmes with components for fostering employability. Programmes: Training and Employment Insurance, the Youth with More and Better Jobs Programs, and the Argentina Works. Extension of social security to informal workers. Social Security Inclusion Plan, Universal Child Allowance and Non-contributory Maternity Allowance, and Tax Categories for the Socially Excluded (*Monotributo Social*). |

Source: Based on Bertranou and Casanova (2013).

of government) that design and implement formalization policies (for example, in the area of work site inspection, which involves different levels of government and institutions).

In the context of slower economic growth, and the concentration of informality in segments that current policy struggles to reach, the Integral Plan to Combat Non-Registered Work was announced in September 2013. Before the plan was announced, a process of social dialogue on informality took place between the government and key actors from the world of labour. Although the plan adheres to strategies in place since 2003, it establishes new policies to further that strategy and to make progress in terms of job formalization. After congressional debate on the plan, the Argentine Congress Approved Law No. 26940 entitled the Promoción del Trabajo Registrado y Prevención del Fraude Laboral (Promotion of Registered Employment and Labour Fraud Prevention) (see Table 8.3).

This new law includes a series of measures to promote formal employment and to formalize informal employment in both the formal sector and the 'partly formal/partly informal' sector. The measures aimed at the formal sector include a plan to consolidate work site inspection and thus dissuade informality. To that end, there is a plan to increase the national government's role in inspections and to create a public registry of offenders (Registro Público de Empleadores con Sanciones Laborales, REPSAL). The names of employers registered as offenders will be made public. Offenders will have to pay the corresponding fines and be subject to a set of sanctions such as the loss of public subsidies and ineligibility for loans from public banks or the federal government's economic stimulus programmes (such as temporary or permanent reductions in social security contributions). The hope is that these measures will help to reduce evasion.[9]

In the formal sector, measures to promote the hiring of workers include both temporary and permanent (in the case of micro-employers) reductions of employer contributions to social security. However, the manner in which social security contributions will be sustainably financed, once this policy is fully implemented, requires consideration.

The Permanent Scheme of Social Security Contributions for Micro-Employers enacts a permanent 50 per cent reduction in employer

---

[9]   Data from the National Job Regularization Programme (Plan Nacional de Regularización del Trabajo, PNRT) reveal that at 58 per cent of the companies where irregularities were detected at an initial inspection, such irregularities were shown to continue by a follow-up inspection. Furthermore, most of the fines ordered by the PNRT go unpaid. Thus, it could be argued that the sanctions associated with work site inspections have not produced the dissuasive effect hoped for.

contribution to social security (the employer still has to pay social health insurance contributions). This new scheme applies to nearly 60 per cent of employers registered in Argentina. The new law also redefines the Scheme for the Promotion of Legal Employment and Registered Work, establishing a limit on the temporary social security reductions for companies with as many as 80 workers and an extended limit for smaller enterprises.[10] These changes in the law are aimed at avoiding the undesirable effects of this type of policy (such as substitution and deadweight loss effects) through impact assessment studies. Studies have revealed that the largest companies had the greatest number of workers hired under the former scheme (which imposed no limits on the basis of number of employees), but that the policy had the greatest impact on smaller firms (Casanova et al., 2015).

For the 'partly formal/partly informal' sector, the plan is to expand the scope of the new permanent scheme of social security contributions for micro-employers (which offers a reduction in workplace accident insurance payments) and to expand the Joint Trade Union–Employer Agreements (Convenios de Corresponsabilidad Gremial, CCG) to other sectors. The CCG were first implemented in 2008 to facilitate compliance with labour and social security regulation in rural employment. These agreements are signed by workers' associations (unions) and rural employers' organizations; they allow the employer to replace monthly social security payments with deferred payments, known as a 'substitute rate' (*tarifa sustitutiva*), that can be paid at a more favourable moment in the production process.

8.5 FINAL CONSIDERATIONS: WHAT TYPE OF STRATEGY IS MOST LIKELY TO REDUCE INFORMALITY?

Argentina's experience in the past few years shows that a comprehensive strategy is necessary to effect important reductions in informal employment. The strategy has covered a wide range of policy areas (Table 8.3), from macroeconomic policies to more specific measures such as the National Work Regularization Programme, economic policies that

---

[10] For enterprises with 15 workers or less, the reduction is 100 per cent during the first year after hire and 75 per cent during the second year of employment. Employers at companies with 18–80 workers receive a 50 per cent reduction during the first two years after hire for all new employees. This scheme is compatible with that of micro-employers.

generate quality employment, and programmes to sustain employment during times of crisis. These measures have contributed to preventing workers from falling into informality, as well as – albeit to a lesser extent – unemployment.

After an important drop in non-registered employment from 2003 to 2008, particular circumstances made it difficult to further decrease informality. Economic growth slowed, and informality has been concentrated in certain entrenched sectors that, due to their economic characteristics (that is, small informal or partly formal enterprises) and social characteristics (for example, unskilled work), are difficult to formalize. Despite advances in reducing some productivity gaps (across sectors and firms), the economic structure continues to be critical to expanding production and to creating quality employment. Regional differences, not only in relation to productive structure but also in institutional terms, are also a necessary condition for formalization. Other factors include social tolerance to informal employment and lack of awareness of the consequences of informality, which may lead many to believe that informality is normal or acceptable in various segments of the labour market. All of this points to a need for strengthening and redesigning the formalization strategy (Bertranou et al., 2015).

Future strategies must take into account the heterogeneous nature of informality, seeking formal employment while fostering economic activity. During the transition to formality, these strategies must also provide social protection for the sectors where informality is entrenched. While the role of the state is fundamental to carrying out this difficult task, the involvement of worker organizations, employer associations and other relevant actors is also critical.

To create decent work, macroeconomic policies must allow for a return to sustained, stable growth. This will not only combat informality, but also foster investment and increase productivity, contributing to the transformation of production. To achieve that last goal, it is necessary to strengthen existing production policies and to design new ones. The goal is to develop a strategy aimed at increasing the economy's overall productivity in the medium and long terms, while reducing gaps between different sectors and types of enterprises.

Another critical factor in formalization is the implementation of specific measures that target segments where informality is entrenched or where, due to the nature of the work or the economic activity, it is particularly difficult for traditional formalization instruments to have an effect. This must be done within the framework of a broader strategy. Law No. 26940 for the Promotion of Registered Employment and Labour Fraud Prevention, passed in 2014, puts into effect a series of integrated labour regulations and labour market policies that have been redefined in order to have greater impact on certain critical segments of the job market, such as small and micro-enterprises.

Finally, to formalize employment in certain critical segments where traditional instruments such as inspection and incentives often prove unsuccessful, it may be necessary to reinforce strategies to communicate information about the issue of informality. The aim would be not only to raise awareness of the need for regularization and of the sanctions associated with non-compliance, but also to support workers if they decide to come forward and report non-registered work. The information should also indicate what tools and measures the state offers companies to facilitate the transition to formality.

REFERENCES

Altimir, O. and L. Beccaria (1999), 'El mercado de trabajo bajo el nuevo régimen económico en Argentina', Serie reformas económicas No. 28, United Nations Economic Commission for Latin America and the Caribbean (ECLAC): Santiago, Chile.

Beccaria, L. (2015), 'Perspectiva de políticas de formalización de la economía informal en Argentina', in Fabio Bertranou and Luis Casanova (eds), *Caminos hacia la formalización laboral en Argentina*, ILO Country Office for Argentina: Buenos Aires.

Bertranou F. and L. Casanova (2013), *Informalidad laboral en Argentina: Segmentos críticos y políticas para la formalización*, ILO Country Office for Argentina: Buenos Aires.

Bertranou F. and L. Casanova (2015), 'Los segmentos críticos de la informalidad laboral', in Fabio Bertranou and Luis Casanova (eds), *Caminos hacia la formalización laboral en Argentina*, ILO Country Office for Argentina: Buenos Aires.

Bertranou F., L. Casanova and A. Beccaria (2015), 'Preguntas, respuestas y nuevos interrogantes sobre la informalidad laboral en Argentina', in Fabio Bertranou and Luis Casanova (eds), *Caminos hacia la formalización laboral en Argentina*, ILO Country Office for Argentina: Buenos Aires.

Bertranou F. and R. Maurizio (2011), *Trabajadores independientes, mercado laboral e informalidad en Argentina*, ILO Country Office for Argentina: Buenos Aires.

Casanova, L., E. Lépore and D. Schleser (2015), 'Profundización y redefinición de políticas para la formalización laboral: Ley de promoción del empleo registrado y prevención del fraude laboral', in Fabio Bertranou and Luis Casanova (eds), *Caminos hacia la formalización laboral en Argentina*, ILO Country Office for Argentina: Buenos Aires.

Cetrángolo, O., A. Goldschmit, J. Gómez Sabaíni and D. Morán (2013), 'Desempeño del Monotributo en la formalización del empleo y ampliación de la protección social', Working Paper No. 4 ILO Country Office for Argentina: Buenos Aires.

Coatz, D. and M. Sarabia (2015), 'La formalización del empleo a través del forta lecimiento del entramado productivo. Cambio estructura y creación de empleo de calidad en los últimos cuarenta años', in Fabio Bertranou and Luis Casanova (eds), *Caminos hacia la formalización laboral en Argentina*, ILO Country Office for Argentina: Buenos Aires.

Contartese, D., X. Mazorra, L. Schachtel and D. Schleser (2015), 'La informalidad laboral: nueva evidencia a partir de la Encuesta Nacional de protección y seguridad social', in Fabio Bertranou and Luis Casanova (eds), *Caminos hacia la formalización laboral en Argentina*, ILO Country Office for Argentina: Buenos Aires.

de Miguel, M. and S. Woyecheszen (2015), 'Estructura productiva e informalidad laboral', in Fabio Bertranou and Luis Casanova (eds), *Caminos hacia la formalización laboral en Argentina*, ILO Country Office for Argentina: Buenos Aires.

ECLAC (2010), *La hora de la Igualdad. Brechas por cerrar, caminos por abrir*, 33rd session of ECLAC, Santiago, Chile.

ILO (2002), *Decent work and the informal economy*, International Labour Conference, 90th Session, ILO: Geneva.

ILO (2013), *Transitioning from the informal to the formal economy*, Report V(1), International Labour Conference, 103rd Session, 2014, ILO: Geneva.

Jiménez, M. (2013), 'La informalidad laboral en el sector formal. Un análisis preliminar', Working Paper No. 10, IELDE, Universidad Nacional de Salta.

Jütting, J. and J. de Laiglesia (eds) (2009), 'Is informal normal? Towards More and better jobs in developing countries', Development Centre Studies, OECD.

Messina, G. (2015), 'Estudio de la inserción de las trabajadoras migrantes paraguayas a partir de las reformas laborales y migratorias en Argentina', Working Paper No. 10, ILO Country Office for Argentina: Buenos Aires.

MTEySS (2013a), 'Trabajo no registrado: Avances y Desafíos para una Argentina inclusivo', Ministerio de Trabajo, Empleo y Seguridad Social.

MTEySS (2013b), 'Diagnóstico de la informalidad laboral, a partir de los datos relevados por la Encuesta Nacional de Protección y Seguridad Social (ENAPROSS)', Ministerio de Trabajo, Empleo y Seguridad Social, presentation during the Jornadas sobre Análisis de Mercado Laboral, Buenos Aires, 25–26 September.

Novick, M. (2007), 'Recuperando políticas públicas para enfrentar la informalidad laboral: el caso argentino 2003–2007', presented at the Interregional Symposium on the Informal Economy – Enabling Transition to Formalization, Geneva, November.

Packard, T., J. Koettl and C. Montenegro (2013), *In From the Shadow: Integrating Europe's Informal Labor*, World Bank: Washington, DC.

Poder Ejecutivo Nacional (2014), 'Ley de promoción del trabajo registrado y prevención del fraude laboral', Bill No. 61/14, http://www.senado.gov.ar/bundles/senadoportal/pdf/pl61_14.pdf.

Schleser, D. (2007), 'El trabajo no registrado en el largo plazo', Serie Trabajo, Ocupación y Empleo No. 7, Ministerio de Trabajo, Empleo y Seguridad Social.

9. Formalizing street vendors: Regulating to improve well-being or to gain control?

Ana Maria Vargas-Falla

9.1 INTRODUCTION

Flor works as a street vendor, selling aromatic water, a kind of tea made from the infusion of different herbs and fruits. Flor had difficulties finding a job when she moved to the city because she had only attended primary school. At the age of 69, and like most senior citizens in Colombia, Flor does not have a pension since she always worked informally. Instead, she hopes to continue working as street vendor for as long as she can. Flor starts her day early in the morning when she goes to the farmers' market and buys the equivalent of 3 USD[1] in herbs and fruits. She goes straight from the market to the 'vending zones' located in front of the hospital in the neighbourhood of Tunjuelito, where she has a tent that she received from the government as part of a programme to formalize street vendors. Inside the tent, there is a small stove, a large pot and a table with some chairs for the customers of Flor's business. She charges the equivalent to US$0.25 for a cup of tea, and from her sales she makes about 10 USD a day. Flor has worked vending tea in front of that hospital for about ten years, but four years ago she was able to formalize her business and enter the vending zone, located only few metres away. Flor is happy to be working in the vending zones because, as she said, 'Here in the tents I have a roof that protects me from the sun and the rain.' However, there are rumours about the government being upset with the vendors for not following the process of formalization all the way. Flor thinks the government may come and take away the tents because she did not manage to save money and move her business into a shopping mall. The vending zones were only a temporary solution for a period of two years, but most

---

[1] USD currency in this article corresponds to an exchange rate of 1 dollar equivalent to approximately 1900 Colombian pesos (as of 31 December 2013).

of the vendors refuse to leave. Their customers are in the streets, and most of the vendors insist that they cannot pay for rent because they make only a small income. However, the government argues that the tents were only a temporary solution and the aim of formalization was to move the vendors into the formal economy.

I met Flor in one of my first visits to a formalization programme called Transitional Vending Zones in the city of Bogotá. Vendors refer to this programme as 'the tents', 'the vending zones' or 'the formalization zones'. Like Flor, most of the vendors I met appreciated the legal status that followed the formalization of their businesses, because now they were not exposed to police harassment or confiscations. They also enjoyed shelter from harsh weather conditions, because in the zones a green tarpaulin protects them from the rain and the sun. The transitional zones appeared as a public policy that enabled vendors to work under better conditions. Yet, Flor was worried about the government dismantling the tents of those vendors who were not able to follow the formalization process, which consisted of saving money and moving into off-street premises. I wondered what the expected outcomes of formalization were, and why vendors and policy-makers seemed to have different views about the process of formalization. Furthermore, understanding whether and how street vendors could improve their working conditions after formalization in the vending zones were some of the questions that inspired this research.

In most cities in the world, street vendors face exclusion, poverty and harsh working conditions due to laws that prohibit selling in public space (Austin, 1993; Bromley, 2000; Crossa, 2009). While street vendors contribute to the economy and constitute an emerging frontier for poverty reduction strategies at the bottom of the economic pyramid, they often work under irregular legal status. Vendors are considered as pre-modern, a nuisance and a source of congestion (Meneses-Reyes, 2013).

Formalization, understood as gaining legal status to develop their businesses, is the mainstream policy to regulate the work of street vendors in most cities in the world. Formalization is also part of a global trend that aims to use legal reforms to improve the lives of the poor (CLEP, 2008). However, formalization policies are criticized by various scholars (Centeno and Portes, 2006; Donovan, 2008; Faundez, 2009; Pena, 2000). According to Pena (2000), formalizing is used by local authorities to recover public space in order to reduce congestion, and many vendors do not see major benefits from being covered by the rule of law. Many vendors go back to the streets after formalization, despite government efforts (Donovan, 2008). It is the assertion of this chapter that there is a gap between what the formalization policies are trying to address and what the needs of the street vendors are.

To contribute to this long-standing debate, this chapter analyses the effects of a recent formalization programme in the city of Bogotá, Colombia. Through an ethnographic approach, the study aims to understand the experiences, ideas and opinions of street vendors and government officials involved in the vending zones in the city. Specifically, this research explores the relation between the formalization of street vendors and the improvement of their well-being. Formalization is addressed from the point of view of the vendors.

I will argue that government officials and street vendors see formalization in different ways. While vendors see formalization as a way to conduct their businesses without fear of police evictions, government officials see formalization as a process to clean up the streets from nuisance and congestion. This study argues the need to consider other outcomes of formalization rather than only the ability of the vendors to improve their income and be able to move off the streets into retail space. To do so, I bring into the debate the work of Amartya Sen, particularly the concept of well-being.

The chapter is organized as follows. Section 9.2 presents a literature review that situates this study within the research on the informal economy. Section 9.3 provides the theoretical framework of the study based on the concept of well-being. Section 9.4 discusses the methodological considerations of this study. Sections 9.5 and 9.6 report the main findings, while section 9.7 gives the analysis. Finally, section 9.8 presents the main conclusions, and the implications for further attempts to regulate the informal economy, particularly street vending.

9.2 LITERATURE REVIEW

There is a long-standing debate about the regulation of street vendors, resulting in a great array of theoretical and empirical research (Bhowmik, 2005; Roever, 2005). Studies in the fields of economics, sociology, urban planning, political science and law illustrate different aspects of formalization such as the entrepreneurial potential (De Soto, 1989), the recovery of public space (Donovan, 2008) and the resistance of vendors to these reforms (Crossa, 2009; Pena, 2000; Steel, 2012; Vargas and Urinboyev, 2015).

Vendors provide a rich variety of affordable goods and services, including food, clothes, shoes, books, flowers, and anything on demand. However, street vendors often experience harassment by the police, mainly because their legal status is informal. A significant argument in favour of formalization of street vendors claims that formalized vendors can achieve economic improvements when the law protects their businesses. In this regard, the most influential study was done by Peruvian economist Hernando De Soto. In his study, De Soto illustrated how street vendors in Lima worked in the shadow of their nation's legal system and therefore had difficulties expanding their businesses and achieving growth (De Soto, 2000). De Soto claimed that facilitating the formalization of small entrepreneurs would support business growth and subsequently improve tax revenues for the state. His work has influenced the global trend regarding the use of rule of law reforms to promote the legalization and formalization of the business of the poor (Banik, 2011).

The entrepreneurial side of formalization has been widely debated. In a study of relocation in Bogotá, Colombia, Donovan (2008) illustrates how many street vendors abandoned relocation programmes after experiencing a considerable decrease in their sales. Similarly, other studies illustrate that the link between formalization and poverty reduction is not clear (Clausen et al., 2011; Lince, 2011; Slocum et al., 2011). In many cases, government authorities use formalization to get rid of the vendors and recover control over public space, as illustrated in the cases of Zambia (Hansen, 2010), Malawi (Kayuni and Tambulasi, 2009), Ecuador (Ferragut and Gómez, 2013) and Mexico (Meneses-Reyes, 2013). Vendors are seen often as a source of nuisance, congestion and lack of development in the cities where they work (Pádua Carrieri and Murta, 2011). However, formalization can generate further exclusion of non-formalized workers, facing harassment not only from the police but also from newly formalized businesses (Lince, 2011; Geenen, 2012). Moreover, vendors find better refuge in their social networks and associations than in the law, regarding legality as control rather than protection (Aliaga Linares, 2002; Lindell, 2010; Steel, 2012).

Nevertheless, there is a renewed interest in the potential of regulation to improve the well-being of informal workers around the world. With the launch of the Sustainable Development Goals in 2015, the formalization of informal workers is seen in connection with poverty reduction and decent work. There is also a growing debate about how to improve the lives of informal workers at the International Labour Organization (ILO), focusing on the need to provide decent work regardless of the legal status of the workers (Sen, 2013). Nevertheless, it is not clear how formalization can positively influence the lives of street vendors.

This chapter will extend the state-of-the-art by exploring the experiences of street vendors and government officials with the Transitional Vending Zones formalization programme in the city of Bogotá. Drawing from data collected among street vendors participating in this programme, the study will examine the specific conditions of formalization in this case, the views of street vendors about formalization, and the opportunities and limits of the formalization approach to improve the well-being and working conditions of street vendors. Consequently, this study will shed light on the debate over formalization and poverty reduction, not from the views of government officials and international organizations, but from the perspectives of those affected, in this case the street vendors that participated in this study.

9.3 WELL-BEING AS A CONCEPTUAL FRAMEWORK TO STUDY INFORMAL WORK

I use the concept of well-being developed by Amartya Sen (1999) to explore how formalization is experienced by the vendors themselves. There are numerous definitions of well-being, and at times even competing perspectives (White, 2010; Taylor, 2011; Sen, 1993). Well-being can be analysed objectively as the result of different economic, social and psychological standards, or it can be defined by each individual subjectively (White, 2010). There are different lists of objective indicators of well-being, including income, employment, having good health, education, housing, security, and good quality of air and food. Subjective aspects of well-being depend on individual self-assessments of one's position in life, including income satisfaction, happiness and satisfaction with one's life.

Amartya Sen has studied well-being in relation to agency, freedom and capabilities. The term 'capabilities' refers to 'a person's ability to do valuable acts or reach valuable states of being' (Sen, 1993: 30).[2] This definition of well-being pays attention to the goals a person can actually achieve (functionings) and the freedom to choose among available choices. It concerns the material aspects of life that produce utility (having food, having good health, access to education) but also about the existence of freedom. Sen pays special attention to the idea of the freedom to achieve well-being, which he calls 'well-being freedom' (Sen, 1985: 203).

For the purpose of this chapter I do not start with objective definitions of well-being, and instead I want to uncover the ways street vendors describe well-being in their own terms. I use Sen's capabilities approach to highlight street vendors' ideas on whether formalization has brought improvement in their well-being, bringing into the debate their voices and

---

[2]   Sen uses the terms 'functionings' and 'capabilities' to define well-being. Functionings are 'the various things that he or she manages to do or be in leading a life. The capability of a person reflects the alternative combinations of functionings the person can achieve, and from which he or she can choose one collection' (Sen, 1993: 31).

experiences. Thus, the concept of well-being and the capabilities approach serve as analytical concepts to investigate the working conditions of informal workers.

9.4   METHODOLOGICAL CONSIDERATIONS

This chapter is based on four periods of ethnographic field research between 2011 and 2014 in Bogotá, the capital city of Colombia. During this fieldwork, significant ethnographic material was collected mostly through observations, informal conversations and in-depth interviews. A total of seven interviews were conducted with leaders of street vendor organizations and nine interviews with government officials working in the formalization programme of the City of Bogotá. The interviews and observations focused on the experiences and opinions of formalized vendors, leaders of the organizations and government officials in relation to: (1) legal status of street vendors; (2) the police; (3) street vendors' associations; and (4) the government and its formalization programmes. The interviews and observations tried to uncover the everyday experiences of street vendors and government officials with formalization and the rule of law. Interviews with formalized street vendors and their leaders were conducted in the 18 districts where the formalization programme was operating in order to ensure a complete geographic representation. Additionally a total of 169 face-to-face questionnaires were conducted among street vendors who formalized their businesses in the transitional zones. The questionnaires raised preliminary questions about the formalization of street vendors and the subsequent fieldwork allowed for the collection of in-depth data. Interviews were conducted at the workplaces of the vendors and during working hours in a flexible manner, allowing me as a researcher to spend time with the vendors.

The interviews with government officials were mainly conducted at the Institute for the Social Economy (IPES), which is the government body in charge of the formalization programmes in the city. I interviewed officials working in the design of formalization programmes, as well as street-level bureaucrats serving as liaison between the government and the vendors. I explored government officials' ideas about the rights of the vendors, the role of the state in the control and regulation of street vending businesses, their interpretations of the rule of law and formality, their thoughts about the advantages and disadvantages of the vending zones, and their general opinions about the work of the vendors.

In the selection of methods, priority was given to spontaneous conversations, observations and long days of fieldwork immersion. I enjoyed buying food from the vendors, sharing time talking, and on many occasions I felt an insider in the street business culture. The interest in understanding what was happening at the street level and how people's ideas about the law influenced their lives shaped the methodology of this research. The interviewees were asked for their consent to participate in the study, and their names and whereabouts have been changed to respect confidentiality.

Access to the street vendors was relatively easy since they work in public spaces. I explained to the vendors my situation as a PhD student in Sweden, and most of them agreed to talk to me. Since I am Colombian, I could communicate with the vendors in Spanish, and I later translated my notes into English. Access to the government officials was more troublesome and I had to use the contact of a friend working at this office in order to get inside the building. While most of my informants inside the government were often busy, drafting reports to the director, I was able to interview them during their lunch or coffee breaks.

Finally, I would like to mention that I myself participated in street vending while I was a university student, particularly for fundraising for school trips. This condition could influence my views on the phenomenon of street vending since I felt a kind of solidarity with the vendors. However, for the purpose of this research I try to present the different sides of the issue, including the government, the vendors and their leaders. The risk of bias in research is always at stake, but honesty is preferred when researchers position themselves in the socio-political space where the research is conducted. For this chapter, I have chosen to present examples of relevant observations, and three informal interviews that represent common views among the three actors interviewed in this research.

9.5 FORMALIZATION IN VENDING ZONES AND WELL-BEING

The situation of street vendors in Bogotá is similar to other cities in the developing world, in which vendors' legal status is often unclear and governments resort to evictions and harassment to control this kind of work. In Bogotá, street vendors are a phenomenon that impacts upon public opinion, with more than 80 000 working on the streets (Donovan, 2008). During the administrations of two city mayors, Peñalosa and Mockus, between 1998 and 2003, street vendors in Bogotá experienced massive evictions and forced relocations, which led to the loss of livelihoods for many workers engaged in this activity. Many vendors were forced to relocate to malls, where their sales decreased; others moved to the city outskirts, or left the street. Yet, new and old vendors came back after evictions and total eradication was never achieved.

There was an important shift in this policy in 2004, connected to the election of a new mayor from the left-wing party Polo Democratico, and the Decision of the Constitutional Court ordering the provision of street vendors with alternative means of work prior to evictions (T-772-2003). The policies implemented between 2004 to 2014 aimed to support street vendors with formalization programmes such as rotating fairs, kiosks, vending in public offices and the Transitional Vending Zones.

The Transitional Vending Zones are one of the formalization programmes that have been implemented in Bogotá since 2006. The vending zones allowed vendors to work in public spaces through a collective permit given to the vendors' associations in each zone. Additionally, vendors received tents that were installed in spaces agreed upon with the vendors, for a period of three years. During these three years vendors were supposed to improve their businesses and then move to the formal economy. Thus, formalization in the vending zones had two main goals: supporting vendors to improve their businesses, and organizing the use of public spaces previously occupied by the vendors, moving them into selected zones. The process to formalize in the transitional zones was simple and affordable because it did not include the payment of taxes or government fees. The only requirement was to be part of an association, because the contract of the zone was given to the associations and not to individual vendors.

In 2012 there were 18 transitional zones established in the city with a total of 455 street vendors. I visited these 18 zones and conducted a short questionnaire among vendors to grasp the general perception of the vending zones among formalized vendors. I was able to interview 169 vendors, 76 male and 93 female. The average vendor in the formalization programme has five or less years of education and has been working in the streets for 15 years. Their age varied between 33 to 69 years old, with an average of 44. Table 9.1 compares the socio-economic profile of formalized vendors interviewed in this study (2012) with the data from a previous census of vendors (2004).

It is commonly assumed that formalization will help street vendors to improve their income since they can access formal credit and invest more to expand their businesses (De Soto, 1989). What happens in fact? Is it true that vendors can improve their businesses after formalization? Do formalized vendors earn more after formalization? Those are some of the main assumptions in the formalization theory. However, the questionnaire applied covered not only income, but also other aspects such as working conditions and membership in organizations.

When asked whether their life has improved, remained the same or

Table 9.1   Socio-economic profile of Bogotá street vendors, 2004 and 2012

	2004 (N = 19315)	2012 (N = 169)
Women (percentage)	48	55
Men (percentage)	52	45
Age (average)	44	50
Years as vendor	10	15
Daily hours of work	10	10
Membership Association	35	100

Sources: Author's research, 2012; Donovan (2008).

Table 9.2   Outcomes of formalization

	N = 169	%
Less than three years in the vending zones	62	37
Three or more years in the vending zone	107	63
Life has improved	138	82
Life remained the same	24	14
Life has worsened	7	4
Experience confiscation of goods by police	0	0
Experience confiscation of goods by police (before formalization)	94	56

Source: Author's survey, 2012.

worsened as a result of formalization, 138 of the vendors (82 per cent) considered that their life had improved; for 24 vendors it remained the same; and seven vendors reported that life had worsened (Table 9.2). The questionnaire had an open question for vendors to explain the reasons for their answer. After coding the answers, the results illustrate that most of the vendors interviewed considered that formalization helped them to gain freedom from police harassment (61, N = 169). Additionally, formalization in the tents gave the vendors protection from the sun and rain (62, N = 169), which was highly appreciated by them. Protection from harsh weather conditions led to improved working conditions for the vendors, and many referred to this improvement as good for their health. Other reasons were: being able to protect their merchandise (20, N = 169), working in peace (23, N = 169) and having a fixed location (10, N = 169). Some of the direct quotes from the answers to this question are summarized in the Appendix. The seven vendors who reported that their lives had worsened explained that this was due to a decrease in their sales. Some of these vendors were thinking about moving out of the vending zone and going back to the streets, while others said that even with lower income it was worth being formalized because they could have more peace at work.

One of the most positive aspects of formalization was the elimination of evictions and confiscations. According to this study, after moving into the vending zones none of the formalized vendors experienced the confiscation of their goods, nor had they experienced police harassment. In contrast, 56 per cent reported experiencing confiscations before moving into the vending zones. The fact that no one had experienced eviction or the confiscation of their goods shows that the police respected the formalization agreement. This result also illustrates that police harassment is a strong threat for many street vendors, and helps to explain why they considered protection from police harassment as one of the most important outcomes of formalization.

Finally, this study found that most of the vendors (63 per cent) had been in the transitional zones for more than three years, passing the limit given by the government. Many vendors considered the time limit of three years as irrational, and they insisted that moving into retail stores after that time was not a realistic expectation. According to the leaders of the associations of vendors, the problem with the transitional zones was that the government failed to provide them with support. Formalization in vending zones for a limited time was not considered appropriate to the conditions of the vendors, and people like Flor claimed the need to have permanent vending zones.

The results of this preliminary questionnaire, although limited in scope, gave a hint as to which important issues should be explored during the subsequent ethnographic fieldwork. The following sections illustrate the results of observations, informal conversations and semi-structured interviews conducted among vendors working in the vending zones, the leaders of their organizations and government officials working at the office of formalization.

9.6 EXPERIENCES, OPINIONS AND UNDERSTANDINGS OF FORMALIZATION

Street vendors, their leaders and the government officials involved in the vending zones interpreted formalization from different standpoints. While vendors considered formalization as a way to stop police evictions and harassment, their leaders complained about the lack of support from the government. Government officials saw formalization as a temporary solution to move vendors into private markets. In this section, I present the results of three informal interviews that illustrate the different meanings of formalization for the actors involved in this process. They illustrate common concerns about formalization. The three interviews presented below were selected for their typicality and representativeness. Lina is one of the government officials in charge of the formalization policy in the city of Bogotá, Ricardo is the leader of an association of street vendors, and Flor is the vendor of herbal and fruit tea.

Lina: 'We gave the vendors everything, support and training, but the only thing they want is to stay in the streets':

> When we started the transitional zones we thought this was a great opportunity for street vendors to move to the formal economy. The vending zones were the result of a process of negotiation between the government and the leaders of the street vendors and the aim was to help the vendors improve their businesses. The original idea was to make a three-year period of transition, in which vendors could work legally in the vending zones and save some money to move to the formal economy. We [the formalization office] gave the vendors tents in defined zones where they could sell and consolidate their businesses. But now after more than five years no one has been able to make the transition and exit the streets. They just like to work on the streets because they don't pay rent, I mean, why would you move to a retail store, when you can have your business on the streets? It is impossible to make the vendors understand that they have to leave the streets. We are now thinking about what to do with this program, but we can't close down the zones, just like that. We have to know what we are going to do with the vendors.

While Lina, working at the formalization office, thinks the vendors just want to stay in the streets, the leaders of the association of vendors tell a different story. Most of the leaders I interviewed in this study considered that moving off the streets was not possible because their economic units were small and they did not have the ability to save money or obtain credit. According to Ricardo, one of the association leaders, they would like to move to the formal economy, but they know this is not easy since it requires large capital investment. Many leaders believe the government failed on the promises of formalization because giving them a tent in the vending zone was not enough to even pretend they could open up stores in the 'formal economy'.

Ricardo: 'You have to be naïve to think a street vendor can suddenly open a store':

> We call the vending zones now, '*zona de traicion*' (betrayed zone), because the conditions of these zones aren't realistic for the vendors. The government

simply gave us some tents and left us to 'God's will'. They organized some training, but the teachers had no idea what it is to be a street vendor and how marketing in the streets works. They came from the formal economy and they wanted to teach us to keep accounting books and that stuff, but that isn't useful when you work on the streets. They also trained us on how to have a bank account and how to get credits there, but the banks denied our credits because we (the vendors) can't show capacity to pay. Additionally many vendors are reported in the Sifin (risk database) for very low amounts, like a cell phone bill they forgot to pay. It is impossible to think that a street vendor can save money to move to the formal sector and pay rent and taxes. Additionally, we are a population in transit, many of us don't work every day and some of us move from formal to informal employment all the time. While we think opening a store or a restaurant is very attractive in reality you need to have a lot of money to open a business in a retail place and vendors can't risk the money of their livelihoods in these kinds of projects. What we need is more support from the government, like seed capital that we can invest in our businesses.

Many leaders of the vendors' association reflected on the government's promises to support them to move to the formal economy. While some considered they needed more support from the government, such as training or credit, others like Ricardo were sceptical about the possibility of a street vendor moving off the streets to start up a shop or a restaurant. Many were aware of the hardships and competition among established businesses, and preferred the flexibility and low amounts of capital needed for street vendors. Yet most of the vendors interviewed for this study considered that they preferred the vending zones, because on the streets they had to endure harder working conditions and the insecurity of working without a legal permit.

The last interview I present in this chapter illustrates some of the positive aspects of the transitional zones and why, despite the failure to move off the streets as expected by the government, many vendors continued working in the tents and did not want to abandon the formalization programme.

Flor: 'Before the vending zones we were outside and had to endure the sun and the rain':

I don't care about the government, I just want to work in peace. I don't do wrong to anyone. I am just trying to survive and I don't understand why the government is always keen to get rid of the vendors. You know I come here every morning to sell my aromatic water, people like it and buy from me because is good and cheap. You know, before the vending zones we were outside and had to endure the sun and the rain. With the weather of Bogotá you never know, it can be sunny and then the next hour can rain as hell. The police used to come here once a week and we had to be ready to run away when they came. The managers from the hospital didn't like the vendors and they were always calling the police, telling them we were crowding the entrance of their building. There was always a fight with other vendors because everyone wanted to be close to the entrance so I had to carry my tea in thermos to be able to move around. For me, I prefer the tents because now I can wake up in the mornings and I know I have my place, I don't have to worry I have to fight with another person to get my space. I also know that the police can't take my things or send me to prison, so I can work in peace. But now I am worried because people around here say the government might take away the tents. I don't imagine going back to the streets at my age.

9.7 TWO SIDES OF FORMALIZATION: ANALYSIS

I started this chapter by asking whether and how street vendors have improved their working conditions after formalization in the vending zones in Bogotá. The results of the preliminary questionnaire gave an indication of two important improvements after formalization: working without fear from police eviction, and protection from harsh weather conditions. However, after spending more time in the vending zones and interviewing government officials, the story of formalization became more complicated, since vendors and the government hold different expectations. While vendors saw an improvement in their lives after formalization, the improvement was not related to the possibility to access credit and expand their businesses as stated by the mainstream theory of Hernando De Soto, but instead it was because vendors could improve their working conditions. Vendors like Flor appreciate the legal status that allowed them to work without fear from police eviction and, additionally in this case, they also benefited from weather protection because of the tents. However, for the government, formalization was a failure because vendors were not able to move to retail stores. Similarly, the leaders of the organizations of vendors claimed formalization was a failure because the government did not give them economic support. While both government and leaders were critical about formalization, their ideas and expectations limit their understanding of other outcomes of the formalization process, and particularly how it helped the vendors to improve their working conditions. Being able to work without fear of the police and with protection from the weather allowed many street vendors to improve their well-being.

The study found that according to the government, formalization was a failure since vendors failed to move off the streets. When interviewing government officials at the formalization office, they appeared unaware of the life situation of the vendors and often referred to the vendors as a problem for the city. The interview with Lina, working at the office of formalization, illustrates some of the views of government officials about the transitional zones. She thinks the transitional zones are a failure because, in her words, vendors 'just like to work on the streets because they don't pay rent'. The government's view on formalization does not consider the vendors' ideas about their own well-being.

In this regard, formalization in Bogotá followed the assumptions of De Soto's (1989) theory about the income improvements and business expansion that should follow after legal status. Like De Soto, the government in Bogotá anticipated that after being in the vending zones, vendors could access credit to further invest in their businesses so that they could move to retail stores. While this was not possible, other positive outcomes followed formalization, such as the improvements in the vendors' working conditions. Yet the government's excessive focus on business expansion and the possibility to relocate the vendors in retail stores led them to think of formalization as a failure.

Like Lina, most government officials considered the vendors as a problem for the city, a nuisance for the rest of the citizens and a source of congestion. In this regard, this research supports the findings of other studies criticizing formalization's hidden aim of getting rid of the vendors and recovering control over public spaces (Ferragut and Gómez, 2013; Hansen, 2010; Kayuni and Tambulasi, 2009; Meneses-Reyes, 2013). When government officials have a hidden agenda regarding getting rid of the vendors, it is hard for formalization programmes to achieve other goals such as the improvement of their working conditions and their well-being.

Formalization for most of the association leaders was also seen as a failure, but for different reasons. While the government complained about the fact that the vendors wanted to stay on the streets, the leaders said vendors needed more time and support to improve their businesses. In this regard, the association leaders were also focused on economic improvements. However, unlike the government they were aware that moving into retail stores required more than 'legal status' as stated by De Soto's (1989) theory. Leaders of the associations were aware of the social conditions of the vendors, the mobility and the economic situations of their businesses. Yet they failed to recognize other basic improvements that came after formalization, such as the protection from the weather.

Finally, the story of Flor and the preliminary questionnaire explain the practical reasons why formalization in the vending zones was not necessarily seen as failure by the vendors. Being able to wake up every day without thinking that the police can come and confiscate your goods was perceived as an important benefit by most of the vendors I interviewed. Additionally, Flor's comment that 'I can wake up in the mornings and I know I have my place' illustrates how formalization generated a sense of security in the vendors about their work and their place of business. This sense of self-worth and living without fear in Flor relates to the idea of 'well-being' proposed by Sen (1985), in which people are able to pursue the life they value.

Apart from being able to work without fear of eviction, most of the formalized vendors in this research considered that they were able to improve their working conditions. However, improvement in the lives of street vendors were not due to access to credit or capital as proposed by the formalization theory, defended by De Soto (1989), but instead due to the tent given by the government and the possibility to have a vending space protected from harsh weather conditions. The vending zones allowed the vendors to keep working on the streets, and their incomes were not drastically reduced as it happened with formalized vendors in relocation programmes (Donovan, 2008). In this sense, the vending zones partially moved away from the ideology that sees vendors as 'out of place', typical of relocation programmes, and instead the zones were established on pavements and in parks. Despite the aim of the government to use the zones as a transitional place, the vendors used them as a place to conduct their businesses with more freedom, and they were not ready to give up their space.

This study has some limitations. First, the conditions of the programme studied, the Transitional Vending Zones, determined some of the outcomes. This study was only able to access vendors in the vending zones, and therefore it is not possible to know whether vendors who quit the zones think the same. However, most of the zones were crowded with vendors, showing a large participation in the programme. Additionally, it is necessary to consider that one of the main reasons why vendors were able to keep up their sales after formalization was the fact that formalization occurred in the streets. The vending zones were located in good selling spots, and the results would have been different if vendors were moved to remote places far away from their customers. In this regard, it is important to keep in mind that street vendors' preoccupation with their working conditions usually comes together with their need to earn an income. After all, they are on the streets in order to provide for their needs. Furthermore, the transitional zones only benefited 450 vendors, limiting the scope of this study. Thus, further research on the largest formalization programmes could reveal other aspects of well-being not covered in this research.

9.8 CONCLUSIONS

The study of the vending zones in Bogotá, Colombia, illustrates how, according to the government, the goal behind formalization was to help vendors to move off the streets. While the government considered this formalization programme as a failure because the transition to the formal economy never occurred, many vendors were protected from the sun and rain, and could work in peace without having to worry about police evictions. In this regard, this study illustrates how formalization can have important outcomes for the well-being of the vendors.

Formalization of workers in the informal economy is a venture that requires a bottom-up approach. The case of formalization of street vendors in Bogotá illustrates that giving vendors a legal status for their businesses can be a tool to improve their well-being. Being able to wake up every day and work in the vending zone, without thinking that the police can come and confiscate their goods, is a major change for vendors. Even though legal status is not a silver bullet that will bring great economic development for small entrepreneurs who are trapped in low-income activities, this research shows that the law is certainly important. It is essential not to worsen the vulnerable situation of street vendors by confiscating their merchandise, or by harassing them with the police and sending them to prison.

Even though many street vendors still live in poverty, most of the formalized vendors in this research were better off after the formalization of their businesses. They gained confidence, self-respect and autonomy. They were empowered by the law that recognized their work and gave them legal status, contrary to previous laws that disempowered them and prohibited their livelihoods. Therefore, formalization can be a tool to enhance well-being when governments use the law to improve the life of the poor, and not as a tool of control.

REFERENCES

Aliaga Linares, L. 2002. Sumas y restas: el capital social como recurso en la informalidad. Lima: Alternative.

Austin, R. 1993. An Honest Living: Street Vendors, Municipal Regulation, and the Black Public Sphere. *Yale Law Journal* **103**, 2119.

Banik, D. 2011. *The Legal Empowerment Agenda: Poverty, Labour and the Informal Economy in Africa*. Farnham: Ashgate.

Bhowmik, S. 2005. Street Vendors in Asia: A Review. *Economic and Political Weekly* **40**(22/23), 2256–64.

Bromley, R. 2000. Street Vending and Public Policy: A Global Review. *International Journal of Sociology and Social Policy* **20**, 1–28.

Centeno, M.A., Portes, A. 2006. The Informal Economy in the Shadow of the State. In: Fernández-Kelly, P., Shefner, J. (eds), *Out of the Shadows: Political Action and the Informal Economy in Latin America*. University Park, PA: Pennsylvania State University Press, pp. 23–48.

Clausen, F., Barreto, M.L., Attaran, A. 2011. Property Rights Theory and the

Reform of Artisanal and Small-Scale Mining in Developing Countries. *Journal of Politics and Law* **4**, 15–26.

CLEP. 2008. Making the Law Work for Everyone: Working Group Reports. LEP.

Crossa, V. 2009. Resisting the Entrepreneurial City: Street Vendors' Struggle in Mexico City's Historic Center. *International Journal of Urban and Regional Research* **33**, 43–63.

De Soto, H. 1989. *The Other Path : The Invisible Revolution in the Third World.* London: Tauris.

De Soto, H. 2000. *The Mystery of Capital: Why Capitalism Triumphs in the West and Fails Everywhere Else.* New York: Basic Books.

Donovan, M. 2008. Informal Cities and the Contestation of Public Space: The Case of Bogotá's Street Vendors, 1988–2003. *Urban Studies* **45**, 29–51.

Faundez, J. 2009. Empowering Workers in the Informal Economy. *Hague Journal on the Rule of Law* **1**, 156–72.

Ferragut, S., Gómez, G.M. 2013. From the Street to the Store: The Formalization of Street Vendors in Quito, Ecuador. In: Hillenkamp, I., Lapeyre, F., Lemaitre, A. (eds), *Securing Livelihoods: Informal Economy Practices and Institutions.* Oxford: Oxford University Press, pp. 214–34.

Geenen, S. 2012. A Dangerous Bet: The Challenges of Formalizing Artisanal Mining in the Democratic Republic of Congo. *Resources Policy* **37**, 322–30.

Hansen, K.T. 2010. Changing Youth Dynamics in Lusaka's Informal Economy in the Context of Economic Liberalization. *African Studies Quarterly* **11**(2/3), 13–27.

Kayuni, H.M., Tambulasi, R. 2009. Political Transitions and Vulnerability of Street Vending in Malawi. *Theoretical and Empirical Researches in Urban Management* **3**, 79–96.

Lince, S. 2011. The Informal Sector in Jinja, Uganda: Implications of Formalization and Regulation. *African Studies Review* **54**, 73–93.

Lindell, I. 2010. Informality and Collective Organising: Identities, Alliances and Transnational Activism in Africa. *Third World Quarterly* **31**, 207–22.

Meneses-Reyes, R. 2013. Out of Place, Still in Motion: Shaping (Im)Mobility Through Urban Regulation. *Social and Legal Studies* **22**, 335–56.

Pádua Carrieri, A., Murta, I.B.D. 2011. Cleaning Up the City: A Study on the Removal of Street Vendors from Downtown Belo Horizonte, Brazil. *Canadian Journal of Administrative Sciences* **28**, 217–25.

Pena, S. 2000. Regulating Informal Markets: Informal Commerce in Mexico City. *International Journal of Sociology and Social Policy* **20**, 37–67.

Roever, S.C. 2005. Negotiating Formality: Informal Sector, Market, and State of Peru. Doctoral dissertation, University of California, Berkeley.

Sen, A. 1985. Well-Being, Agency and Freedom: The Dewey Lectures 1984. *Journal of Philosophy* **82**(4), 169–221.

Sen, A. 1993. Capability and Well-Being. In: Nussbaum M., Sen, A. (eds), *The Quality of Life*. Oxford: Oxford University Press, pp. 30–52.

Sen, A. 1999. *Development as Freedom.* New York: Knopf.

Sen, A. 2013. Work and Rights. *International Labour Review* **152**, 81–92. doi:10.1111/j.1564-913X.2013.00164.x.

Slocum, S.L., Backman, K.F., Robinson, K.L. 2011. Tourism Pathways to Prosperity: Perspectives on the Informal Economy in Tanzania. *Tourism Analysis* **16**, 43.

Steel, G. 2012. Whose Paradise? Itinerant Street Vendors' Individual and Collective

Practices of Political Agency in the Tourist Streets of Cusco, Peru. *International Journal of Urban and Regional Research* **36**(5), 1007–21.

Taylor, D. 2011. Wellbeing and Welfare: A Psychosocial Analysis of Being Well and Doing Well Enough. *Journal of Social Policy* **40**(4), 777–94.

Vargas, A.M., Urinboyev, R. 2015. Everyday Forms of Resistance to the Law: An Ethnographic Study of Street Vendors in Bogotá, Colombia. *Droit et Société* **91**, 623–38.

White, S. 2010. Analysing Wellbeing: A Framework for Development Practice. *Development in Practice* **20**(2), 158–72.

APPENDIX   QUOTES FROM STREET VENDORS' QUESTIONNAIRE

BOX 9A.1   LIFE IMPROVEMENTS AFTER FORMALIZATION, STREET VENDORS, BOGOTÁ 2012

'I feel better here because I can develop my business; I would like to become formal one day' (Survey No. 2)

'I am free from the sun and the rain' (Survey No. 8)

'I have now the recognition from the local authorities' (Survey No. 18)

'We can work without fear, they let us work' referring to the police (Survey No. 19)

'Now my work is stable and safe' (Survey No. 24)

'I am not an ambulant anymore' (Survey No. 29)

'I can work here with my son (a baby) and this is more safe than in the streets' (Survey No. 34)

'This is very good for us, we are protected from the weather, don't have to look for the police, and we don't have to pack up our products at the end of each day' (Survey No. 38)

'I have a roof and I don't have to pay much rent' (Survey No. 164)

'I have more dignity here' (Survey No. 146)

'Before the police treated us like criminals, now I can work in more peace' (Survey No. 142)

'I feel like these tents are our shopping centre, I feel like a real merchant now' (Survey No. 137)

'My health is better because I don't get wet every time rains, I can sit while I work and don't have to stand all day' (Survey No. 90)

'The streets are a hard place to work, here we are more safe' (Survey No. 73)

'The police is not harassing us anyone, we used to work with fear' (Survey No. 55).

Source: Author's study, 2012.

---

10. Working conditions of urban vendors in Indonesia: Lessons for labour law enforcement

Alex de Ruyter, Muhammad Irfan Syaebani, Riani Rachmawati, David Bailey and Tonia Warnecke

10.1 INTRODUCTION

> A good job can change a person's life, and the right jobs can transform entire societies. Governments need to move jobs to center stage to promote prosperity and fight poverty
>
> (Jim Yong Kim, President of the World Bank, 2013)[1]

With the onset of a global economic downturn during 2008, the incidence of informal employment and vulnerable employment has increased across developed and developing countries alike (ILO, 2012). The incidence of informal employment is now estimated to be more than 40 per cent for two-thirds of developing countries (ILO and IILS, 2013: 12),[2] and in some South and South-East Asian countries, 'informality rates reach up to 90 per cent of total employment' (ILO, 2014a: 13). More than half of developing-country workers (approximately 1.45 billion people) are engaged in vulnerable employment; in South Asia and sub-Saharan Africa, vulnerable employment rates are greater than 75 per cent (ILO, 2014b: 9). Such outcomes have renewed the debate over the impact of labour standards in facilitating a shift to 'decent work' (De Ruyter et al., 2012; ILO and IILS, 2009), and the problems involved in enforcing labour standards in developing countries (Warnecke and de Ruyter, 2012); particularly for women, who are over-represented in vulnerable work (ILO, 2014b).

---

[1]   Commenting on the 2013 *World Development Report* (see https://www.one.org/us/2012/10/05/world-development-report-2013-finds-jobs-essential-for-development/).
[2]   For which such data are available.

As the problems associated with globalization became more apparent, policy-makers re-evaluated the Washington Consensus deregulatory approach to development (Bergsten and Williamson, 1994; Williamson, 2004), shifting to a broader focus on good governance and capability endowment as encapsulated in the Millennium Development Goals (Maxwell, 2005). Scholars increasingly noted the negative economic impact of a large informal sector, hampering the development of diversified export sectors and limiting the ability of workers to develop generic skills that can be applied productively in a variety of occupations (WTO and ILO, 2009). However, this evolution in thought has not done enough to tackle social exclusion (ibid.), and given the recent economic crisis, pressure has only increased to reduce government spending and further deregulate labour markets across countries.

Indonesia represents a particularly illustrative example of these trends: on the one hand, after the downfall of the Suharto regime in 1997 following the onset of the Asian financial crisis, the country democratised and moved to ratify key International Labour Organization (ILO) standards such as the Freedom of Association and Protection of the Right to Organise Convention, 1948 (No. 87) (Tjandra, 2009: 8). However, Tedjasukmana et al. (2008) argue that the broader thrust of labour legislation after 1997 had been to complete a shift from a highly corporatist set-up under the Suharto regime to a flexible, market-based system. The country also required assistance from the International Monetary Fund and the World Bank to counteract the impact of the crisis on the banking system, which further added to pressures for marketisation (Tjandraningsih, 2013). The bailout conditions imposed by these bodies included privatisation of state-owned assets, cuts to government spending, and the subsequent liberalisation of labour laws pertaining to contract employment and outsourcing (ibid.). These macro-level developments have posed considerable challenges to efforts to develop sustainable institutions for labour law enforcement, despite a more solid economic performance since 2004. As such, employment and labour regulation policies have been heavily influenced by a neo-liberal agenda.

Accordingly, this chapter explores the labour market experiences of urban vendors, a key group of informal sector workers in Indonesia. Of key importance here is their interaction with customers and authorities, and the actions of other labour market intermediaries seeking to improve their welfare. The following sections of the chapter explore these issues, drawing primarily on interview findings with vendors.

10.2   PRECARIOUSNESS AND VULNERABILITY

The economic downturn that began in 2008, together with persistent labour market stagnation, have provoked renewed emphasis on issues of underemployment, hidden unemployment and insecurity of employment in developed and developing countries alike (ILO, 2013; ILO and IILS, 2013). These issues in turn have been intimately linked to the labour market phenomenon that has been described as 'vulnerable employment' (ILO and IILS, 2013). Very simply put, the ILO (2013: 39) defines vulnerable workers as comprising the labour market categories of own-account workers and contributing family helpers. This is because these types of workers are far less likely than waged or salaried workers to benefit from social protection measures (ibid.). However, vulnerability as a concept has many dimensions, and thus obtaining a precise measure of vulnerable workers (or informal workers in general) can be problematic. As Folkerth and Warnecke (2011) note, informal sector workers are likely to work at more than one location, further compounding the difficulties in recording the extent of such work. Given the nature of such work, it is often unregistered, or clandestine, and hence falls outside official scrutiny (Nazara, 2010).[3] The clandestine nature of much informal work in turn makes such workers far more vulnerable to exploitative work practices or otherwise very low wages and poor working conditions, as they are not covered by labour laws (De Ruyter et al., 2012).

An emphasis on social protection thus highlights the link between vulnerability and labour market precariousness. Vosko (2006: 3–4) argues that labour market precariousness is typified by 'forms of work involving limited social benefits or statutory entitlements, job insecurity, low wages and high risks of ill health'. In a similar fashion, Kalleberg and Hewison (2013: 273) denote precarious work as work that is otherwise typified by 'uncertainty, instability, and insecurity'. In this sense, precarious work and informal work can be regarded as largely synonymous, and a majority of work in developing countries is precarious, since informal work is characterised by being excluded from the scope of regulatory coverage.

As such, vulnerability as a concept seems synonymous with labour market precariousness (although the debate on precariousness has largely been framed in the experience of developed countries). It extends beyond

---

[3]   It is not the purpose of this chapter to provide a comprehensive definition of the informal sector. Readers are invited to see Nazara (2010) for this purpose. The key characteristic is its unregulated and undocumented status (for example, unregistered enterprises).

the objective conditions of work to cover an individual's wider physical, economic, and social and social-psychological circumstances. It calls into question their position within the home, their relationships to other individuals and to the authorities, as well as access to social benefits (and, as such, the ability to participate in society). Vulnerability arises because an individual is somehow disadvantaged in terms of their position within a society. Vulnerability can be seen as concomitant with social exclusion. Thus, vulnerability as a concept arises because of social relations that generate inequality; and hence it has explicit dimensions in terms of class, race and gender.

To be a vulnerable worker, then, is to be vulnerable in terms of unequal distribution of income and power; unequal gender relations within the home, having lack of adequate representation or recourse before the law, or otherwise suffering exclusion and gendered or racialised discrimination, as well as a lack of access to social benefits. It stands to reason that vulnerability becomes more acute in those societies where there is a distinct lack of democratic mechanisms and accountability and where corruption is endemic, as disadvantaged groups have less redress to assert their rights. In this sense, 'informalisation' of the formal sector (Bhattacharya et al., 2013; Hewison and Kalleberg, 2013; Tjandraningsih, 2013) should be seen more in terms of power relations (Chang, 2009; cited in Arnold and Bongiovi, 2013: 295), rather than the existence (or not) of regulations and their enforcement (or not). Historically, this has been a particular problem for developing countries.

Hence, whilst one can refer to family workers and own-account workers as being highly vulnerable workers, as per the ILO definition, it is evident that aspects of vulnerability can occur in other categories of employment, even for those engaged in seemingly secure employment in the formal sector. Brata (2010: 51), building on the earlier work of Dabir-Alai (2004), attempted to construct an index of vulnerability by looking at the working conditions of street vendors, which incorporated an examination of an individual's wider work–life circumstances. These ten elements of vulnerability (the first seven of which were adopted by Brata from Dabir-Alai) are reproduced below, namely:

- Low(er) net profit: more hours are needed to attain a given level of income.
- Experience of bullying: individuals are more likely to feel threatened in their relations with authorities.
- Have at least one dependent: lowers an individual's mobility and hence reduces scope for risk-taking (entrepreneurial) behaviour.
- Have no formal education: less ability to take advantage of economic opportunities.

- Long working hours: suggests a low hourly earnings rate.
- Dependent on supplier or creditor: more likely to face a 'usurious' trading environment.
- Family members not working within same locality: less opportunity for family protection or other support.
- Long commute to place of work: increases the risks (and costs) of travel.
- Not a full owner or just an operator of a business: reduces the scope for decision-making in operating a business.
- Not a member of an association: results in lower bargaining power.

Whilst these elements of vulnerability were denoted for street vendors, it is apparent that they can be readily applicable to other workers (regardless of formal or informal status), along with other factors originally considered by Dabir-Alai, such as gender, age, race, migrant status and principal/agent status (as cited in Brata, 2010: 50). Vulnerability, then, arises from a various mixture of economic and social factors and is shaped by both the supply and demand sides of the labour market. These factors are depicted in Figure 10.1.

The gendered elements of vulnerability are manifest in that it is women in developing countries who are far more likely to be working in unpaid labour or as highly insecure own-account workers (Antonopoulos, 2009). Within this context, the diverse nature of production arrangements (capitalist and non-capitalist; Bhattacharya et al., 2013: 343), the nature of linkages between different types of enterprises, and the impact of globalisation (that is, domestic or part of global supply chain) on a business's production and employment decisions needs to be critically reassessed. There is thus a need to move beyond a simple dichotomy of 'formal' and 'informal' sectors (as the presence of informal workers in formal sector enterprises attests) and recognise that there is a more nuanced gradation of vulnerability across the spectrum of employment arrangements in developing and newly industrialised countries (see Arnold and Bongiovi, 2013). Within this, issues pertaining to class, gender, ethnicity and migrant status all have an impact.

Whilst much of the discourse on vulnerable employment has stemmed from the labour law literature that assesses vulnerability in terms of exclusion from protective regulation and social benefits, and non-compliance, as inferred from the previous discussion, it is also important to recognise the geography of vulnerability. As Vosko (2006: 3–4) pointedly reminds us, labour market precariousness is 'shaped by geography'. Vulnerability will be higher in rural areas, where infrastructure is poor, education standards are lower and opportunities to seek gainful employment else-

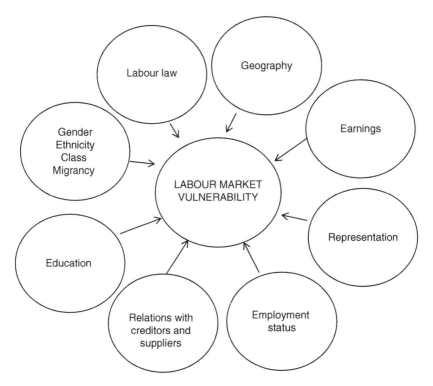

Source: Adapted from Brata (2010).

Figure 10.1   Factors shaping labour market vulnerability

where are more difficult due to a lack of waged employment. This process is exacerbated by attendant urbanisation, where recent jobs growth in export sectors and tourism has left rural areas increasingly disadvantaged (Antonopoulos, 2009: 15). Similarly, deeply ingrained cultural attitudes that work against women and other disadvantaged groups are likely to be more persistent in rural areas. Globalisation and the subsequent movement of people also raise issues peculiar to migrant workers, particularly those who face constraints on their entry and exit into a work arrangement (such as passport confiscation). Such 'unfree' labourers (Barrientos et al., 2013) can also be regarded as particularly vulnerable. Hence, as economies develop and open up to global influences, migration, urbanisation and structural change transform the nature of vulnerability experienced by individuals moving from agriculture to emergent sectors in the urban economy.

It is apparent that some factors, such as the nature of regulation, will operate at a national level, whilst other factors shaping vulnerability will be more place-specific or localised in their impact. As such, it is important that any analysis of vulnerability must be able to 'connect with the emergent local spaces of the contemporary service economy' (Cumbers et al., 2010: 129). The traditional focus of industrial relations and labour law researchers on the implementation of national policies and agendas (ibid.) has been poorly placed to deal with these developments. However, this is not to understate the impact of national factors on regional and local developments. The key point to consider is that the various factors shaping the degree of vulnerability faced by workers in a particular locality will necessarily involve interaction between local, regional and national (and indeed international) influences.

However, the relative invisibility of such workers makes any aggregate analysis difficult. What evidence there is suggests that daily conditions can be difficult, where workers such as street vendors regularly face harassment from local government authorities for purportedly conducting activities that may be illegal, or merely constructed as 'illegal' (for example, through the use of 'clearance operations' to drive street vendors away from the busiest areas of cities; Brata, 2010: 48). However, it is unclear how this translates into other areas of the work experience, and importantly, how measures of policy bodies designed to improve the livelihood of such workers are regarded by the workers themselves. As Arnold and Bongiovi (2013: 293) note, 'knowledge of the informal economy is extremely limited in most developing Asian countries and researchers have paid little attention to the subject'. This necessitates an approach that can capture the daily work experience that such individuals face, if a genuine understanding of the impact of economic developments and policies on the well-being of informal sector workers is to be attained. Such an understanding is of importance not only for those interested in the immediate well-being of informal sector workers in Indonesia, but also for those more generally interested in promoting economic development and well-being. In the sections that follow, we explore these issues, by examining the experiences of street vendors in the Jakarta area.

10.3   CONTEXT: INFORMAL AND VULNERABLE WORKERS IN INDONESIA

The Indonesian economy has enjoyed considerable economic growth in recent years, after a long period of stagnation in the wake of the 1997 Asian financial crisis. The period leading up to the 1997 crisis was char-

Table 10.1 *Population 15 years of age and over by main employment status, 2007–14 (%)*

Main employment status (%)	2007	2008	2009	2010	2011	2012	2013	2014
Employer with permanent workers	2.95	2.97	2.84	3.01	3.4	3.52	3.4	3.6
Employee	27.72	26.94	27.09	29.16	34.36	36.33	36.68	36.97
Formal work	*30.67*	*29.91*	*29.93*	*32.17*	*37.76*	*39.85*	*40.08*	*40.57*
Self-employed	20.89	20.81	20.49	19.6	17.46	16.66	17.0	17.9
Self-employed assisted by family member/temp. help	21.56	21.81	21.43	20.44	18.34	17.1	17.2	16.8
Casual employee in agriculture	5.43	5.41	5.18	4.95	4.94	4.81	4.01	4.44
Casual employee not in agriculture	4.10	4.92	5.3	4.67	5.15	5.53	5.71	5.59
Unpaid worker	17.35	17.12	17.59	18.17	16.36	16.05	16.19	14.67
Informal work	*69.33*	*70.07*	*69.37*	*67.83*	*62.25*	*60.15*	*60.11*	*59.4*

Note: Figures for August of each year. Technically, even the categories of 'employer' and 'employee' can display elements of informality (e.g., contract work).

Source: Calculated from BPS Indonesia. Accessed 14 May 2015 at http://www.bps.go.id/.

acterised by strong growth of the export-oriented manufacturing sector under the authoritarian Suharto New Order regime that saw growth in 'formal sector' jobs (De Ruyter and Warnecke, 2008). After the 1997 crisis the export-oriented manufacturing sector shrank and many workers returned to agricultural jobs or otherwise engaged in precarious forms of work in the service sector (ibid.). This long period of relative stagnation only began to end in 2008, after recovery from the recent world economic downturn, and the period since 2008 has been characterised by strong growth in waged employment, as evidenced by growth in the share of the 'employee' category in Table 10.1. However, precarious forms of work remain dominant, with significant proportions of workers in the vulnerable worker categories of self-employed/own account workers and unpaid family helpers. The need to consider a more nuanced spectrum of vulnerability in employment arrangements is also evident in the recent growth of contract work and outsourcing, in effect contributing to the informalisation of the formal sector.

Within the overall national context, the DKI Jakarta region is one of Indonesia's wealthiest regions, as might be expected from its capital city status and platform for foreign investment. The relative affluence of those living in Jakarta is evident in the nature of employment, with employers and employees comprising a greater share of employment than Indonesia as a whole. This is reflected in the fact that formal sector employment accounts for a higher percentage of jobs than in Indonesia as a whole: in 2009 only 26.4 per cent of workers were reported to be in informal work (Nazara, 2010: 31). The minimum wage is also relatively high, at 2.7 million Rp per month in 2015 (Department of Labour and Employment, 2015). Given that there has been a marked shift of economic activity to Jakarta in recent decades, with its population more than quadrupling between 1975 and 2015 to more than 10 million (McCarthy, 2003; Central Intelligence Agency, 2015) and its share of gross domestic product (GDP) doubling after 1975 to become one-sixth of total Indonesian GDP (Hill et al., 2008: 117; HVS Global Hospitality Services, 2013), it should not be surprising that Jakarta should figure as the most developed region of Indonesia, a fact reinforced by its urban, capital city status. If anything, the gap between Jakarta and the rest of Indonesia has only widened since the enactment of decentralisation in 2001 (Matsui, 2005: 175).

However, the same attraction of Jakarta as a magnet for economic growth has led to an influx of migrants from other parts of the country, despite decades of official attempts to resettle people in less-populated parts of Indonesia under 'transmigration' programmes (McCarthy, 2003). This has placed consequent strain on already poor infrastructure (for example, lack of effective public transport or sewerage systems) in a city prone to severe flooding and heavy traffic jams (Wilhelm, 2011; Bunnell and Miller, 2011). This has led to the associated problem of slum development, and the widespread use of land clearance operations on traditional urban neighbourhoods, or *kampongs* (Davidson, 2009: 305, as cited in Bunnell and Miller, 2011: 39). These operations were often violently conducted by 'gangs of thugs', who were reported even to have resorted to rape and murder (ibid.). It was for these reasons that the Jakarta region was selected to undertake the fieldwork.

10.4   METHODS

The research methods used were predominantly qualitative, consisting of interviews and observations. Interviews were conducted with nine vendors. These consisted of two market stallholders (Vendors 1 and 5), four railway platform vendors (Vendors 2, 3, 6 and 8) and three street vendors (Vendors 7, 4 and 9). Table 10.2 provides a summary of supply-side characteristics of each of the vendors. In addition, interviews were conducted with two members of ILO staff in the Jakarta office (in English), and three student activists working with street vendors (and other informal sector workers). The interviews with vendors were conducted with the assistance of local interpreters. They took place in a semi-structured questionnaire format, so

Table 10.2   Vendors by supply-side characteristics

Vendor	Gender	Age bracket	Educational attainment	Marital status	Children
Vendor 1	Male	45–54	Senior high school	Married	4 (3 independent)
Vendor 2	Male	16–20	Junior high school	Single	None
Vendor 3	Male	55–64	Senior high school	Married (to 6)	6 (all independent)
Vendor 4	Male	55–64	Junior high school	Married	6 (all independent)
Vendor 5	Male	21–34	Junior high school	Single	None
Vendor 6	Female	55–64	Elementary school	Married (to 3)	6 (all independent)
Vendor 7	Male	45–54	Elementary school	Widower	4 (2 independent)
Vendor 8	Female	45–54	School teacher	Married	3 (all independent)
Vendor 9	Male	21–35	Junior high school	Single	None

as to enable further exploration of any particular issues that arose, but still allowed for a modicum of comparison and generalisation across responses. The issues covered included basic income and working conditions, access to welfare, role in the home, childcare (if any), access to advice and impact of the state (for example, interaction with authorities). The interviews were conducted so as to minimise disruption to the worker's schedule, and were carried out in a discreet manner in a location that was acceptable to the participant. The interviews were then transcribed by local interpreters upon the conclusion of the fieldwork phase. At all times the process adhered to ethical principles of voluntary participation, full disclosure, confidentiality and anonymity.

10.5   FINDINGS

The interviews revealed that the street vendors and railway platform vendors displayed a high degree of vulnerability in terms of the facets of labour market vulnerability expounded in previous sections, as explored below. These vendors generally had a relatively low educational attainment (with only three vendors having attained a senior high school matriculation), low income and long work hours. Ambiguous legal status was a theme that was particularly pressing for those vendors interviewed at railway platforms. Below, particular aspects of vulnerability are further explored.

Work–Life Trajectories: On the Periphery of the Urban Economy

Echoing the earlier discussion, for most of the respondents working as a vendor was seen as providing the only way of earning a living in the urban economy, given the low levels of educational attainment. Indeed, for most, it was the only work they were able to obtain. Vendor 3 commented that 'it's hard to find a job for a high school graduate, with more people with undergraduate and bachelor looking for jobs – it's easier to start their own business rather than to find a job in office'. Only Vendor 8 (a qualified school teacher from Semerang) cited a different reason for working as a vendor: namely, to move with her husband to support him in his work (also a vendor). Turning to work hours, all of the respondents reported long work hours, with vendors 1, 3, 5, 7, 8 and 9 reporting that they worked 'every day'. For those with family responsibilities, it often meant relying on other family members or neighbours to assist with child care:

> I serve customers every day – it's about 6 am I start maybe. I take care of the children first, then I just go to the market. I close around 6.30 pm . . . There's someone who helps me when I take my pray time, it's my neighbour – he also sells something near here. In the morning my children have to go to school then they will have Quran learning in afternoon. For me, I have to prepare them to go to school every morning and I have to wash the dirty clothes in the evening. (Vendor 7, 11 April 2013)

However, the pathways into such work varied among the individuals interviewed, in turn highlighting the different ways in which the informal sector functions within the wider economy. A majority of the respondents (five) had migrated from other parts of Indonesia to the Jakarta area. For these individuals, working as a vendor in Jakarta represented an improvement from their previous work circumstances, or provided better opportunities for their children. This was evident from interviews with those who had worked as agricultural labourers, for example Vendor 7, a street vendor selling fruit, who reported that:

> I was a farmer . . . when I was a farmer, once my rice field was attacked by insects so I failed to harvest the rice. Besides, the kids only could only do farming in the village . . . but here they can go to school. In here I still can fund my children for their school, even in worst condition. I still can do many things here, to fulfil my family needs. (Vendor 7, 11 April 2013)

Agricultural work was seen as physically demanding and as the ageing process set in, consequently was too physically exhausting to maintain. In this context, a precarious existence as a street vendor was seen as preferable (Vendor 7).

Table 10.3 Earnings and hours worked

Respondent	Daily earnings	Hours worked (daily)
Vendor 1	n/a	9-hour shifts (but has 3 workers)
Vendor 2	$2/day on average	Unclear
Vendor 3 and 6	$5/day on average combined	6 am until 10 pm
Vendor 4	$3/day on average	unclear
Vendor 5	n/a	11-hour shifts (but has 1 worker)
Vendor 7	$5/day less school fees	6 am until 6.30 pm
Vendor 8	$10/day	12-hour shifts
Vendor 9	$1.60/day	12-hour shifts

For others, the informal sector served as a sink for those displaced from formal sector jobs. Vendor 4 used to work in real estate until he lost his job during the 1997 Asian financial crisis. Given the continued lack of unemployment benefits in Indonesia (Schmitt, 2011) he had no recourse but to fall into some kind of paid activity, no matter how low-paying; in this case, selling boxes of tissues to students at the university railway station:

> Let's say if today I can sell all tissues in this box I will get Rp.60 000 (approx. $6) . . . then I spent 12 000Rp on transportation fare . . . then I have to set some money aside for paying the rent. But usually I just get Rp.30 000 – I still have to spend the same transportation fare . . . then there will be 18 000Rp left. I think I would have to do fasting if I only got Rp.18 000. (Vendor 4, 9 April 2013)

This variability of income was something that all respondents reported. Given the internationally recognised World Bank poverty threshold of US$2 per day, five of the respondents lived at (or near) the poverty line, as shown in Table 10.3. Only vendor 8, whose husband was working, appeared to have earned a higher income (data was not available for the registered stallholders, vendors 1 and 5).

However, the precarious nature of the work was exacerbated by the unequal social relations faced by vendors.

Ambiguous Legal Status: Problems of Harassment and Corruption

As mentioned above, the undocumented or unregistered status of the majority of respondents has rendered them vulnerable in terms of their legal rights. The ambiguous legal status of many vendors has led to problematic relations with authorities. Street vendors, for example, are argued to be a source of traffic congestion, as their activities can (and often do) spill over onto roadways (Dimas, 2007), prompting disproportionate responses from authorities, as noted earlier (Brata, 2010), often in the form of bullying and harassment, which have become endemic to working as a vendor in the informal sector.

For the respondents in this study, this was a particularly pertinent issue, and arose in two distinct but related ways: (1) alleged corruption on the part of officials and police officers; and (2) alleged harassment and physical intimidation in the name of upholding the law. Both of these issues were in turn exacerbated by the relatively weak organising ability of vendors (despite attempts by vendors to form an association).

The railway station vendors were particularly vulnerable as they were considered by the train operating company to be illegally occupying their premises, although it should be noted that the issue of legality was contested, difficult to understand, and appeared to involve two sides claiming different things. The victims, however, were the vendors who, even if they were legally occupying their premises, were being asked to leave. At both stations where interviews with railway platform vendors took place, it was reported that the train operating company planned evictions (and was indeed planning evictions for all remaining vendors in stations in the Jakarta area run by the state railway operator, PT KAI, hereafter referred to as the Company). The Company's goal was to improve profitability by clearing space in and around train stations in order to construct more car parking space, promote more train travel and ease traffic congestion (Student Activist 1). However, the Company was alleged to have argued that the vendors were 'disturbing the passengers', despite no apparent evidence at either of the stations visited to support this proposition (Student Activist 1). Vendor 6 asserted that '[t]hey said that we disturbed the passengers, but as a matter of fact we are not on the railroad platform'. The legal position underpinning the Company's right to evict the traders was based on their interpretation of Law Number 2 Year 2012, which concerns Land Procurement for Public Purposes, ostensibly allowing the Company the right to evict traders in and around stations (Interseksi.org, 2013).

However, the railway station vendors claimed to have paid rent for their premises beyond the stated eviction date:

> Actually [the threat of evictions] started at the end of [last] December when the train company came up with a plan for a clearance operation of the vendors … you know … they argued about making the station more comfortable and cleaner, so that no street vendor would be allowed to operate a business there. But we came up to talk to the vendors about what really happened. [The Company] give them formal letters that stated that the vendors had to leave in just only 2 weeks. However, this was a shock to the vendors, who argued that 'we paid to be here'. Maybe they paid for 3 or 5 years to operate their vendor in

the stations, but [the Company] as the owner of the station said that they had to go in 2 weeks. (Student Activist 1, 18 April 2013)

What appeared to have transpired was that the vendors were actually paying 'brokers' or middlemen to rent premises at the stations, and were not communicating directly with the Company. In turn, the Company was only issuing rights to the broker. Apparently, brokers were charging vendors to rent premises for a particular period, but instead of forwarding the money to the Company, the brokers pocketed it. So a lease that a vendor believed was legal for two years beyond the stated eviction date was not recognised by the Company, and no compensation would be forthcoming upon eviction. Since some of the brokers were allegedly Company employees (Student Activist 1), this raised concerns about corrupt behaviour within Company ranks.

In an attempt to lobby together to try and prevent the evictions, the vendors formed an association and enlisted the help of local university students to try to publicise their situation and negotiate with the Company. However, at the time of this research, no satisfactory outcome had been achieved. This had led to acute distress for the vendors as it was their only source of income, and the notion of relocation would be problematic at best for most of them. For one couple (Vendor 3 and Vendor 6), their station premises also served as their home (upstairs in a very small room, up a ladder) so the threat of eviction was particularly distressing, as the following interview dialogue demonstrates:

Interpreter: 'What has the association done, Mam?'
Vendor 6: 'We do demonstration everywhere . . . we ask . . .'
Vendor 3: 'From the students, just to help us not to be removed. From the National Commission of Human Rights, to help us.'
Interpreter: 'They try to facilitate between the trader and the train company. They tried to find the solution. No, no result yet. So they're . . . actually they're still afraid, as you can see that she's crying.'
Interviewer: 'I'm sorry. Please say I'm sorry.'

In turn, the fears of station vendors were realised: an eviction took place at the university station on 29 May 2013 (*Jakarta Post*, 2013). Some 81 stalls were demolished as part of the eviction, resulting in scuffles between vendors (supported by local university students) and security staff hired by the Company. At least one student was injured during the altercation, which was alleged by students to have been started by station staff.[4] The

---

[4]   See also video footage of the eviction at http://www.youtube.com/watch?v= e06vVbpys6k.

Company in turn stated that it had 'no responsibility' to relocate the vendors (ibid.), the concerns reported above about alleged corruption notwithstanding.

Even without the threat of forced evictions, for street vendors interaction with authorities can still be marred by corruption and harassment. Evidence suggests that local police officers, for example, were not averse to taking payments off vendors to not harass them:

> In the past, when I was a street vendor, it was often . . . We had to pay money to the Satpol PP [police officer] as we were not supposed to be there . . . If we paid, we would not be harassed by them. But if we didn't pay, then they would harass us, they might expel us from where we were selling. Sometimes they would even beat us or kick us, whatever (Vendor 5, 11 April 2013)

Whilst it can be difficult to generalise such findings, such comments do reinforce previous studies that point to continuing widespread problems with corruption and selective interpretation and enforcement of the law in Indonesia (von Luebke et al., 2009). This is particularly problematic for the workers in this study who have ambiguous legal status. For those workers engaged in 'illegal' practices (for example, Vendor 2, who was a hawker selling magazines on the train, a practice forbidden by the Company), little – if any – adequate recourse before the law could be expected. As such, companies and/or authorities often claim that vendors are engaged in illegal activities, even if there is no legal ruling to this end. They then use this socially constructed 'illegality' as part of their argument to move or alter the conditions of vendors. In this situation, vendors themselves appear to have no recourse to legal redress on the matter.

Lack of Access to Finance

Another important issue is the nature of relations with creditors. Lack of access to finance has been a problem reported by own-account workers, as they typically lack collateral. Hence, banks are highly reluctant to lend to them and they are forced to seek out moneylenders, who typically charge high rates of interest on their loans (Tribunnews.com, 2013). This is often the only option, since moneylenders stipulate less rigid procedures than banks do, and moneylenders do not require borrowers to put up collateral, in contrast to banks (ibid.). In this context, it is not surprising that only one respondent, Vendor 5, had sought out (and obtained) a loan from a bank. Rather, the typical comment on obtaining finance was more in the order of:

for now I just use my own money, I'm afraid with the interest if I borrow money from a bank, I still have to find money to eat for my family so it will be better for me not to borrow anything from the bank . . . instead of paying high interest for the bank. (Vendor 7, 11 April 2013)

Also apparent was a general lack of awareness by respondents on even how to obtain a bank loan. In this context, other potential sources of finance for respondents could be family members, highlighting the importance of informal (social) networks.

10.6 DISCUSSION: LESSONS FOR POLICY

Our research findings strongly illustrate that vendors exhibit a high degree of vulnerability, as per the indicators developed by Brata and Dabir-Alai. The street vendors and station vendors faced harassment from authorities, had low incomes and lacked access to finance. For such individuals, neighbours, family members and community networks were more important sources of assistance (Sirojudin and Midgley, 2012) than the state. For those respondents who were street vendors (and the station vendors, excluding Vendor 8), lack of capital made it problematic to grow their businesses. In this context, self-employment served as a 'refuge' for those who would otherwise be unemployed, and for recent migrants from rural areas (echoing Mandelman and Montes-Rojas, 2009, cited in Bhattacharya et al., 2013: 341). Any income received would be spent immediately, primarily on food.

A particular aspect of vulnerability highlighted in this chapter was the reporting of harassment by authority figures, and making payments in order to avoid harassment. This is particularly concerning amidst wider issues about corruption. This reiterates previous findings suggesting that despite considerable pressure and lobbying by international bodies, attempts to facilitate improvement in vulnerable working conditions continue to be undermined by corruption at various levels of government: local, regional and national (von Luebke et al., 2009: 286). This has been a concern with continuing links demonstrated between elements of the police and paramilitaries, government officials, and domestic and multinational businesses (Kristiensen and Trijono, 2005: 249). As von Luebke et al. (2009: 270–71) have noted, 'although Indonesia's regime change has introduced formal good-governance structures, local policy realities continue to be dominated by informal and particularistic relationships'. Such relationships place workers such as street vendors at severe disadvantage if the law is only selectively enforced. Hence, 'enacting new labor regulations, or making workers "formal" or in an SER [standard employment relationship], will not improve the lot of workers if they have no power of enforcement' (Arnold and Bongiovi, 2013: 295). Thus, government needs to exert a greater willingness to tackle corruption and hold those charged with enforcement to account.

In addition, at a very basic level, improving the working conditions of urban vendors means improving the physical and social infrastructure available to them, and suggests a wider focus on capability endowment (as per Amartya Sen's notion of positive economic freedom; see Warnecke and De Ruyter, 2010 for a discussion; see also Vargas-Falla, Chapter 9 in this volume). In particular, this means free education and extending health care and social security coverage. However, the ongoing dispute over reform of current social security coverage in Indonesia highlights just how problematic this can be. The central government has balked at reforming and extending (ostensibly for cost reasons) the existing institutional arrangements. Four funds, managed as state-owned corporations, cater to government employees and military personnel. The Jamsostek covers formal workers in the private sector (Sirojudin and Midgley, 2012: 126). The current Social Welfare Insurance Program targeted at informal workers (Asuransi Kesejahteraan Sosial, or Askesos) is limited in its scope (for example, to local residents in their own neighbourhood, who earn no less than approximately $35 per month) and hence only covers a small proportion of workers, at some 350 000 by 2011 (ibid., 130–31). A study of the informal economy estimated that more than 32 million paid informal workers in Indonesia would not 'be covered by any health insurance scheme in 2014' (GIZ, 2013: 1). Thus, more needs to be done to address lack of management capacity in community organisations that administer such programmes, improve the adequacy of benefits and better link such local initiatives to national initiatives (ibid.).

This highlights the important role that civil society can play (particularly at a local and regional level) to support vulnerable workers. Evident from this study was the support that university students had given to station vendors.[5] However, attempts to improve the working conditions of informal sector workers must be accompanied by an approach seeking to generate growth in decent waged employment, so as to reduce the need for individuals to engage in marginal activities such as that of street vending. Failing this, as a fall-back measure at least, those vendors who

---

[5]   Parallels were seen in other areas visited during the research, such as volunteers providing free education provision to children in slum areas, enabling women to engage more in paid work.

faced eviction needed further assistance in order to be able to afford alternative premises (such as those of market traders) to conduct their business. In addition, improving access to finance could be considered, for example by simplifying administrative arrangements (Warnecke and De Ruyter, 2010: 400) and reducing collateral requirements. All of these measures would reduce the nature of vulnerability experienced by urban vendors and contribute to an agenda of facilitating 'decent work'. Nevertheless, this agenda is in itself contingent on the emergence of political movements that can successfully challenge the current neo-liberal hegemony.

10.7 CONCLUSION

This chapter has explored the working conditions of urban vendors in the Greater Jakarta area of Indonesia. As own-account workers, the vendors are vulnerable workers according to the ILO definition. Brata's (2010) typology (as adapted from Dabir-Alai, 2004) illustrating aspects of vulnerability was utilised in order to explore the nature of working conditions experienced by vendors. In this study, the nature of vulnerability experienced by the vendors was particularly acute in terms of their low income, potential for harassment by authorities (in a context of evidence of corrupt behaviour exhibited by some local officials) and also lack of access to capital.

The findings suggest that more pressure needs to be brought to bear on authorities by labour organisations and international bodies such as the ILO, and non-governmental organisations, to ensure that highly vulnerable workers such as urban vendors are given adequate and just recourse before the law, and that their grievances are given due consideration. In turn, more needs to be done by authorities to eliminate corrupt and unaccountable practices by officials with whom these workers interact. In a wider context, improving the poverty of urban vendors can only be accomplished through an approach that seeks to extend adequate social welfare coverage to all vulnerable workers. Such measures would also broadly correspond with the recommendations of the World Trade Organization and the ILO (WTO and ILO, 2009) that a multidimensional approach is needed to promote formal employment and support those still in informal employment through, for example, specific social security schemes that reach outside of the formal economy. Moreover, such an approach necessitates supporting political movements that will be better placed to challenge the current orthodoxy.

REFERENCES

Antonopoulos, R. (2009) 'The Current Economic and Financial Crisis: A Gender Perspective', Working Paper, Levy Economics Institute, No. 562.

Arnold, D. and Bongiovi, J.R. (2013) 'Precarious, Informalizing, and Flexible Work: Transforming Concepts and Understandings', *American Behavioral Scientist*, **57** (3): 289–308.

Barrientos, S., Kothari, U. and Phillips, N. (2013) 'Dynamics of Unfree Labour in the Contemporary Global Economy', *Journal of Development Studies*, accessed 17 June 2013 at http://dx.doi.org/10.1080/00220388.2013.780043.

Bergsten, F. and Williamson, J. (1994) 'Introduction', in J. Williamson (ed.), *The Political Economy of Policy Reform*, Washington, DC: Institute for International Economics.

Bhattacharya, R., Bhattacharya, S. and Sanyal, K. (2013) 'Dualism in the Informal Economy: Exploring the Indian Informal Manufacturing Sector', in S. Banerjee and A. Chakrabarti (eds), *Development and Sustainability*, New Delhi: Springer India.

Brata, A. (2010) 'Vulnerability of Urban Informal Sector: Street Vendors in Yogyakarta, Indonesia', *Theoretical and Empirical Researches in Urban Management*, **5** (14): 47–58.

Bunnell, T. and Miller, M.A. (2011) 'Jakarta in Post-Suharto Indonesia: Decentralisation, Neo-liberalism and Global City Aspiration', *Space and Polity*, **15** (1): 35–48.

Central Intelligence Agency (2015) 'Indonesia', *CIA World Factbook*, accessed 17 May 2015 at https://www.cia.gov/library/publications/the-world-factbook/geos/id.html.

Cumbers, A., MacKinnon, D. and Shaw, J. (2010), 'Labour, Organisational Rescaling and the Politics of Production: Union Renewal in the Privatised Rail Industry', *Work, Employment and Society*, **24** (1): 127–44.

Dabir-Alai, P. (2004) 'The Economics of Street Vending: An Empirical Framework for Measuring Vulnerability in Dehli in the late 1990s', Paper presented at the EDGI and UNU-WIDER Conference, 17–18 September, Helsinki, Finland.

Department of Labour and Employment (2015) 'Comparative Wages in Selected Countries', accessed 17 May 2015 at http://www.nwpc.dole.gov.ph/pages/statistics/stat_comparative.html.

De Ruyter, A., Singh, A., Warnecke, T. and Zammit, A. (2012) 'Labor Standards, Gender and Decent Work in Newly Industrialized Countries: Promoting the Good Society', in J. Marangos (ed.), *Alternative Perspectives on the Good Society*, New York: Palgrave Macmillan.

De Ruyter, A. and Warnecke, T. (2008) 'Gender, Non-Standard Work and Development Regimes: A Comparison of the US and Indonesia', *Journal of Industrial Relations*, **50** (5): 718–35.

Dimas, H. (2007) 'Street Vendors: Urban Problem and Economic Potential', Working Paper, Center for Economic and Development Studies, Universitas Padjadjaran, Bandung.

Folkerth, J. and Warnecke, T. (2011) 'Organizing Informal Labor in India and Indonesia', Paper presented at the Global Labor University Conference, Johannesburg.

GIZ (2013) 'Expansion of Social Health Protection for Informal Workers in

Indonesia – Main Challenges and Recommendations', Policy Brief, Bonn: Deutsche Gesellschaft Fur Internationale Zusammenarbeit.

Hewison, K. and Kalleberg, A. (2013) 'Precarious Work and Flexibilization in South and Southeast Asia', *American Behavioral Scientist*, **57** (4): 395–402.

Hill, H., Resodusarno, B. and Vidyattama, Y. (2008) 'Economic Geography of Indonesia: Location, Connectivity, and Resources', accessed 23 May 2011 at http://www.rrojasdatabank.info/wdr2009/regeas09p115-134.pdf.

HVS Global Hospitality Services (2013) 'Indonesia Hotel Watch: Indonesia Overview', Jakarta: HVS.

ILO (2012) *From Precarious Work to Decent Work: Outcome Document to the Workers' Symposium on Policies and Regulations to Combat Precarious Employment*, Geneva: ILO.

ILO (2013) *Global Employment Trends 2013: Recovering from a Second Jobs Dip*, Geneva: ILO.

ILO (2014a) *Global Employment Trends 2014: Risk of a Jobless Recovery?*, Geneva: ILO.

ILO (2014b) *World of Work Report 2014: Developing with Jobs*, Geneva: ILO.

ILO and International Institute of Labour Studies (IILS) (2009) *World of Work Report 2009*, Geneva: ILO and IILS.

ILO and International Institute of Labour Studies (IILS) (2013) *World of Work Report 2013: Repairing the Economic and Social Fabric*, Geneva: ILO and IILS.

Interseksi.org. (2013) 'Penggusuran penggiat usaha di stasiun Jabodetabek', accessed 20 June 2013 at http://interseksi.org/blog/files/gusur_stasiun.php.

Jakarta Post (2013) 'Station Clean-Up Turns Ugly as UI Students Join Evicted Vendors', 30 May, accessed 21 June 2013 at http://www.thejakartapost.com/news/2013/05/30/station-clean-turns-ugly-ui-students-join-evicted-vendors.html.

Kalleberg, A. and Hewison, K. (2013) 'Precarious Work and the Challenge for Asia', *American Behavioral Scientist*, **57** (3): 271–88.

Kristiensen, S. and Trijono, L. (2005) 'Authority and Law Enforcement: Local Government Reforms and Security Systems in Indonesia', *Contemporary Southeast Asia*, **27** (2): 236–54.

McCarthy, P. (2003) 'The Case of Jakarta, Indonesia', Understanding Slums: Case Studies for the Global Report on Human Settlements 2003 series, World Bank, accessed 19 June 2013 at http://www.ucl.ac.uk/dpu-projects/Global_Report/pdfs/Jakarta.pdf.

Matsui, K. (2005) 'Post-Decentralization Regional Economies and Actors: Putting the Capacity of Local Governments to the Test', *Developing Economies*, **43** (1): 171–89.

Maxwell, S. (2005) 'The Washington Consensus is Dead! Long Live the Meta-Narrative!', London: Overseas Development Institute.

Nazara, S. (2010) 'Ekonomi Informal di Indonesia: Ukuran, Komposisi dan Evolusi', Jakarta: ILO Country Office for Indonesia and Timor-Leste.

Schmitt, V. (2011) 'Promoting Unemployment Benefits and Income Security Measures for Workers in Asia: Current Debate, Situation and Way Forward', Paper presented at the Expert Meeting on Building Social Safety Nets for Employment – Strategies in Asia, 21–22 February, accessed 24 June 2013 at http://www.mhlw.go.jp/english/topics/conference/15th_ILO/dl/em.pdf#page=103.

Sirojudin and Midgley, J. (2012) 'Microinsurance and Social Protection: The

Social Welfare Insurance Program for Informal Sector Workers in Indonesia', *Journal of Policy Practice*, **11** (1/2): 121–36.

Tedjasukmana, I., Djoen, O.H. and Tjandra, S. (2008) 'Watak politik gerakan serikat buruh Indonesia', Trade Union Rights Centre.

Tjandra, S. (2009) '9.2 Understanding Workers' Law Reform in Indonesia, 1998–2004', *Labour and Management in Development*, **9**.

Tjandraningsih, I. (2013) 'State-Sponsored Precarious Work in Indonesia', *American Behavioral Scientist*, **57** (4): 403–19.

Tribunnews.com (2013) 'PKL gantungkan nasib ke rentenir', accessed 20 June 2013 at http://www.tribunnews.com/2013/05/11/pkl-gantungkan-nasib-ke-rentenir.

von Luebke, C., McCulloch, N. and Patunru, A. (2009) 'Heterodox Reform Symbioses: The Political Economy of Investment Climate Reforms in Solo, Indonesia', *Asian Economic Journal*, **23** (3): 269–96.

Vosko, L. (2006) 'Precarious Employment: Towards an Improved Understanding of Labour Market Insecurity', in L. Vosko (ed.), *Precarious Employment: Understanding Labour Market Insecurity in Canada*, Montreal: McGill-Queens University Press.

Warnecke, T. and De Ruyter, A. (2010) 'Positive Economic Freedom: An Enabling Role for International Labor Standards in Developing Countries?', *Journal of Economic Issues*, **44** (2): 385–92.

Warnecke, T. and De Ruyter, A. (2012) 'The Enforcement of Decent Work: Developing Sustainable Institutions? A Comparative Study of Indonesia and India', *Journal of Economic Issues*, **46** (2): 393–401.

Wilhelm, M. (2011) 'The Role of Community Resilience in Adaptation to Climate Change: The Urban Poor in Jakarta, Indonesia', in K. Otto-Zimmermann (ed.), *Resilient Cities: Cities and Adaptation to Climate Change*, Proceedings of the Global Forum 2010, Local Sustainability 1, DOI 10.1007/978-94-007-0785-6_5, Springer Science+Business Media.

Williamson, J. (2004) *A Short History of the Washington Consensus*, Washington, DC: Peterson Institute for International Economics.

World Trade Organization (WTO) and International Labour Organization (ILO) (2009) *Globalization and Informal Jobs in Developing Countries*, Geneva: WTO and ILO.

Index

access to employment, rights of 43, 45,
  50–51
Act on the Protection of Fixed-
  Term and Part-Time Employees
  (Republic of Korea) 163
age, and employment 50
Aged Care Award (Australia) 142–3
agriculture
  Argentina 184–5, 188, 191
  Indonesia 221, 224
  see also women, informal work in
    developing countries
Angola
  agricultural work 99, 102
  commerce sector work 112
  female employment shares, selected
    sectors 112
  informal work 100, 104
  labour participation rate (LPR) 111
Argentina, economy 33, 176, 185
Argentina, formalisation of work, *see*
  formalisation of work, Argentina
Arnold, D. 220, 230
Arthurs, H. 34, 35
articulation work 128–9
austerity 33, 38–9, 66
Australia
  enforceable undertakings (EUs)
    80–82, 82–3
  Fair Work Ombudsman (FWO)
    72–3, 80–82
  see also home care workers, Australia
Australian Competition and Consumer
  Commission (ACCC) 80, 81
Australian Unity 138
Ayres, I. 67
Azerbaijan
  agricultural work 99, 102, 105
  commerce sector work 103, 112
  female employment shares, selected
    sectors 112

informal work 100, 104
labour participation rate (LPR) 111

basic income guarantee 36
Beccaria, L. 185
Belarus
  agricultural work 99, 102
  commerce sector work 112
  female employment shares, selected
    sectors 112
  informal work 100
  labour participation rate (LPR)
    111
benefit recipients, fair treatment 52–3
Blofield, M. 50
Bogotá, formalisation of street
  vendors, *see* formalisation of
  street vendors, Colombia
Bongiovi, J.R. 220, 230
Bosch, G. 34
Botswana
  agricultural work 99, 102
  commerce sector work 103, 112
  female employment shares, selected
    sectors 112
  informal work 100
  labour participation rate (LPR) 111
Boyer, R. 54
Braithwaite, J. 67
Brata, A. 217–18, 220
Brazil
  agricultural work 99, 101, 102–3,
    105
  commerce sector work 101, 103, 106,
    112
  female employment shares, selected
    sectors 112
  informal work 96, 97–8, 100, 101,
    104, 105, 106
  labour participation rate (LPR)
    111

/